THE ARTS OF MAN

An Anthology and Interpretation of Great Works of Art

THE ARTS
OF MAN

Eric Newton

Published by NEW YORK GRAPHIC SOCIETY *Greenwich, Connecticut*

Published in 1960 by New York Graphic Society

Planned and produced by

CHANTICLEER PRESS, NEW YORK

N
7435
N45

ACKNOWLEDGMENT

My grateful thanks are due to Miss Sylvia Schweppe for advice, assistance and a great deal of research: to Miss Elizabeth Brown for her gentle refusal to allow my own careless proofreading to reach my publishers: and to Milton Rugoff for raising a pair of shocked eyebrows whenever my choices seemed to him unpardonably wild.

Library of Congress Catalog Card No. 60-8920

 Text and plates printed by Amilcare Pizzi, Milano, Italy.

Designed by ANDOR BRAUN

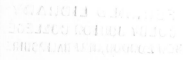

CONTENTS

The Reawakening of Humanism

The Baroque and the Worldly

The Nineteenth Century   *211*

The Century We Live In

Introduction

I N S T R E N G T H the human being is no match for the tiger, in speed he can be outstripped by the gazelle; as a swimmer his performance is childish compared with that of a dolphin; his sense of smell is far less acute than that of the dog; his eyes, in the daytime, are less serviceable than the hawk's, and at night, than those of a cat. Yet in one major respect he outstrips them all—he is capable of what is known as civilization. That is not merely a short way of saying that he has invented cooking and weaving, the telephone and the plough, the automobile and the hydrogen bomb. Civilization involves more than the power to make and use tools, to understand and master the forces of nature.

One of the basic differences between man and the animals is his power to stand outside himself. Doubtless the tiger and the eagle are capable of the major forms of experience—love, hate, hunger, lust. But they do not *contemplate* their experience, marvel at it as something precious or beautiful in its own right. Therefore they have no will to communicate their experience. For them emotion is a mere spur to action—the building of a nest, the defeat of an enemy or the search for food or a mate. Man, like the animals, builds his nest, destroys his enemy and seeks his mate, but unlike them, he takes surprising and infinite pains to express his experience and record his emotions—his relationship to his gods, his fellows and his environment.

To note that man is a recorder of his own experience is important, for that is equivalent to saying that man is an artist. To create a record of experience involves more than a will to record. It involves skill in the making and considerable deliberation long before the act of creation can begin. For experience is invisible, inaudible. It cannot be shared until its equivalent has been found in a sensuous symbol. Joy when the spring returns, loneliness when love dies, elation when difficulties are overcome cannot be communicated until they have been translated into the movement of the dance, the melody and rhythm of a song, or the form and color of a work of visual art. And at the precise moment when man undertakes this task of *11* translation he is beset by a new urge—the urge for *harmonious* organization which aestheticians call form or design and which the average man calls beauty.

Beauty has never been satisfactorily defined despite the labors of generations of aestheticians. Yet we recognize it when we see it or hear it, and the more we see and hear, the more sensitive we become to its appeal, whether we meet it in a saucepan or in the Sistine Chapel, in doggerel rhyme or Dante's *Divina Commedia.* Its preciousness for us in extreme cases cannot be measured, yet we acknowledge that preciousness when we remember that not all the wealth of the nations of the world could purchase the contents of the Louvre, the Prado, the Uffizi and the National Galleries of London and Washington.

This book is concerned with a fraction of a fraction of the records man has left behind him and in which human experience has been communicated in terms of beauty. It is an anthology, frankly personal, and therefore incomplete: woefully restricted, considering the mass of accumulated records that man, for the past 20,000 years and throughout the inhabited earth, has produced. And even though, in reproduction, these records must be divorced from their environment, and for the most part inevitably reduced in size, and, in the case of three-dimensional works, seen from one only out of a hundred possible points of view and in one only of a hundred possible effects of light, yet what is essential remains. It is true that the stained-glass window no longer shines like an illuminated jewel in a comparatively dark interior; the surface of the statue cannot be stroked; the tesserae of the mosaic can hardly be sensed; some at least of the delicacy of the illuminated manuscript is lost and much of the monumental scale and solemnity of the Romanesque tympanum; yet our eyes are at the service of our imaginations, and it is not difficult for us to reconstruct, as we turn each page, the appearance and quality of the original work.

What I have had in mind in making my final choice (out of how many thousands of strong claimants the reader can easily guess) is the multiplicity of means at the artist's disposal. We no longer suffer from the illusion that art, in its profounder levels, must always involve the use of pigment. Or that it was only with the invention of oil paint at the close of the 15th Century that man became fully able to express his deeper emotions. In mediaeval Europe, throughout all of Asia, and among what we glibly call primitive peoples, "easel painting" has been unknown. Yet the windows of Chartres, the mosaics of San Vitale in Ravenna, the ritual masks of Africa can leave as deep an impression on the memory as a mythology by Titian or a portrait by Rembrandt. As records they can be equally authentic; as formal inventions they can be equally satisfying.

This book, then, is an anthology of works of art chosen without prejudice or preference for one medium over another. What has finally been
12 included, after a long process of selection and rejection, has had to pass

three tests—the test of sincerity in what was to be expressed; the test of skill in the expression; and the test of aesthetic or formal harmony. Once these tests have been passed, a Limoges enamel or an ivory crozier head has as strong a claim to inclusion as Raphael's Sistine Madonna.

So much for the principles of choice. But principles are less important than preferences. The reader will doubtless note that this book does contain an ivory crozier head but not the Sistine Madonna. And having begun to search in vain for old favorites among the world's masterpieces and having discovered, in their place, minor and less familiar works, the names of whose authors are not even known, he may find himself wondering on what capricious and seemingly irresponsible system these works have been chosen.

That is a question that every anthologist must be prepared to answer. Asked by what right he has included an anonymous 6th-Century mosaic from Ravenna and rejected Paolo Veronese, the anthologist's answer is not simply that both are perhaps equally worthy but that the former had a special personal appeal which he is prepared to justify in his explanatory text. But an even more valid answer is that the anonymous mosaicist achieved something utterly beyond Veronese's power, and that to omit him would be to omit the expression of an emotional mood that no other century but the 6th, and no other medium but mosaic, has been able to achieve. To stand in the sanctuary of the Church of San Vitale in Ravenna is an experience none of the world's art museums can supply.

Nor is profundity the only quality to be taken into account. The ceiling of the Sistine Chapel and the cumulative power of Tintoretto's tragic narrative in the Venetian Scuola di San Rocco make demands on the spectator which he is certainly prepared to meet at certain moments of unusual awareness, but by no means all the time. This book would have failed in its purpose if it had excluded the playful, the exquisite, the decorative, even the merely skillful. For there is a strange minor satisfaction in contemplating those examples of extreme mastery of a difficult medium that one finds all over the civilized world—miracles of patient control in a Flemish · 16th-Century boxwood carving no larger than a billiard ball, or a page in the Book of Kells, or certain Chinese jades. As for what is addressed purely to the delight of the eye—the rich patterning of a Persian illumination or its Western counterpart in the color orchestration of a painting by Matisse—or to the sense of gaiety to which delight is closely related, or to our appetite for fantasy—these are aspects of human experience which cannot be ignored in a book whose purpose is not to gather together the great masterpieces of the world but to show how man has recorded the whole variety of his moods as a civilized being, from the making of a child's toy or the setting of a jewel to the creating of memorable symbols of the deity. Offenbach must take his place beside Wagner, Edward Lear beside Shakespeare, Rock 'n Roll beside the Sarabande if the complexity of human moods is to be understood. *13*

If such an anthology as this is regarded merely as yet another potted history of the world's greatest art, it must be regarded as a failure. The reader must not expect anything so ambitious and at the same time so futile. What Malraux has called the "museum without walls," which modern curiosity about the past or the distant, and modern means of reproduction have made available, should not be a museum that contains nothing but the skimmed cream. Such a museum would, in the end, become nauseating. It might impress and overwhelm but it would soon cease to surprise and delight. Also it would be a "safety first" museum, containing only what the connoisseurs of the world have all agreed to call works of genius.

I have tried, in making my choices, to forget these easy and universal agreements. Even though no sensitive man could deny that Michelangelo is profound, that Rubens is exuberant, Watteau nostalgic, Picasso passionate, it is still necessary to cultivate the unjaded eye, to be capable of delight whether confronted by the unfamiliar and the unexpected or by the universally acknowledged masterpiece.

I have no means of guessing how many of these plates will seem unfamiliar to my readers. But at least their inevitable divorce from their context has one advantage. It makes them self-reliant. The Syon Cope is no longer a vestment designed to be an integral part of a Catholic ritual: it becomes a specimen of Opus Anglicanum—the high watermark of mediaeval embroidery. A slipware dish by Thomas Toft or a red-figure kylix from Athens cease to be objects of use. They are removed from the life of action to take their place as objects to be contemplated in the same way that a modern easel painting asks for nothing but contemplation.

By this means it acquires a slightly different significance. Our sense of its usefulness or its purpose is minimized. If, in that process, it loses its hold over the eye, it has failed as a work of art. Emptied of wine, and displayed in a case or between the covers of a book, the amphora ceases to be a vessel and becomes polychrome sculpture, and as such it can be compared with the works of other sculptors in polychrome, simpler in form, less ambitious in content, but still asking us to judge it by the potter's sensitivity to shape and the painter's handling of line.

Isolated on the page we begin to see it with new eyes. My own attempt has been to use new eyes before isolating it. Another pair of eyes would have isolated a different object. Some of my choices may seem perhaps capricious, but the reader will find in my notes on the individual plates my written justification of what, among a million strong candidates, has pleased me most.

The Medium and Its Effect on the Work of Art

The invisible, inner world of experience, the artist's secret possession, is limited only by his capacity for experience. But once the artist crosses the frontier between emotion and creation, choice is forced upon him. The main problem is no longer the end but the means. For him the "what?" of his creative imagination is gradually invaded by the "how?" of his creative hand. Briefly, he has to choose a medium (usually it is chosen for him by the requirements of his patron or the nature of the task imposed on him) and once he has done so the age-old struggle between opportunity and limitation begins. Out of that struggle the work of art is born. Stubbornly the medium imposes its will on the artist while he, like a skillful jujitsu wrestler, turns its stubbornness to account, making each medium work *for* him to produce effects unattainable by any other means, even while it is working *against* him by refusing to behave as his creative imagination would perhaps have liked.

Media vary considerably in their degrees of stubbornness. The most flexible of all is that of oil paint, whose capacity to obey the artist's will has produced styles as different as the meticulous smoothness of a Van Eyck and the furious rhythms of a Van Gogh. Powdered pigment, whether mixed with oil (oil paint) or with water (water color) or egg (tempera) or wet plaster (fresco) has always tempted the artist for this reason. Being obedient to his will, its range of stylistic expressiveness is almost limitless; the Tachistes and the action painters of today are still discovering possibilities in it that were unsuspected even half a century ago.

No wonder, then, that about 60 per cent of the color plates in this anthology consist of reproductions of paintings or details from paintings. The preponderance was inevitable. It has always been in the medium of painting that the struggle between the will of the artist and the opposing will of his medium is least dogged and least apparent, and the range of different temperaments and personalities widest.

Yet a glance through these pages will reveal at once how many startling possibilities are denied to the painter. To take an obvious example, the most brilliant of colorists in pigment—a Carpaccio or a Matisse—is powerless to compete with the intensity of color so readily available to the artist who works in stained glass. Transmitted light and reflected light are as different in kind as song and speech, though inevitably in the reflected light of a color reproduction representing a 13th-Century Gothic window the difference is less striking.

Each medium imposes its will on the artist, thereby limiting his range; and each medium, by way of compensation, enables him to explore possibilities (and therefore establish a mood) peculiar to itself. The brilliance of a

Limoges enamel casket, with its juxtaposition of blues and greens against the golden sheen of molded metal, never fails to produce in me a special thrill. The Chinese artist who carves a figure in translucent rock crystal cannot, unless he is completely insensitive, carve an identical figure in opaque stone. The etcher whose needle glides easily across the metal surface of his plate conveys a different message from the engraver whose burin acts as though it were a miniature plough.

Every artist knows from experience, but few laymen ever realize, the constant interplay between mind and hand as a work of art progresses. The layman might suppose that all the artist has to do is to call up in imagination an image, as complete as he can make it, of the work he intends to produce, and then to translate it into his chosen or prescribed medium. But that is by no means an accurate account of the creative process. The original, imagined image is actually far from complete, and as soon as the artist sets to work, his medium begins both to modify and to clarify it; and unless he is a bad artist, he will accept and take advantage of those modifications.

It is unlikely, for example, that the mediaeval artist in stained glass saw in his mind's eye the network of lead lines that cut across his design. But as soon as those lead lines begin, as they eventually must, to appear in his work, his whole conception of the saint or the Madonna he is portraying begins to depend on the magic of that black network that divides color from color. He seizes every opportunity for using them to intensify the mysterious glow of his blues. He will even allow them to cut across a face or an arm in order to keep the pattern consistent.

The etcher, finding how easily his needle can convey tremulous hints and with what reluctance it makes harsh or forcible statements, begins to rely on hints and to repress his desire for statements. Had he chosen to make an engraving the opposite would have happened.

Some of the most significant leaps made by the artist's imaginative mind have been the direct result of a purely technical discovery in the use of media. It is certainly true to say that the change-over from a love of line to a love of surface that occurred in Venetian painting at the end of the 15th Century was due to the introduction of oil paint which, by its physical consistency, was incapable of a finely articulated Botticellian line, but could easily achieve the most breath-taking modulations of surface. What we are accustomed to call the Venetian feeling for the shimmer and dapple of light on surfaces— the very essence of the Venetian attitude to the physical world—may, it is true, be an expression of inherent Venetian sensuousness, but it is the direct result of a simple innovation in the use of the painter's medium.

It follows, therefore, that every artist is both the master and the slave of the material he uses. His inspiration is the direct result of its limitations.

He ignores them at his peril and any attempt on his part to evade or bypass the discipline imposed on him is bound to detract from his power. The designer who attempts to evolve the shape of a glass goblet by drawing with his pencil on paper, instead of trusting to molten glass and a blowpipe, is denying himself the nourishment on which his creative vitality depends. Such short cuts are always weakening and sometimes fatal. To model in clay and then copy the modeled forms in marble is to think in one language and speak in another. Yet this betrayal of the medium is frequently practiced by artists today who are unwilling to acknowledge the meaning of the word craftsmanship, or who even regard the drudgery of craftsmanship as something to be avoided.

It is not entirely a disease of today if it involves tiresome technical procedures. When Leonardo drew a comparison between the painter and the sculptor and argued that painting was a higher form of art because it involved the artist in a less messy struggle with his medium, he was making one of the earliest protests against the old tradition that the artist is primarily a workman. Leonardo was one of the first of the self-consciously romantic theorists. For him inspiration was entirely a product of the mind, and the best medium was the one that most readily obeyed the mind's commands. It is hardly surprising to find him a miraculous and indefatigable draftsman, an impatient painter, and a reluctant sculptor. His mind easily conceived images of solid objects which his hand was unwilling to make. Ingenious as is his famous flying machine, he would very quickly have modified it had he been craftsman enough to work in wood and metal rather than with pen and paper.

This plea for close contact between artist and medium is, of course, a familiar one, but certain modern artists and art philosophers have misused it by drawing the wrong conclusion from it. It is true that the artist must never ignore the nature of his medium. But it is certainly not true to say, as some extremists have said, that the artist must never impose his will on it. If all that were required of a block of wood or a piece of jade was that each should express, with the maximum of clarity, its own nature—the comparative softness and the sinuous grain of the former, the hard translucency of the latter—it would be enough to polish a sawn-off section of a tree or a jade pebble. But that is *not* enough. Such procedures are the exact reverse of the designing of a glass goblet on paper; they would produce nothing but a formless lump of glass that had never been worked on by the blowpipe. Both extremes avoid the struggle between mind, hand and matter that lies behind all good art. It might be thought that the virtuosity of a Bernini who can turn his block of marble into the semblance of flesh, hair, metal and even a cumulus cloud was skill misplaced. Perhaps Bernini went too far in the direction of *trompe l'œil*. Perhaps he moves us too little by his sincerity and astonishes us too much by his skill. But the other extreme is equally suspect.

In choosing most of my examples I have searched for the middle way between arrogant mastery of a medium and abject obedience to it, especially in the case of the more stubborn of the media. The Limoges enameler must retain in his mind the image of a saint while doing justice to the shine of polished metal and the pattern of colored patches of inlay.

The reader may notice that even though the work of thousands of centuries had to be compressed into less than two hundred illustrations, certain artists appear more than once. That is not due to an unreasonable enthusiasm on my part but to the fact that these artists have been willing to experiment with more than one medium, and that in each case they have achieved an extraordinary understanding of the possibilities of various media. Picasso, for example, has not been given too much but too little space. His sculptures in bronze, his etchings, his aquatints and lithographs, his ceramics as well as his paintings and drawings all point a moral. It is the central moral of this book, that the artist who is master of his ends must also be the servant of his means.

The Temperamental and the Racial Factor

Behind the medium is the man who manipulates it. Skill in the manipulation is, of course, essential, but skill is no more than a servant of his intentions; the speed of an automobile depends on the efficiency of its engine but its destination, once it is on the move, can only be decided by the man at the wheel.

Every work of art reproduced in this book is, therefore, both an example of skill and the expression of an intention. And that intention, despite the limitations imposed on the artist by his patron or by the particular demands of the task undertaken, is ultimately decided by the artist's personality. The stained-glass window must admit light into an interior, it must be intelligible as narrative and harmonious as decoration, yet the difference between two stained-glass windows by different artists, both of which deal equally effectively with light, with subject matter and with the problem of pure decoration, is the difference between two human beings—their personalities, their sense of values, their decisions about clarity or mystery, their choice between the strange and the ideal, or between the imagined and the real, their solutions of the problem of visual harmony, even their muscular habits: the purely physical "handwriting" that betrays an artist's style and which is, in fact, another manifestation of his personality.

Sooner or later the word "style" was bound to appear in these pages. It is the key to the situation. Yet it is not a word to use lightly, for its
18   ingredients are infinitely complex.

The 20th-Century eye is perhaps more sensitive to style than that of any other period in history. All the artistic creations of man, in whatever medium, at whatever period in history and in whatever portion of the earth, are now available to us in the form of reproduction. Malraux's "museum without walls" is limitless in its extent. And we, wandering casually along the corridors of this gargantuan record of man's hopes, fears and loves all expressed in visual terms, can only come to grips with it by observing stylistic differences, grouping it into stylistic families, noting the turbulent vigor of one family, the reticent understatements of another, or finding that one set of artists speaks in prose, another in poetry.

Without some such instinct for grouping we are lost. And as soon as we begin to divide the world's art into categories we begin to need a vocabulary to describe and identify them. The "museum without walls" requires a dictionary if we are to find our way without too much bewilderment in its mazelike structure. That dictionary is today in the making. We begin to know just what is meant by "Expressionist," "Surrealist," "Impressionist," "Realist," "Cubist," "Fauve" and so on. Such words are mainly 20th-Century inventions called into being by our increasing sensitivity to style and our decreasing sensitivity to subject matter. Where the 19th Century responded to a painting by John Constable by identifying its subject as Salisbury Cathedral seen from the meadows, we examine the surface of the painting to find out with what technical means Constable was able to render the freshness and the movement of tossing foliage or the fitful play of light on a brick wall or the surface of a pool. Having done so, we begin to establish new connections. We look for derivations from Rubens or influences on Delacroix or Monet. Unexpected stylistic family likenesses begin to appear, and as they do so we are forced to draw, in our minds, a new diagram of the many family trees that force themselves on our attention.

This book is a museum without walls in miniature, and like all museums, its contents will remain unintelligibly chaotic if they are not first of all submitted to at least a rough stylistic grouping. But what system of grouping will impose an intelligible pattern on the whole?

Style, as already noted, is the outward manifestation of personality. But personality is, to a greater extent than we are aware, the product of a cultural environment. It is not by accident that there is a stylistic similarity between artists living at the same moment in time, surrounded by the same everyday sights, reading the same books, accepting the same social conventions. Temperamentally, perhaps, no two personalities could be more different than Leonardo and Michelangelo—the former a scientist at heart, the latter a poet, the former consumed with curiosity about the universe and the laws it obeys, the latter so indifferent to everything but the spiritual and physical magnificence of man that he virtually ignored his environment, placing the newly created Adam on a featureless rock instead of in the Garden of

Eden. Yet the similarity in style between the two artists in their approach to draftsmanship is startling.

Almost the first impression made on the student of art history is the "period style" of a work of art, provided it occurs within the geographical limits of a national culture. In Italy, it is fairly easy to date any painting or carving to within a comparatively narrow margin of time, despite the slight variations that reflect the cultural divergencies between Florence, Siena, Venice and Milan. As we travel outward from the cultural centers, the period begins to leave a weaker stamp on the work. When we look at the art of Germany at the turn of the 15th Century, we note the gradual emotional change that reflects a different habit of mind. Grünewald is no longer a member of the Italian family. His handwriting is more agitated, his tone of voice more restless and agonized. We travel to England and discover a culture, and therefore a style, that has not yet succumbed to the Italian spell, has not even, like Germany, had the opportunity to produce a restless, agitated variation of it.

We travel further afield—westward to America—to find that at the very moment when Michelangelo is painting in the Sistine Chapel and Leonardo is finishing his Last Supper, strange pre-Columbian cultural traditions are producing works of art that still claim a place in our wall-less, timeless museum, but have no family likeness at all. Or we make our way eastward to India, China and Japan, where a set of interrelated civilizations, which were already old when Europe was culturally adolescent, are manifestly based on a series of fundamental axioms which no European could possibly accept but which the sensitive European eye cannot fail to admire.

Once we have established our right to look for the expressive, the memorable and the beautiful at any moment in time, or in any position in space to which curiosity leads us, the chronological sequence that would produce a comfortable stylistic pattern in Europe becomes useless.

It becomes useless not only because the development of civilization has reached different stages in different parts of the world, but for the even more basic reason that the very concept of development must be defined differently in Florence and in Peking. To look at the joyful energy of a 15th-Century Italian cassone panel and then to turn the page to find ourselves confronted by a precisely contemporary product from China or Japan would shed no light on either. There is a more valid connection between a bison by the palaeolithic artist of Altamira and a 20th-Century bull by Picasso than there is between a Sicilian mosaic of the 12th Century and a Chinese painting of the Sung Dynasty produced, perhaps, in the same decade.

We fall back, therefore, on the more fundamental concept that all the works of art in our museum were made by men bound together by the common bond of humanity. All of these works came into being under the stimulus of emotions we can understand and sometimes share. Awe, for example, is an emotion that few human beings have not experienced at some moment in their lives and that is responsible for powerful visual images in every corner of the earth. The 12th-Century mosaicist, who imagined and executed the great head and shoulders of Christ Pantocrator that overwhelms the visitor who enters the Cathedral of Cefalù in Sicily, felt it and communicated it unforgettably. But there are equally unforgettable images of awe, stylistically unconnected with Christianity (images of gods to be placated, spirits to be feared), to be found in primitive Africa or in hypercivilized China. Surely the "museum without walls" could advantageously group them together, not under a *family* heading but under the heading of a common human response to a common human emotion.

Occasionally, therefore, the reader will find that the arrangement of the plates in this book is frankly opportunist. The civilized or semicivilized human being is far too complex an organism to submit readily to such crude classification as chronology,· although chronology can easily clarify some aspects of his journey from animal to philosopher.

If it were not that "style" is so dependent on the behavior of the medium and the purely traditional conventions of a common craftsmanship, I have sometimes wondered whether a less obvious but in some ways more fundamental classification of works of art would not be made in terms of temperament. It is here that modern psychology could offer valuable assistance.

We know, well enough, that there is a romantic attitude of mind which always seeks to heighten emotion, which dwells sometimes fiercely, sometimes tenderly, on all that is strange and abnormal, that underlines the macabre and rejoices in the fantastic. We know equally well that there is also a classic point of view that is at pains to eliminate all these overtones of excess, of strangeness and emotional intensity, and that seeks, behind these variations from the normal, the hidden ideal. We are familiar with this classic point of view in the sculptures of the Parthenon, in the paintings of Raphael's middle period, in the whole of Poussin, in the untroubled silences that Vermeer of Delft seems to create in his paintings and finally in Mondrian's Calvinistic reduction of the world to a series of vertical and horizontal lines, a purity of black and white broken by an occasional square of primary color.

Why, then, should not Pheidias, Raphael, Poussin, Vermeer and Mondrian find themselves, in defiance of chronology, side by side in our museum as brothers—not in time but in temperament—where they would certainly be joined by one or two Chinese painters and one or two Egyptian sculptors to form a more or less homogeneous group?

That is perhaps a sensible question, but alas, it is a rhetorical one. I have been tempted in certain cases to use an occasional juxtaposition by temperament in order to establish an unsuspected connection between works that are otherwise remote from each other chronologically, geographically and culturally. But as a firm basis for rearranging the world's art, I have found it hardly practical. The vertical stratification by temperament is too often contradicted by the horizontal stratification that cuts across it, of period or of racial culture. Leonardo and Michelangelo are still too close to each other by virtue of their common ground in Florentine thought and vision to justify their separation on the ground of opposing temperament.

East and West, on the other hand, rarely feel happy in each other's proximity. Or perhaps it would be truer to say that they could not be made to settle down together between the beginning of the 13th and the end of the 19th Centuries. For that there is a good reason. The Western eye, consumed since the beginning of the Renaissance with visual curiosity about the world of phenomena, was always attempting to solve the problem of *how* to interpret such aspects of that world as light, space, and structure and was continually "developing" toward a completer realism as it solved those problems.

The Eastern eye is troubled by no such quest. Logically, for example, it could easily have discovered and applied those laws of optical perspective which enabled the European artist to produce, scientifically, an illusion of recession and space. Artistically it did no such thing; for the Eastern eye, a scientific solution of such a problem would seem absurd. For the Oriental artist, the dimensions of a tree, a mountain or a man do not depend on their physical distance from the artist's eye. In the eyes of the gods, size and distance are not interdependent.

What applies to the "accident" of remoteness in space also applies to the "accident" of the impact of light (so dear to the European artist) and to all the other accidents of appearance which, to the Oriental, merely interfere with and obscure fundamental truth.

If, therefore, there are no optical problems to solve, the word "development," in the European sense, becomes meaningless; and consequently the idea of a chronological sequence becomes almost equally meaningless.

An attempt at chronological arrangement in the art of so-called primitive peoples would be even less meaningful. Here visual curiosity plays an even smaller part than in Asia. All that concerns the African or the Polynesian is to discover the most powerful possible symbols to express his attitude to his gods or to design a ritual that will placate them or identify him with them. Perhaps some of those symbolic images are among the most powerful ever made. And it is only in the 20th Century that their imaginative power has begun to be understood in Europe.

Early in our century we began to recognize that power; European art has undergone a significant change. We are no longer the slaves of visual curiosity, we no longer subscribe to a mimetic theory of art. At last, and for the first time since the Middle Ages, the arts of Asia, Africa, Europe and America can sit happily side by side in our imaginary museum.

Vision and Style

Born at a given moment in time into a given cultural environment, heir to fixed traditions of craftsmanship, trained in the skillful use of whatever medium may be appropriate to his task, the artist is distinguished only by his personality from such of his contemporaries as have shared his local culture and inherited the same studio traditions within the narrowest limits. Indeed, his personality can fully manifest itself only at certain favorable periods—periods when civilization has agreed that the artist's personality is more precious than the traditions imposed upon him, and that he is to be praised rather as a rebel or a genius than for his obedience and conformity.

Genius, in fact, is a comparatively recent concept in Europe. Even the most famous of the Greek sculptors were admired by their contemporaries more for their mimetic skill or their power to evolve a physically ideal human type than for their originality or for their creative imaginations. The Greek critic who praised Zeuxis pointed out that the bunch of grapes he had painted deceived the very birds into picking at it. It is hardly in those terms that we praise Van Gogh or Picasso, nor was it in those terms that Vasari praised his idol, Michelangelo. The cult of the individual, the concept of "genius," was a product of the Renaissance.

The notion that the artist's style rather than his skill is precious because it is the visual symbol of *himself* is familiar enough to us. But it was not always familiar. Almost the whole of the bewildering mass of sculpture that enriches the Romanesque and Gothic churches of Europe, the temples of India, the tombs of Egypt is anonymous. It was made by individuals to whom it had not occurred that art could be an expression of individuality. To them, what we regard as a work of art, whether a candlestick, a crucifix or an illuminated page of a Psalter, was either an object of use or a symbol of faith. In every case, what mattered was not that it should be original or unique but that it should be well made. It is a sign of our own excessive preoccupation with the personality behind the work of art that the many anonymous masterpieces the world contains have been given too little attention by art historians, simply because the names of their authors are unknown.

What is true of the whole of mediaeval Europe is even truer of primitive African sculpture. We may sometimes catch ourselves wondering what kind of man conceived the windows of Chartres, but we are not even curious about the personality of the man behind a Benin bronze.

The cult of the personal in the arts and crafts of China and Japan certainly exists, but is different in kind from that of Europe. To the Western eye, a Chinese landscape or a Japanese color print are such complete expressions of a point of view which we cannot share, and they obey a set of artistic conventions so alien to our own, that at first sight the personality of the artists seems to be submerged under a veneer of orientalism that gives to all Chinese or Japanese art a family likeness. That is an illusion that must be attributed partly to unfamiliarity. Only the shepherd can distinguish between his sheep, and only the orientalist can trust his eye to recognize the difference between genius and talent in a Chinese scroll or to see at a glance the difference in personality between Hiroshige and Hokusai. But our unfamiliarity with them is not the only reason why the arts of the East seem impersonal.

Oriental art, as already noted, mistrusts the "accidents" of the fall of light on objects; it ignores the fact that shadow and distance can interfere with the local color; it mistrusts the illusory laws of optical perspective so dear to the Western mind. The oriental could, conceivably, find the vision of a Simone Martini or a Fra Angelico sympathetic, for early 15th-Century Italy had not yet succumbed to the European disease of visual curiosity or the scientific study of "appearances as opposed to the more basic understanding of essentials." Therefore the extraordinary devotion to purely visual truth which we admire in a Rembrandt or a Velasquez can have no counterpart in China or Japan. Nor could the medium of oil paint, so necessary to them both, ever gain a foothold in the East. For the expression of oriental vision it would be useless.

But it does not follow that personality plays a less decisive part in oriental painting than in occidental. It plays a different part and one that the Western critic finds difficult to define. Where the Western artist always seeks to build up new traditions and the Western critic is on the lookout for stylistic innovations, the Eastern artist's ambition is to perfect traditions, to increase his sensitivity and make his hand more obedient than ever to the quality of his vision. Hence the oriental veneration for brushwork as such, so that calligraphy itself becomes an art. One cannot but feel that beside any Chinese painting on silk or rice paper even the most masterly of European painters is clumsy. There is nothing in European art to match those Chinese renderings of bamboo leaves in which the brush, loaded with Chinese ink, trails off at the end of a stroke as it rises from the paper leaving behind a record of its passage like a gradual decrescendo in music.

Since, therefore, sensitivity rather than discovery is the mark of genius in the East, it would be foolish and meaningless to attempt a chronological order in the oriental plates in this book. Illuminating juxtapositions, when they occur, must be based on a system that leaves "development" out of account.

But it is worth while examining briefly the "development" in European art which positively compels the anthologist to arrange his selected specimens in a rough chronological sequence. Fra Angelico, at the beginning of the 15th Century, and Rembrandt, in the middle of the 17th, may both choose to interpret the same theme—a Nativity or an Annunciation—but the two interpretations cannot be compared; therefore, they cannot be set side by side. Naturally, the Italian and the Dutch minds have little in common beyond an attitude of reverence for the chosen theme. But what accounts for the depth of the gulf between them is not the reflecting mind but the searching eye. In the interval of nearly three centuries between our two artists, so many discoveries had been made, so many problems solved about the *appearance* of the world and its inhabitants that what seemed "truth" to Fra Angelico was no longer "truth" to Rembrandt. The problem of volume and structure had been solved by Michelangelo, that of color and the play of light on surfaces by the Venetians, that of tonal relationships and the interplay between light and shade by later artists of the 16th Century, who had also mastered the difficult problem of space. Rembrandt, inheriting, as he did, the fruits of all this research, *saw* his world in terms unsuspected by Fra Angelico.

I have called this gradual shift in purely optical experience "development," which is by no means the same as "progress." Rembrandt may be generally considered a greater artist than Fra Angelico, but not because he happened to be born in a later century. Glancing casually through the pages of this book we shall, I hope, be struck by the power of the artist's expression rather than by the completeness of his optical and technical equipment. If "development" were synonymous with "improvement" most of the plates in this book would have to be chosen from the art of our own century.

Development, however, is not entirely the product of research. Certainly, when we look at a Romanesque carving from Bourges of the 12th Century and then at one by that archtechnician Bernini, we are conscious of having moved from a spiritual to a worldly climate. Man's relationship, not only to his visible environment but also to his God, has undergone a complete transition. Bernini, we may say, has gained nothing in his grasp of the spiritual world. Nothing that the 17th Century produced in the way of sculpture has the solemnity of the tympanum of the Last Judgment at Vézelay or Autun. Those gaunt, fluted folds of drapery that run in vertical rhythms up and down the saints of Chartres, or in geometrical spirals round and across the Isaiah of Souillac, are vivid affirmations of the human soul—equally potent if they appear in stained glass or an enameled casket or a statue. They are the channels that drain away every trace of the worldly or the sensuous.

In that sense, the chronological development of style bears witness not only to the development of *seeing* but of *feeling*. Between the anonymous sculptor of Bourges and Bernini, spiritual aspiration has been replaced by physical beauty. Between a Nativity by Fra Angelico and one by Rembrandt the spirit of democracy has appeared, turning the shepherds into Dutch peasants, the manger into a Dutch barn, the star in the East into a lantern that only half illuminates the dark interior.

Art can perform the miracle of translating all these complex values. The inner, visionary life of man has found, through art, its equivalent in tangible 25 matter and that tangible matter has received the imprint of style.

It is for the reader, with a minimum of help from the essays that accompany the plates in this book, to translate style back again into vision. Each plate in this book is a photographic reproduction of an *object*. But before that object came into being under the artist's creative hand, it had to be envisaged in the artist's creative mind. What the reader has to do is to reverse the process, using the object as a kind of window through which he is enabled to look curiously into that mind, divine what kind of a man it inhabited, what was the religious or worldly climate that produced him, what type of civilization he belonged to.

The Earliest Historical Records

R EADABLE RECORDS enable us to look backward through time. But records need not be written, and even though they were made before writing had been invented and while spoken language was in its infancy we can still hazard a guess at what man was doing—and even what he was thinking—at a distance of time that is not to be measured in centuries but in hundreds of centuries.

What we have inherited from paleolithic man—flint tools, carvings on bone and, above all, paintings on cave walls—tell us that he was a hunter and an artist. It is less surprising that he should have made primitive weapons to help him with his hunting, than that he was able to train his visual memory to such a pitch that he could record the precise appearance of the animals he hunted.

Those painted records, hundreds of which have now been discovered in the caves of Western and Southwestern Europe, make it quite clear that the first proofs of civilization are to be found, not in writing or weaving or building, but in drawing and painting; and the first artists were not merely good but first-rate recorders of the appearance and behavior of the larger animals, even though they were ineffective and probably uninterested recorders of the shape and the activities of men and women.

It is for the student of anthropology to explain why this should be so. The student of art can only wonder at and admire the earliest of all historical records. Their purpose may be obscure but the quality of the best of them is unquestionable.

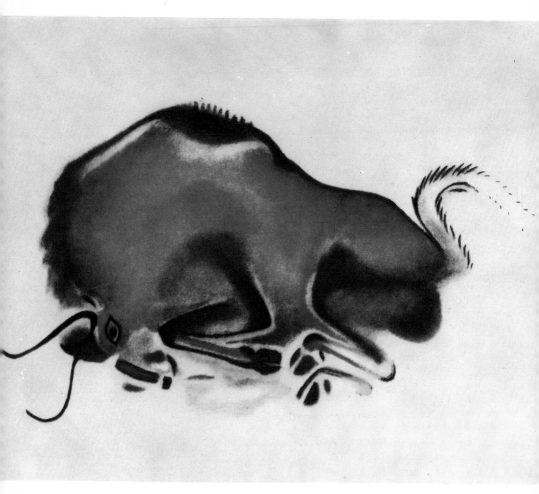

1. *Crouching Bison. Prehistoric rock painting.*
Cave of Altamira.

Crouching Bison from the Cave of Altamira

BEFORE LANGUAGE as we know it had been invented, before man could weave or cook or build, he was a draftsman and a painter. The distance in time between the bisons in the Cave of Altamira in Spain (and other caves scattered about the Dordogne district in France) and the horses of Degas or the bulls of Picasso has to be measured not in centuries but in thousands of years—just how many thousands is not known. Yet the paintings done by palaeolithic man on the walls of his cave often seem a good deal nearer to us in spirit than many a masterpiece of later ages.

"How vividly observed and how confidently drawn!" is our natural exclamation when we first meet these creatures painted on the bare rock by the hands of unknown men before the beginnings of recorded time. We are never tempted to add "considering that they lived before the dawn of civilization." Civilization may have refined man's sensitivity but, apart from one or two instances of outstanding genius, it has generally blunted his visual responses.

Yet, if we could meet the artist who painted this bison and see into his mind, I think we should be surprised. "Art" was certainly not one of the few words in his vocabulary. I doubt whether it would have been possible to convey to him the faintest idea of the meaning of the word.

On the other hand, if he could express himself in words, he might endeavor to make it clear to us that what we mistake for *art* is in reality *magic*: that the image he made of the bison on the wall of the cave was not done to please our eyes or provoke our admiration or even to supply documentary evidence about the appearance of bisons, but to give him, as hunter, power over the animal he hunted. The fact that other paleolithic artists, coming after him, would often superimpose another unrelated image on top of his, and for the same purpose, would not have disturbed him at all. It would not have occurred to him to complain, "You have ruined the composition of my picture," for though he was certainly what we would call an artist, and an exceptionally able one, he had no suspicion that he was creating a "work of art." He was not concerned with "composition" but with exercising his powers as a magician in order to turn himself into a more efficient hunter.

2. *Mycerinus and his Queen.*
IVth Dynasty, c. 2800 B.C.
Schist. Museum of Fine Arts, Boston

Egypt and State Religion

THERE IS SOMETHING rather frightening in the imperturbable perfection of Egyptian official art—and the bulk of it is official to a degree never achieved before or since. It is an art that enshrines a system, half political, half religious, so deeply rooted in the power of the gods, of the king and his hierarchy of priests, that it seems to have no purpose beyond that of evolving a set of invariable symbols of state religion. For that reason it is impressive, awe-inspiring and, for the most part, impersonal.

Almost all art, as this book will prove, draws its strength from its concern with human ambitions, dreams and struggles. But the strength of Egyptian art springs from its unquestioning acceptance of human decrees. It is the ultimate expression of obedience to authority. Hence its changelessness, its stiffness and its grandeur. It is, in itself, a ritual, and like all ritual it is both solemn and repetitive. Over a period of 3,000 years and through thirty dynasties, the "official" art of Egypt repeats with rare exceptions its hypnotic message in material chosen for its indestructibility and with a degree of subtle craftsmanship that combines unusual sensitivity with infinite patience.

Mycerinus and his Queen.   Egyptian IVth Dynasty.

WITH THE Fourth Dynasty, about 2600 B.C., Egyptian carving reached a formalized maturity, an impersonal grandeur, that it did not quite achieve again till the time of King Rameses II in the Nineteenth Dynasty, 1500 years later. But for all its ceremonial stiffness there is a touch of humanity in the Fourth Dynasty tomb statues of the kings, especially those of Mycerinus and Kephren. They give the impression of having *assumed* the authority of sovereignty for the purpose of art and of retaining the power to relax into informality when occasion permitted: Rameses, on the other hand, gives the impression of having been cast in an unchangeable mold.

Like all the best ceremonial statuary from Egypt, this wonderful group gives a first impression of mathematical simplicity, but after a moment's contemplation the eye discovers, beneath the rigid framework of these two bodies, a subtlety of surface that only occurs in the most sensitive sculpture. There are no unrealized passages, no meaningless conventions, no awkward transitions between torso and pelvis or pelvis and thigh, such as can always be found in archaic Greek figures. Nor is there any sense of strain, as though the king and queen were forcing themselves into a pose of authority that compelled them to hold their breath. Their gentle forward movement is not "frozen" despite the strict frontality of the two bodies.

Like the best Greek sculpture of the age of Pericles, pride of body is inherent in this king and queen. The difference between Egypt and Greece lies not in a different attitude to physical beauty but in a different attitude to authority. For Mycerinus and his queen, democracy is unthinkable. They are "on parade."

3. *Seated Figure.*
    XVIIIth Dynasty,
    c. *1500 B.C.*
    Granite. British Museum

Seated Figure. Egyptian XVIIIth Dynasty

ONLY AFTER a long and gradually developing submission to a set of traditional conventions could a sculptor have arrived at so perfect a compromise between humanity and geometry as this. Egyptian sculpture was notoriously conservative, except for one brief moment of uneasy freedom under the "heretic" king, Akhenaton. It was the servant of state religion and as such was concerned with symbols of power rather than with personalities. Hence it dealt in abstractions, but an abstraction as complete as this could only have been invented comparatively late (this statue was carved about 1500 B.C.) in Egyptian history. It is impossible to say whether the artist attempted to turn a cube into a man or to reduce a man to the form of a cube.

The statue "represents" (if anything so formalized can be described as a representation) a superintendent of the treasury under Hatshepsut and Thothmes III and the inscription gives us his name and station, but it is not a portrait, nor is there anything but the vaguest indication of the clothes he wore or the construction of his headdress. The function of the statue is to mark the position of the Treasurer's tomb.

The shaping of the cube, the subtle indication of arms folded across the knees, the diagonal of the concealed thighs, the curve of the shin, the diagrammatic indication of the extended hands are indications of complete mastery of sculptural form. Even the ears are formal abstractions.

Such a figure, the timeless symbol of impersonal officialdom, had to be carved in timeless material. The polished granite has proved impervious to the ravages of the years. It is exactly what it was when the sculptor completed it thirty-four centuries ago.

33

Greece. The Gods in Man's Image

EGYPTIAN ART extols authority; Greek art celebrates humanity. Slowly, as one turns the pages of history, the rigid crust of officialdom softens, the individual emerges. Democracy breaks through the polished surface. Bodies relax. Gestures begin to express human will rather than human obedience.

Yet, despite the Greek discovery that the human being was an individual and not a cog in the state machine, the development of that individual in Greek art was not in the direction of character or personality but of physique. What slowly evolved in Greek art from the archaic statues of the 7th Century to the mature sculpture of Pheidias and, later, Praxiteles, was a canon of physical perfection which, almost unconsciously, was to dominate the art of the Mediterranean basin for centuries to come. What the Greeks invented was a physical ideal—serene and, even in tragic situations, graceful. It was in Greece that the notion of standards of human beauty—the enemy of human character—originated. It was Greece that formulated the two theories to which the "classic" artist has always subscribed: that man is the measure of the created world, and (2) that though the created world in general and mankind in particular can never achieve perfection in any given example, it is the artist's task to discover and portray the physical perfection that is latent throughout the whole of creation. In doing so he evolves not individuals but types, and even his types must be few. They are limited, in fact, to four, the perfection of adolescence and of maturity, each of which can be divided into male and female.

In this pursuit of a canon of beauty, men become gods and the gods themselves become embodiments of the four types—Artemis and Hermes of adolescent perfection, Zeus and Hera of maturity. Greek literature can be permitted to refer to wilfulness and passion, to conflict and mental suffering: Greek sculpture, even when it describes energy, can rarely allow itself to look farther than the gymnasium. Hellenic man's faultless body was seldom regarded by the sculptor as a vessel to contain a soul, as it was to be later by the sculptors

34 of the Renaissance.

Greek Amphora and Kylix

T H E B E S T Chinese ceramics are beautiful in their own right. It is for their exquisite shape, their color, the texture of their glazes that we value them. Greek pottery has none of this oriental refinement. Its shapes are satisfying but pedestrian : its color—almost invariably a terra cotta inclining to orange-red—is unadventurous and monotonous. But when the Greek potter finished his work and handed it over to the vase-painter it came to life.

The surfaces of the amphora or two-handled jar, the lekythos or wine jar, and the inner and outer surfaces of the kylix, a shallow drinking cup with a base, afford the vase-painter an opportunity for practising an art which looks simple enough at first sight, but presented problems which were by no means easy to solve. The subjects, taken from mythology or epic poetry, or later from everyday life, in which figures are painted in black silhouette on a plain terra cotta ground or stand out in terra cotta on a black ground, are often composed with extraordinary skill and ingenuity. So much so, indeed, that our memory of even the best of the great Panathenaic amphorae (presented to the victors in the Panathenaic athletic contests) is not of their shape but of the paintings that adorn them.

Simple though these silhouettes may be, with a minimum of interior modeling of limbs and muscles and a mere linear indication of the fall of drapery or patterned embroidery, they had always to be designed on a curved surface, and the problem of overlapping figures in scenes involving crowds in action was one that would tax any painter's ingenuity.

The amphora and the interior of the kylix shown in Plates 4 and 5 were both Attic ware of the same century. Only about forty years separates them, but in that forty years the change-over from the "black-figure" to the "red-figure" style had taken place. The earlier method of imposing a black silhouette on to the plain red surface began to be supplanted by the more flexible red-figure style some time before 510 B.C.—which is the approximate date of the youth and girl in the circle of the kylix.

The black-figure amphora dates back to about 550 B.C. It is a good example of an elaborately decorated vase with borders running round the shoulder and the edges of the handles and a figure panel on both sides.

On the side which cannot be seen in the illustration is the wedding of King Peleus and the nymph Thetis—a ceremony which the gods attended. The side which we see (Plate 4) shows one of the vase painters' favorite subjects, a scene from the adventurous life of Herakles. The fight with Cycnus, the son of Ares, god of war, and Pelopia, is one of the less well-known phases of his

4. *Black-figure Amphora.*
c. 550 B.C. *Vase Painting.*
British Museum

crowded career, but the complicated action, involving no less than five figures, is described with masterly skill.

Herakles—as always, identifiable by his lion's skin and quiver—draws his sword to attack his adversary, who is armed with a tall plumed helmet and a circular shield. Between them stands Zeus with arms raised in a gesture of intervention. On the left, Athene, helmeted and richly attired in embroidered robes, urges Herakles on. Balancing her on the right stands Ares with a huge Boeotian shield and a visored helmet.

The spacing of the figures, their vigorous silhouettes, the scratched indications of drapery and brocaded patterns are in the best traditions of black-figure Attic ware.

The kylix (Plate 5) is a far more refined product of the Athenian potteries. It has been signed not only by the painter, Epictetus, but also by the potter, Python. The boy who plays a double flute and the girl dancing

5. *Red-figure Kylix.*
   c. 510 B.C. Vase painting.
   British Museum

with castanets are placed with delightful precision and balance within the circle that surrounds them. Their limbs are lighter and their movements less frozen than those of the black-figure painting.

But both red and black are instructive examples of the difficult art of silhouette. The indication of muscles on legs and arms by the finest of brush lines or delicate scratchings down to the background color have been reduced to a minimum. Without them and without the sparing use of a middle tone, a dull purple, on the amphora, the figures would have looked thin and papery. On the kylix the linear additions are almost nonexistent and there is no use of a third color. The effect of lithe movement has been achieved by line alone; one senses the rhythm of the dance that moves the two young bodies to the same musical tempo.

The Parthenon Pediment

EVER SINCE Lord Elgin, in 1812, shipped the sculptures of the Parthenon away from their home in Athens and deposited them in the British Museum they have remained in magnificent isolation, torn from their context but convincing enough to need no context.

6. *Diana and Aphrodite. Fragment of the Parthenon pediment.*
c. *440 B.C. Pentolic marble. British Museum*

If we think of any given cycle of art as inevitably moving from archaic to mature and from mature to decadent, it is impossible not to place the Parthenon sculptures at the exact climax of the progression, to fix that climax, as far as Athens is concerned, about the year 440 B.C., and to connect it with the sculptor Pheidias. It is not a question of regarding Pheidian sculpture as "better" than that of an earlier age (for until recently, owing to the constantly swinging pendulum of taste, the archaic boys and girls of 6th-Century Athens more easily satisfied our aesthetic appetites) but of feeling that the Parthenon is the inevitable destination towards which the Greeks were working and beyond which they could not progress without a sense of anticlimax.

It is significant that we do not know (and if we did the knowledge would be unimportant) whether these two monumental specimens of womanhood represent Diana and Aphrodite or two Fates or embodiments of Earth and Sea. They are idealizations of the mature human body in serene relaxation. Compared with them almost every other representation of the human figure in this book is uneasy, restless, imperfect, unsatisfied. Whether we are anxious to contemplate perfection or not, this is the nearest approach to it in art that we are likely to find.

Covering the magnificent limbs of these two women is an organization of drapery that reminds us sometimes of a cataract flowing over rocks, as in the tumbling folds between the breasts of the right-hand figure; sometimes of the contours on a map that explain the lie of the land, as in the drapery that stretches over her stomach or the thigh of her sister on the left; sometimes

of bodily movements, as in the ridges of drapery that are stretched between her knees. But in each case they form a pattern that contrasts with and enhances the smoothness of the bodies that emerge from them. The fact that the goddesses have lost their heads robs them of none of their impressiveness and, we may be sure, very little of their meaning. For this is the moment when it is the body and not the soul that demands human worship.

Flute Player of the Ludovisi Throne

THE EARLY Greek Ludovisi Throne (so called because it was discovered when the old Villa Ludovisi was demolished in 1887) in the Terme Museum in Rome and the similar set of reliefs in the Museum of Fine Arts in Boston are enigmatic both in style and in purpose. If they were indeed the back and sides of two carved marble thrones they must have been uncomfortably large; or perhaps they were intended as bases for seated statues.

Stylistically they are equally puzzling. There is a strange mixture in them of archaism and sophistication, as though some provincial sculptor—

7. *Flute Player from the Ludovisi Throne.*
   Early 5th Century B.C. Marble.
   Museo delle Terme, Rome

probably Ionian—who was familiar with mature Greek sculpture, had deliberately copied the mannerisms and the naïveté of an earlier age. It is humiliating to have to confess that one cannot solve the problem of so attractive a group of works, but they are the only ones of their kind that we know. They produce on us the effect of great lyric poetry which has surprisingly adopted a slightly colloquial turn of phrase. We find them all the more endearing for that reason, yet "endearing" just fails to describe their tender perfection. They are much more human in gesture and movement than any other surviving work of the period—the early 5th Century B.C.—and we have, in their presence, none of that sense of respectful admiration that most Greek carving of the figure inspires.

The central relief shows Aphrodite rising from the sea. On the right a shrouded woman tends a lighted lamp; on the left is the girl in the illustration, naked, playing a flute. One thinks of her, as of no other Greek female nude, familiarly, as a "teenager." She sits so casually, with crossed legs, and her playing is utterly free from self-consciousness. She is amusing herself and has no thought of impressing a spectator. The outline of her limbs is firm and simple, and the sculptor has deliberately contained her hair in a cloth so as not to break the simplicity by having to solve that eternal sculptor's problem, the discovery of a sculptural convention for hair.

Symbolically, she and her companion, the shrouded woman, together suggest some such meaning as Sacred and Profane Love. That in itself, in a carving dedicated to the cult of Aphrodite, is a concept more typical of Renaissance Italy than of pre-Christian Greece.

If one searches for a literary counterpart to the carvings on the Ludovisi Throne, the lyrics of Herrick come to mind, with their polished perfection and their irresponsible charm.

Coins from Syracuse and Acanthe

I N 1870 John Ruskin, in a lecture as Slade Professor at Oxford, selected the head of Arethusa on this silver coin (Plate 8), struck in Syracuse in celebration of a Syracusan victory over the Etruscans, and described it to his students as follows. "The relief... simplifies itself into a pearl-like portion of a sphere with exquisitely graded light on its surface... and each smaller portion, cheek or brow or leaf or tress of hair, resolves itself into a rounded or undulated surface, pleasant by gradation of light... That these intricately modulated surfaces present some resemblance to a girl's face, such as the Syracusans imagined that of the watergoddess Arethusa, is entirely a secondary matter."

8. *Arethusa: Coin from Syracuse.*
   c. 430 B.C. Silver.
   American Numismatic Society

Thus forty years before the appearance of the first abstract painting, Ruskin was already insisting on the abstract basis of all art. Today we are accustomed to read the abstract meanings of any representational work of art. Arethusa's four dolphins are there, we know, to impart a clockwise rotating movement to the static head. The circle that encloses it and echoes the circle of the coin itself also underlines the sphere of her head. The lettering *Syrakosion* adds a new element of crisp pattern to the gradations of light on the dolphins. Even her earrings and the string of pearls at the base of her neck contribute to the abstract elements that make the coin—no more than an inch in diameter—so profoundly satisfying as an essay in pure design.

To the Syracusans themselves there was the added satisfaction of symbolism. Dolphins reminded them of the seagirt island of Sicily on which they lived, the wreath worn by Arethusa was for them a proud symbol of victory against their enemies on the mainland. She herself was their patron goddess and her head appears on a long series of Syracusan coins in which her hair is dressed in a surprising variety of elaborate coiffures. Sometimes it is contained in a net, sometimes it breaks out into a riot of little curls. The Syracusans were as proud of their coin-engravers as were the Athenians of their vase-painters, so that frequently the signature of the artist is to be found on the coins of Syracuse.

41

9. *Lion Attacking Bull:*
   Coin from Acanthe.
   c. *424 B.C. Silver.*
   American Numismatic Society

The second specimen of a ten-drachma silver coin is of about the same period but comes from Acanthe in the Calchidice. Its date is about 424 B.C. The vigorous design of a lion attacking a bull was the emblem of the city. All that Ruskin said about the abstract perfection of the Arethusa coin is equally true of this more compact study of violent action. Each animal retains its own character and its own characteristic behavior. The sagging, wrinkled folds of the bull's dewlap, its desperate struggle to raise its head in order to gore with its horns the belly of the lion, the modeling of the lion's claws and the bull's hoofs and the bold indication of the lion's mane—all these are indicated in a kind of sculptural shorthand within a circle one inch in diameter, exactly the same size as the Syracusan coin, but the problem of design and the need for realism make even more demands on the artist of Acanthe.

The Mediaeval World

THE RECOGNITION of Christianity by the Emperor Constantine, in the first quarter of the 4th Century A.D., produced the most far-reaching revolution that had ever happened in the arts of Europe. It was inevitable that it should do so. Physical beauty was gradually ousted by spiritual striving. The soul, not the body, was the preoccupation of the newly established religion, and since the Church had almost a monopoly in the patronage of the arts, the arts themselves (and especially the arts of painting and sculpture) abandoned their concern with the beauty of this world in order to explore the soul of man and its destiny. Even aesthetic philosophy acknowledged this new set of standards in the visual arts when Plotinus (A.D. 203-270) announced that "beauty" in art was not to be achieved by the imitation of beauty in nature but was the direct outcome of divine inspiration.

That inspiration could take many forms. In Southwestern Europe the Byzantine mosaicists formalized and simplified their figures but presented them to the eye with a richness of color and a complexity of decoration and design that would have puzzled and dismayed an Athenian of the time of Pericles. The mosaics of Ravenna have an oriental gorgeousness; the Book of Kells a delicate but tortured elaboration; the Romanesque carvings on French cathedrals a set of ascetic vertical or spiral rhythms; the 12th-Century mosaics of Sicily an awe-inspiring starkness that had never been seen in art before.

The Middle Ages all over Europe, for all their preoccupation with the unseen, the spiritual and the symbolic, produced art of extraordinary richness and gaiety. It was an age in which the crafts flourished; once the imitation of physical appearances had become unimportant, stained glass, inlaid enamel, tapestry, mosaic and jeweled metalwork could be just as capable of expressing the artist's intentions as paint or carved stone. For that reason flowered tapestries, the glowing colors of glass, the richness of mosaic are among the most precious and satisfying things the mediaeval world produced.

Perhaps the most revealing contrast—and one that cannot be illustrated in this book—between the classicism of Greece and Rome on the one hand and the restless romanticism of the Middle Ages, would be the juxtaposition of a Greek temple, solid, static, clear-cut and noble, and a Gothic cathedral, fretted, restless, dynamic, mysterious and often playful.

43

10. *Abraham and the Three Angels. Mid-5th Century. Mosaic. Santa Maria Maggiore, Rome*

The Mosaics of Santa Maria Maggiore, Rome

I T I S S T I L L uncertain whether the long series of mosaics high up on the walls of the nave of Santa Maria Maggiore in Rome were commissioned by Pope Liberius (A.D. 352-366) or by Sixtus III almost a century later. If Liberius was responsible then they are by far the earliest Christian mosaics reproduced in this book; if not they would have been executed at about the same time as the Mausoleum of Galla Placidia in Ravenna (see Plate 11).

Whatever their date they are more "Roman" in style than the Good Shepherd mosaic in Ravenna. The artist has been more interested in narrative and in the gestures that explain his story. They are more spirited, less hieratic.

The cycle, which once consisted of forty-two separate mosaic pictures, of which only twenty-seven now exist, deals entirely with Old Testament history and the stories of Abraham, Jacob, Moses and Joshua. The panel shown in Plate 10 describes three stages: the meeting of Abraham and the three angels, Abraham commanding his wife, Sarah, to prepare a meal and (on the right) the angels seated at the table on which the meal is served, as described in the eighteenth chapter of the book of Genesis.

What is remarkable about the execution of the panel is the almost Impressionistic use of the tesserae to suggest the light on the robes and the landscape, and the expression on the faces of the angels as they gaze sideways at their host. A single tessera of white set beside another black tessera are sufficient to render the eye and the pupil and the direction of the glance. Abraham himself has the air of a Roman senator and the tent in which he lived with his wife has become a Roman house.

The lower portion of the mosaic, including the amphora of wine below the table, has perished and has been clumsily restored in painted stucco, but the upper portions are still in good condition

Mausoleum of Galla Placidia, Ravenna

T H E S M A L L , cruciform brick building that occupies a modest corner near the Church of San Vitale in Ravenna and is known as the Mausoleum of Galla Placidia, was, in the middle of the 5th Century A.D., part of an ambitious architectural ensemble that included an Imperial Palace. Today the mausoleum is all that is left from a century in which Ravenna was the western capital of the empire.

To enter this unostentatious little brick box is to experience the most

11. *Good Shepherd. Mid-5th Century. Mosaic.*
Mausoleum of Galla Placidia, Ravenna

startling change of mood that awaits the traveler to Ravenna, that strange, decayed city of surprises. The cruciform ground plan with its squat central tower at the crossing (no more than thirteen feet square) is as clear from within as from without, but once the eyes have adjusted themselves to the dim light that filters in from the small sheet-alabaster windows, the effect is of an indescribable complexity of design and an unparalleled richness of subdued but saturated color. The barrel vaults are thickly patterned with rosettes of pink, green and gold on a ground of what has been aptly described as "moonlight blue." Borders of densely crowded foliage, fruit and flowers enclose these curved spaces. Eight apostles, arranged in four pairs, occupy the interior walls of the central tower, and the four tympanum-shaped ends of the cross are filled with mosaics of which the most familiar is that of the Good Shepherd—a beardless Christ seated among his sheep on a rocky mound covered with stunted bushes.

Galla Placidia, daughter of Theodosius the Great, sister of the Emperor Honorius and mother of the Emperor Valentinian III, arrived in Ravenna in

46

the second decade of the 5th Century and lived there most of her life. A few years before her death she must have built this little church and caused it to be filled with what are still aesthetically the most satisfying and technically the most accomplished 5th-Century mosaics in existence. The lower walls are covered with slabs of golden yellow marble. The mosaic is continuous through-out the upper portions.

Although it has been assumed, until recently, that the Mausoleum is the actual burial place of Galla Placidia, it is most probable that she was buried in Rome, where she died in A.D. 450. Mediaeval documents refer to a monas-tery of St. Lawrence near to the Church of San Vitale. As one of the mosaics in the mausoleum depicts St. Lawrence with his grill and the flames beneath it, the mausoleum may, in fact, be an oratory dedicated to the saint and martyr. None the less, the mosaics belong to the epoch of Galla Placidia and are certainly the earliest in the great series for which Ravenna is famous.

The design of the Good Shepherd tympanum (placed inside the building over the entrance door) is characteristic of a transitional era when the idioms of classic art were still familiar, but Christianity, established as an official religion by the Emperor Constantine little more than a century earlier, was beginning to tackle the difficult problem of working out a system of icono-graphy and a set of symbolic images that would express the new teaching and the new ideals without making too sharp a break with the stylistic tradi-tions of Greece and Rome.

As we know, the problem was solved slowly and the Byzantine style was the result. But in the earliest Christian mosaics in Ravenna and Rome, the new style and the old, the Christian wine and the pagan bottle, are sufficiently tolerant of each other to cause no feeling of contradiction in the spectator. The beardless Christ of the Good Shepherd tympanum has the ease of a pagan Apollo. The landscape and the sheep have all the inherent natural-ism of Hellenistic art. Yet the golden nimbus proclaims the divinity of the Shepherd: His rich garment suggests an attempt to symbolize a divine being by clothing Him as an emperor.

The treatment of the landscape and the depth and richness of color throughout both the decorative and the representational portions of the mosaics are manifestly derived from Eastern art. The mosaics are, in fact, a surprisingly successful attempt to create a new style out of three almost contradictory elements: oriental opulence, Hellenistic naturalism and Christian symbolism. In theory such an attempt would seem doomed to failure. In practice it is one of the most memorable instances of early Christian art and one of the most convincing of all Italian mosaics.

The Empress Theodora

THE SANCTUARY of the Church of San Vitale in Ravenna is probably one of the most satisfying examples of interior decoration in the world. The Church itself, built in the reign of the Emperor Justinian, early in the 6th Century, is modeled, in plan, on the great edifice of Santa Sophia in Constantinople. Seen from the outside it is a modest octagonal brick structure almost devoid of ornamentation. Inside, the octagonal space, with its seven symmetrical recesses and elongated sanctuary has a refinement of proportion and detail that arrest the eye at once, but the scale is spoiled by the addition of baroque motives awkwardly placed over the seven arched recesses. It is only when one enters the sanctuary that the full meaning of Byzantine mosaic, in relation to its architectural setting of marble columns with their intricately carved capitals and the complexity of wall spaces leading to the climax of the semidome, becomes clear.

The light is dimmed by small windows filled with transparent sheet alabaster and it requires a few moments to adjust one's eyes. But once that has happened the effect is breath-taking. In the semidome itself, a beardless Christ is seated on the globe of the world, flanked by saints, on a background of gold. Above, the vault rises, in green and gold, ornamented with garlands of leaves, flowers and peacocks, while four standing angels in white support the medallion where the garlands meet. On either side are rocky landscapes with groups of figures, half symbol, half narrative, representing the sacrifices of Abel and Melchisidech. Below these and nearer to the opening of the sanctuary are two panels: on the one side the Emperor Justinian with his guards and deacons, on the other, the Empress Theodora with her ladies in waiting. Our plate shows the head, with its magnificent barbaric crown, of the Empress.

Some such brief description of the whole scheme is necessary if one is to visualize the relationship of this tiny part to the whole. The color of the sanctuary mosaics have an oriental richness not to be found in mosaics elsewhere. But what matters—what makes the interior impossible to illustrate in any color reproduction—is its cumulative power.

That, of course, is lost in a detail, but the detail must stand for the whole. Certain painters—notably Seurat—have attempted, by the device of *pointillisme,* to find an equivalent to the vibrating surface of mosaic but the attempt was bound to fail. For in mosaic, each of the tesserae, besides having its own color, also has its own angle and its own power to catch and reflect the light. Mosaic is a method of incrustation. The effect is of a wall built of semi-precious stones.

48

12. *Empress Theodora (detail). Early 6th Century. Mosaic. San Vitale, Ravenna*

It is a stubborn medium which imposes its own slow, deliberate tempo on the artist who uses it. Each cube of cut colored glass or each square of gold (gold leaf diffused between a solid glass base and a paper-thin covering of clear glass) has to be bedded separately into the mastic which dries slowly and, once dry, becomes an integral part of the wall itself.

Such an art defies realism and is therefore bound to be used either as decoration or symbolism. Figures executed in mosaic tend to be static and awe-inspiring. It is therefore astonishing to find, in San Vitale, these two large commemorative panels, celebrating the presence of the Emperor and Empress at the dedication of the church around the year 547, filled with portraiture—and portraiture of a convincing kind. Among this complex of decoration and supernatural beings are a man and a woman with their attendants, full of character, ablaze with crowns and jewels and brocaded dresses.

Secular mosaics at this period are rare. And without their larger architectural context of symbolism, these two panels would lose much of their effect—the effect of a documentary voice intruding into an awe-inspiring incantation. Yet the unity of the medium seems to lift them, despite their subject matter, onto a symbolic plane. They ought to strike a slightly jarring note. In fact they do the reverse. The two earthly rulers in their imperial robes take their place quite comfortably below Abel and Melchisidech in their mountain settings and the Christ in His glowing golden dome who dominates the whole sanctuary.

The Raising of Lazarus. Sant'Apollinare Nuovo, Ravenna

THREE personalities dominate the early history of Ravenna and make it a place of pilgrimage for students of the early history of mosaics—Galla Placidia, who died in 450 A.D., the Emperor Theodoric (493-526) and his successor, Justinian, who built the church of San Vitale. If the mosaics of Justinian are the most gorgeous, those of Theodoric, as seen in the interior of the church of Sant'Apollinare Nuovo, are the most solemn.

The church itself is a basilica, long and narrow, and the walls of the nave, supported on graceful arches, are filled with mosaics arranged in three horizontal bands. The lowest zone, immediately above the arches, consists of a hypnotic procession of figures, martyrs on the right, who move from the Emperor's palace at the west end of the church toward the enthroned Christ: virgins on the left, who leave the seaport of Classis and proceed, with the same measured tread, to an enthroned Virgin.

Above this zone, set between the windows, are isolated single figures of prophets and authors of the Bible. And above these again, in the space between the windows and the cornice, a series of mosaic panels, smaller in

13. *The Raising of Lazarus. Early 6th Century. Mosaic.*
Sant'Apollinare Nuovo, Ravenna

scale, livelier and more dramatic in design, and narrative in content. Those
on the left show scenes from the Miracles and Parables of Christ: those on
the right illustrate His Passion. Our plate shows the miracle of the raising of
Lazarus.

Its extreme simplification makes it evident that the artist was anxious
in this, as in all the other panels, to concentrate on essentials in the interests
of narrative clarity. Nothing could be more explicit than the relationship of
the three figures—the dead Lazarus in his white shroud, framed by the darkness of the tomb, the commanding, outstretched arm of the Christ and the
awestruck gesture of the nameless third figure who must symbolize the onlookers.

The medium is handled with wonderful economy both of line and color,
so that although the whole series is placed high up on the wall, each panel
clearly delivers its separate message. Each one is, as it were, a diagram—a
visual equivalent of shorthand—yet each is an essentially human interpretation
of an event.

Illuminated Initial from the Book of Kells

IN THE whole corpus of masterpieces of the illuminator's art, the Book of Kells, probably produced at the little town of Kells in Ireland some time in the 9th Century, is as exquisite in its way as anything done at a later date, even including the Hours of Turin with its miniature paintings by Jan Van Eyck or the Très Riches Heures of the Duc de Berry by Pol de Limbourg (Plate 39), both done six centuries later.

Its origins are mysterious, the names of the artists responsible for it are unknown. They were men of extraordinary skill and patience and their capacity for containing the minutest of detail within the framework of monumental design is surprising. At least two enthusiastic students in our own century have attempted to copy the page reproduced here and have been defeated by the minuteness of the ornament and have lacked the patience required to finish the task. The book has suffered many adventures, including its abduction from the Church of Kells where it was displayed as early as 1006, the removal of its golden binding studded with jewels, its burial in the earth and its recovery some months later, with many of its vellum pages discolored and others (which might have revealed the names of the artists) missing.

It consists of 339 pages, each measuring, even after being ruthlessly trimmed by a 19th-Century binder, 13×9½ inches. It contains eight pages of elaborately ornamented Eusebian Canons, a miniature of the Virgin and Child, seventeen pages of "summaries" of the four Gospels, a few pages of legal documents, and, lastly, the four Gospels in Latin, including symbols and portraits of the Evangelists and certain full pages of exceptional splendor, of which the *Christi autem* page is one. The text is written in the large script typical of early Celtic illumination with decorated capitals.

The passage beginning with the eighteenth verse of the first chapter of the Gospel according to St. Matthew—the words *Christi autem generatio* ("Now the birth of Jesus Christ was on this wise...")—was the Gospel for the Christmas Mass and so received special attention. No photographic reproduction can do justice to the intricacy and precision of the ornament, which sums up the whole vocabulary of the Celtic decorative style with its interlacings and its "trumpet" patterns. But to isolate a detail for enlargement would be to destroy the magnificent flow of the huge X (the first letter of the word Christ) which swirls across the page and encloses in its finials nine large circles and many smaller ones, packed with spiral ornament. The remainder of the wording consists of the interlocked *rho* and *iota* and the abbreviated *autem* joined to the *generatio* relegated to the bottom right hand

14. *Initial from the Book of Kells.*
9th Century. Illumination.
Trinity College, Dublin

corner of the page. There is a wealth of subsidiary detail, both representational and formal, clinging precariously to the firm outline of the initial.

Almost too small to be deciphered in a reduced reproduction are the angel at the top; groups of angels at the side, below and to the left of the diamond-shaped crossing; and at the bottom a touch of theological comedy where two rats nibble the Eucharistic Bread while two cats look on.

It is not the most richly colored page in the book, for the portraits and symbols of the Evangelists are carried out in the saturated blues and reds of enamel. But it is the noblest, the most flexible in design and the most crowded —but never overcrowded—in detail. The colors, in view of the artist's exceptional self-imposed task, must have been quite deliberately muted. One feature of the page is the purple that forms the plain band which runs round the whole of the *chi* and detaches it from the rest of the design without interfering with the wonderful unity of the whole effect.

53

15. *The Adoration of the Magi.*
    c. 1120-30. Whalebone.
    Victoria and Albert Museum,
    London

The Adoration of the Magi (Whalebone Carving)

THIS REMARKABLE little carving—fourteen inches high and only six inches wide at its base—is evidently the work of a monumental designer forced to work on a small scale, but unwilling to omit anything that he would have put in had his Virgin and Child been life-sized. The result is
54 an effect of tremendous compression: not a square millimeter of the available

surface has been wasted, not a fold of drapery or a detail of embroidered borders or a jeweled headdress has been shirked. Yet the amount of detail—the gathered curtain above her head and the formalized flowers at her feet—is not just the result of a restless desire to fill every corner: it is part of a controlled design and they are bound together by a set of rhythms that takes little account of human anatomy or relative human scale.

In the middle of this fretted arabesque of intricate carving, the Virgin's head and the halo that surrounds it (hardly more than two inches in diameter in the original) dominate the whole design. It was dramatically inevitable, one feels, that her head should be too large for her body; that her body should dwarf those of the Magi who gather round her, offering gifts to her Divine Child; that the Child should be framed in a kind of niche formed above, by the borders of her cloak, and below, by the *V*-shaped fall of the drapery between her knees.

The more one examines this little masterpiece of carving, the more satisfying and inventive it becomes—the pattern formed by the legs of the Magi, the frame made by the fanlike folds of the curtain, the general tendency to rigid lines which make the occasional sweeping curves all the more significant, the slowly rising diagonal of the four cupped hands in the center.

There is something hypnotic in the expression of the Virgin's face. It, and the area to the left of it where the sculptor has placed the guiding star, are the only smooth areas in the whole of the carved surface. Her eyes seem to stare sadly into the future.

It is not known whether the anonymous carver came from England or from Northern France, though the architecture above the canopy suggests an English origin. Nor can it be guessed whether this was a small, self-contained object of devotion or part of a larger assemblage of carvings for an altar.

The Apse Mosaic of Cefalù Cathedral

S U C C E S S I V E civilizations have left a more decisive mark on the island of Sicily than on any other corner of Europe. The Greeks built temples at Syracuse and Selinunte, at Agrigento and Segesta which hostile Phoenician invaders damaged but did not completely destroy. The Romans colonized the island and built the famous amphitheatre at Taormina; later, the Arabs conquered it and were, in turn, subdued by the Normans.

Throughout the Middle Ages and the Renaissance, Sicily produced interesting though never magnificent architects, sculptors and painters. But the golden age of Sicilian civilization was the 12th Century when three successive Norman kings of Sicily built the great palace in Palermo and that

gem of architecture, the Cappella Palatina with its Arab ceiling, and filled it with the loveliest mosaics in Southern Italy.

Less lovely but more inspiring than the Cappella Palatina, or the huge church of Monreale in the hills above Palermo, is the Cathedral of Cefalù, built on a rock and backed by a granite precipice, dominating the little town.

All the mosaics in the cathedral are concentrated in the apse. The rest of the church is a vast, gray, austere and empty monument of Sicilian Gothic. And because of its spacious emptiness, the mosaics of the apse are overpowering. The head and shoulders of Christ, Pantocrator, high in the semidome is both alarming and uplifting, not only by virtue of sheer size (the head alone is over fifteen feet high) but also because of its strange fusion of calmness and severity. It is the symbol of passionless justice untempered by mercy. Below, on the curved walls of the apse are three superimposed rows of single figures of saints, less powerful but equally passionless.

No photograph can convey the effect of the contrast between the tomb-like emptiness of the nave and the crowded austerity of the apse to which it forms a prelude. For no photograph can relate a visual climax to its context. One has the impression of finding oneself unexpectedly in an empty court of justice in which the judge, motionless and silent and clothed in the full panoply of divine law, awaits the arrival not of a single sinner but of the whole of mankind. The only concessions to the eye's search for charm and glitter that mosaic can alone achieve are in the decorative borders that frame the whole unit of the apse.

Isaiah from the Abbey of Souillac

HERE, in the portal of the Benedictine Abbey of Souillac, is a more dynamic example of Romanesque carving than the preceding plate. Its date is possibly a little earlier, and the single figure of the prophet Isaiah has a fiercer movement, for he has not only more room to move in, architecturally speaking, but there is more reason for his powerful gesture as he strides forward and proudly displays the scroll on which his prophecies are written.

Something of the angry poetry of his writings can be felt in the zigzag movement of his body, the sweeping folds of his cloak, the tension of his fingers holding the scroll and the backward turn of his head.

The linear folds of his robe and cloak are more thinly spaced than in the whalebone Adoration of the Magi. That is not surprising, for here the sculptor has attempted to give his figure a bulk and rotundity that is not common in French Romanesque. Although his cloak clings to the flat surface of the wall behind him, he himself seems to struggle to achieve the fully three-dimensional existence of a free-standing figure. Where the designer of

57

16. *Christ Pantocrator. 12th Century. Mosaic Apse of Cefalù Cathedral, Sicily*

the "Adoration of the Magi» carved the sharp furrows of drapery in order to produce a pattern that is almost independent of the limbs beneath them, here the finely drawn lines that indicate the tension of the drapery actually emphasize the roundness of the limbs: curving across the torso, pulled tight across the extended left arm, stretched across the thigh and loosely festooned where the cloak hangs free.

17. *The Prophet Isaiah. c. 1110. Stone. Abbey of Souillac*

18. *Chasse of St. Valerie. 12th Century. Champlevé enamel. British Museum*

Limoges Enamel

THE CRAFT of fusing colored glass onto a metal base was familiar to the Greeks. In mediaeval Europe it became popular for small, highly colored objects, especially plaques and reliquaries, and the two main centers of production, Cologne and Limoges, were active from the early 12th Century. In the work of the Limoges enamelers of the late 12th and early 13th Centuries, a limited but brilliant range of color—lapis lazuli, turquoise blue, greens and dull yellows and a range of bright reds—was used, contrasting with the engraved metal grounds with a startlingly rich effect.

Doubtless the craftsmen of Limoges paid unusual attention to the design and execution of certain reliquaries belonging to local saints and this Chasse, designed to contain a relic of St. Valerie, is not only one of the most beautiful of its kind but also one of the most explicit and elaborate in its iconography. The story of the saint's martyrdom is set forth in considerable detail on the front of the casket (which is about twelve inches in length) and on its movable lid.

The story of St. Valerie, patron saint of Limoges, the rich and virtuous daughter of an early governor of Aquitaine of the time of the Emperor Nero, 59 is not lacking in incident. She was affianced to her father's destined successor, but before her marriage she was converted to Christianity by St. Martial, took vows of chastity, decided to devote her life entirely to religion and broke off her engagement. Enraged at this insult, her betrothed ordered her execution, and the left half of the casket depicts his commanding gesture to the executioner who seizes her by the wrist, brandishing his sword. As she is led away, the story relates, she predicts to the executioner that his death will occur shortly after her own. The right hand side of the casket describes how, in the presence of the amazed citizens, she is beheaded, but her body remains upright and she catches her head (which now acquires a nimbus) while the hand of the Almighty, issuing from a cloud, blesses her. With her head in her arms she walks, so the chroniclers tell us, to the Cathedral, where she presents it (on the right hand end of the lid) to St. Martial as he is celebrating Mass. Meanwhile the astonished executioner returns to his master (see the left hand end of the cover) to report the event and is struck by lightning, represented by a red arrow emerging from a highly decorative thunderstorm.

The subsequent conversion of the rejected fiancé and the restoration to life of the executioner are not described in this spirited narrative, nor the miracles performed by her remains after burial.

This is surely one of the loveliest examples of what is essentially a small-scale craft, jewel-like in its distribution of color and metal but closely allied to mosaic in its power to tackle narrative on a decorative level. The date of the casket is about 1170. The hidden side of the cover and the back of the casket are treated with equal elaboration but are purely decorative.

The Youths in the Fiery Furnace

THE LITTLE PLAQUE shaped like a large fish scale, which tells the story of Shadrach, Meshach and Abednego, who disobeyed King Nebuchadnezzar when ordered to worship his golden image, is even finer in craftsmanship.

It comes from the area between Cologne and the Meuse Valley. Though there is no means of telling exactly where it was made, since enamelers' furnaces were easily transported, this is almost certainly made by the most famous of the Cologne enamelers, Godefroid de Claire of the town of Huy, between Liège and Namur. It was probably the lowest section of a set of four similarly shaped plaques arranged round a rectangular central panel. It is exceptional in that the faces, instead of the usual engraved and chased metal, are also carried out in enamel. The design is particularly spirited and the angels' wings sweep magnificently across the curve of the border.

19. *Youths
in the Fiery Furnace.
12th Century.
Champlevé and cloisonné enamel
on copper. Museum of Fine Arts, Boston*

The story of the three youths begins in the third chapter of the book of Daniel and is continued in the Apocrypha. Having been cast into the fiery furnace, in which they remained unscathed, the angel of the Lord came down into the oven and smote the flame of fire out of the oven. Whereupon the three broke into the song of praise whose beginning is inscribed on the scroll that lies across them—"Blessed art thou, O Lord God of our fathers: and to be praised and exalted above all for ever."

The Mosaics of St. Mark's, Venice

THE RADIANCE of the western façade of St. Mark's basilica in Venice is broken only by the five dark doors, each flanked by clusters of 61 columns in colored marble, leading to a kind of wide corridor—the atrium—in which pilgrims assembled and waited before penetrating into the interior of the church. It is a spacious but, by contrast with the dazzling brightness of the façade, a dark enclosure, whose vaults and shallow overhead domes are filled with mosaics, crowded with symbolism and narrative, all drawn from the stories and narratives of the Old Testament, completed for the most part in the 11th Century.

Here the pilgrims, seated on the tessellated pavement and looking up into the domes, learned the stories of the Creation, of Noah and the building of the Ark, of Joseph and the exile in Egypt. The intention of the designers and craftsmen responsible for these mosaics was to pack as much incident as possible into the available space, and to give the maximum simplicity and vivacity to each separate section of the narrative.

As one enters the atrium by the door on the far right, the dome containing the narrative of the Creation is directly overhead, arranged in a sequence of panels in neat, concentric circles and treated as a chronological sequence, rather in the manner of the comic strip cartoon of today.

Each of the successive days of creation is given its own essential pattern —the dividing of light from darkness, the undulating rhythms of the sea, the sparkle of the newly created sun, moon and stars, the arrival of birds and animals, the making of Adam, the first man, and of Eve, his partner in the Garden of Eden, the temptation and disobedience, the introduction of clothes (this amounts to the earliest fashion plate in the history of civilization) and the expulsion from the Garden.

When the mosaics were made, an illiterate population must have regarded this combination of visual symbol with a minimum of text as a delightful form of instruction. Today, familiar as we are with the story told, we can regard these mosaics largely as decoration and admire them for their startling economy and explicitness. For example, the sequence of days is indicated by the number of attendant angels that denote each division in that critical first week in the history of the world. The 11th Century was an ideal moment for such an undertaking. The solemnity of early Byzantine iconography was giving place to the new Gothic interest in the fascinating details of nature. Each animal has its own shape and its own personality. Adam and Eve, a little uncouth and bewildered, still belong to the innocent animal world. The complex struggles between the forces of good and evil, prosperity and adversity portrayed in the other domes of the narthex, have not yet begun. The dawn of human history has been reduced to a delightful and colorful diagram.

The interior of the basilica is even darker and richer in decoration than the atrium. Panels of streaked Cippolino marble form a continuous dado above which the vaults rise upward, surmounted by domes coated with mosaics, most of which were carried out in the 11th and 12th Centuries which understood the problems of how to handle the medium. Those portions of the

20. and 21. *The Days of the Creation (detail). 12th Century. Mosaic.*
St. Mark's, Venice. BELOW, *view of the dome*

22. *The Baptism of Christ. 12th Century. Mosaic.*
St. Mark's, Venice

walls that remained unfinished in the 12th Century were completed in the
16th, which notoriously did not have the understanding. They were designed
by great masters—Tintoretto among them—and carried out by efficient craftsmen. But while the earlier mosaics in the basilica are among the best in Italy
outside Ravenna, the later ones are a cumulative aesthetic *faux pas* which can
only be forgiven because of the grandeur and dignity of the interior as a whole.

In one section of the basilica, however, the earlier style is not interfered
with by the artistic mistakes of a later age. The baptistry, with its series of
mosaics of the life of St. John the Baptist, is the most satisfactory single
ensemble in the church. The sprightliness of the dance of Salome before Herod
and the solemnity of the baptism are equal claimants in any anthology of
Italian mosaics. Of the two I have preferred the baptism, because of the
comparative simplicity of its composition and its special use of an accepted

64

Byzantine iconographical tradition which includes the hand of God emerging from clouds, the descending Holy Ghost, the ax laid at the foot of the vine, the God of the River Jordan and the three attendant angels holding towels on the bank of the river.

In the whole of the great interior there is no single panel with a grander design or more subtly harmonized color.

The Pala d'Oro of St. Mark's

THE INTERIOR of St. Mark's basilica in Venice is one of the most sumptuous spectacles in Europe. Its tessellated pavements, its marble dadoes and columns, its intricately carved capitals, and its mosaics that fill the upper walls and domes with a rich but subdued glow of gold and color offer a bewilderment of decorative detail to the eye which only achieves unity because of the simplicity of the basic architectural plan. One would have thought that no single item in such an interior could have caught and held the eye by virtue of its special intensity of richness, yet the Pala d'Oro,—the screen that rises behind the high altar, filling the space between the two eastern columns that support the ciborium, or architectural canopy overhead— succeeds in establishing itself as a decorative climax to the whole interior.

Nearly four feet in height and six in breadth, it consists of a gold ground fretted with chased metalwork, encrusted with jewels and inlaid with panels of brightly colored enamel. In the top section three scenes from the New Testament are arranged on either side of a quatrefoil of the Archangel Michael. Below, divided by jeweled borders, are thirty-two figures of prophets, apostles and angels, and in the center is the most elaborate section of all, in which an enthroned Christ is seated between four medallions containing the four Evangelists. It is this section that is shown in Plate 23.

It would be impossible to imagine that a work of sheer craftsmanship could contain more elaborate or more ornate workmanship, and from a detailed description of the Pala one might guess at a final effect that was positively vulgar in its glittering showmanship. Yet the design of the whole is so firm and steady that the result, far from being vulgar, is even solemn in its unity.

The Pala consists largely of Byzantine work from Constantinople, done at various periods between the 11th and 12th Centuries, with subsequent additions as late as the 14th. In fact it was slowly built up, changing its form as successive doges added to it or reorganized it. It did not achieve its final form until 1345, under Doge Andrea Dandolo, though is existed in the church in its present position, though smaller, under Doge Pietro Orseolo I, late in the 10th Century.

Chartres Cathedral.   The Last Supper

THE ART of the stained glass window is hardly a thousand years old and the possibilities of the medium were not fully exploited until the 12th and 13th Centuries. It is an art that belongs to northwestern Europe. It was, in fact, an inevitable by-product of Gothic architecture which increasingly stressed the importance of the window; whereas mosaic was a necessary corollary of Byzantine architecture, of which the essence was the wall.

Technically, stained glass depends on two factors, the manufacture of transparent colored glass and the discovery that small pieces of such glass could be held together by strips of lead. Aesthetically it differs from every other medium in that it uses transmitted instead of reflected light and can therefore achieve a chromatic intensity denied to every other medium. This intensity is increased partly by the network of black leadlines that lies across the window and isolates each fragment of colored glass from its neighbour; and partly (and more important, since the window is the source of illumination of the interior in which it is seen) it must always have the effect of a luminous area surrounded by darkness. In order fully to realize the emotional impact of such an effect it is necessary to stand, say, at the transept crossing of the Cathedral of Chartres and look at the two rose windows high up to right and left. There, one is dazzled by the saturated intensity of the blues and reds of the 13th-Century French craftsmen. Only in the art of the stained glass window is visual drama of this kind attainable.

Realism, as understood by the Italian Renaissance, is impossible in such a medium. Consequently the art of stained glass fell into decay in the centuries that followed, and not until our own has a successful attempt been made to take advantage of those qualities which the mediaeval world understood so well. The reader will find in this book no example of stained glass between the 13th and the 20th Century and he will probably be impressed by the similarity of effect between the windows by French artists of the 13th Century in the Cathedral of Chartres and those by John Piper in the chapel of Oundle School in England. It is a similarity partly imposed by the demands of the medium itself but largely by the modern full acceptance of symbolism and the modern discovery of spiritual potentialities in stubborn media.

Because stained glass is the only important medium that depends on transmitted light seen in comparative darkness no reproduction on a printed page and seen by reflected light can do more than approximate justice to it. Yet to omit it altogether would be absurd. I have limited the examples of it to two plates, whereas it deserves, on its merits, a dozen.

23. *The Pala d'Oro (detail).* c. 1345. *Enamel, gold, jewels.*
St. Mark's, Venice

24. *The Last Supper. 13th Century. Stained Glass.
Chartres Cathedral*

Partly in order to break their surfaces into manageable decorative areas and partly in order to create a multiplicity of subsidiary spaces to be filled with narrative or imagery, the glass of the larger windows of the great French cathedrals is split up into a geometrical patterning of diamond shapes, circles and quatrefoils, surrounded by borders, thus giving the eye a double delight, first in reading the all-over pattern and then examining in turn each smaller panel.

This detail, which shows a Last Supper from Chartres, is an example of 13th-Century French glass at its best. Yet its quality could be matched by a hundred similar details both in Chartres itself and in the equally magnificent though less familiar windows of Sens and Bourges. The artist's respect for the problem of scale in design has prevented him from attempting to crowd thirteen figures into the space at his disposal, yet the full meaning of the Last Supper is preserved. Each of the figures has its own character, from the monumental dignity of the Christ in the center to the awkward gesture of the disciple (presumably Judas) on the near side of the table.

Yet one feels that the problem uppermost in the artist's mind is not that of iconography but of color distribution and particularly the difficult balance of white as against the main masses of red, blue and golden yellow. For the secret of the brilliance in such panels lies in the sparkle given by small areas of plain, uncolored glass. The double border of minute white circles, like two strings of pearls, that contains the broader leaf-pattern border in which areas of darker color alternate, forms a strong framework to what lies within the circle. Here the whites are still used sparingly but they are distributed with wonderful skill, and the central halo, of vivid red relieved by a white cross, forms the climax of the design. No single area of color has been left unbroken. The table is patterned with a Gothic diaper design, the tablecloth hangs in conventional folds. The more closely one examines the composition the more one realizes the artist's unerring sense of color balance.

Drunkenness of Noah. Palace of the Doges, Venice

I T I S a sad but essentially human weakness that makes us look less closely and feel less deeply about works whose authors are not known to us. The mediaeval world produced many masterpieces that are just as powerful as those of a later date by artists whose names are familiar. No one knows, for example, who carved the three groups at the angles of the Venetian Ducal Palace, yet two of them—the Drunkenness of Noah and the Judgment of Solomon—deserve a place in any anthology of memorable European sculpture. They, and the elaborately carved capitals of the long arcade below them, offer inexhaustible material for the study of late Venetian Gothic sculpture.

Of the three "angle" groups, the Drunkenness of Noah is both the most familiar and the most human. Every day, crowds that drift along the Riva degli Schiavoni toward the Piazzetta pause as they mount the steps of the bridge over the little canal, which divides the prison from the palace. They glance to the right at the Bridge of Sighs that links the two buildings, and 69 then, as they begin to descend again, find themselves unexpectedly at eye level with this group and almost within touching distance of it.

Although it performs no architectural function, it marks the angel of the great building without weakening it. The drama inherent in the group of three men, the swaying, half-naked body of the father as he empties the bowl of wine, the sturdy figures of his two sons, the younger of whom discretely replaces the loin cloth while the elder frowns disapproval of his father's unseemliness— all this is immediately arresting as narrative. Later on in the 15th Century Italian sculpture began to be so conscious of grace of gesture and beauty of form that these half-humorous touches of human drama tended to disappear. Sculpture became more impressive but less lively.

Gothic too in its crisp detail, but Italian in its amplitude, is the carving of the vine that separates Noah from his sons and carries the angle of the building upward. Its foliage is disciplined yet its growth is free and vigorous. Perhaps this naturalism is a reflection of influences percolating across the Alps from Germany and Austria. Certainly the three figures remind us of the statues of Bamberg and Naumberg. They are not types but personalities, and their expressions and gestures remind one of the realism of German Gothic at its best. Yet behind that realism is the Italian sense of controlled classic design.

25. *Drunkenness of Noah (detail).*
Late 14th Century. Istrian stone.
Palace of Doges, Venice

26. *Madonna and Child. Early 14th Century. Ivory.*
Victoria and Albert Museum, London

Madonna and Child.   Ivory Crozier

HARDLY LARGER than the reproduction shown here, this little pastoral staff is typical of the perfection that Gothic carving could achieve in the first half of the 14th Century. The sweep of the containing curve has in it the grace and strength of an unfolding frond of fern and the leaves that break its regularity have the regular rhythms of all good decoration, combined with a vitality that comes from close observation of nature. The same can be said of the four figures enclosed in the circle. They are composed in a densely packed design in which every curve is in close, calculated harmony (note, for example, the canopy formed by the angels' wings over the Virgin's head), yet each figure has its own movement. The angels move gently inward, the Madonna leans back to balance the vertical of the Child on her knee, the folds of drapery between her knees festoon downward and are caught up at the base in the swinging circular rhythm of the whole. The flowing design and the tender sentiment are perfectly attuned to each other—we could say that each is an aspect of the other and that form and content fit each other like hand and glove.

71

One cannot imagine such a carving better done. Yet it is by no means unique. It is not the expression of an exceptional artist but of an exceptional moment when art and religion had each found the perfect stimulus in each other. In its grace it is typically French, but in its underlying spirit it is Gothic—and the Gothic spirit could find its outlet in every corner of North-western Europe.

On the reverse side is a Crucifixion. The horizontal arm of the cross can be seen behind the head of the Virgin.

The Syon Cope.   English Embroidery

E M B R O I D E R Y is the least impressive of the crafts, although certain oriental embroideries can dazzle us with an intensity of color unattainable in paint and some Elizabethan and Jacobean embroideries are enchanting as decoration. The Bayeux Tapestry—which is technically not a tapestry at all, but a unique example of needlework used for the purpose of describing an historical event—has an innocent charm but owes too much to the story it tells and too little to its inherent qualities to be taken seriously as a work of art.

One thinks of embroidery as an essentially feminine craft, requiring patience and practised control of the needle but rarely capable of moving us deeply. But the reason it has become so Cinderella-like among the arts is surely the fact that the most impressive specimens of it were divorced from their function when they found their way into museums where, the more carefully displayed they are, the more lifeless they become.

Consider, for example, the famous Syon Cope as we see it today, pains-takingly spread out like a tablecloth, its fragility protected by glass, in a huge fan-shaped case specially built for it. Seen thus, we can marvel at the boldness of the design and the skill of the workmanship, even though we can no longer admire the colors which have now faded to a set of discreet creams, browns and golds. But we can no longer see it, as it was meant to be seen, playing its part in the pageantry of Christian ritual. Worn by a priest, hanging in heavy folds, constantly altering its form with each movement and each shift of light, against a background of 14th-Century Gothic architecture whose shapes were echoed in its design, the effect must have been remarkably moving.

It was made in the first quarter of the 14th Century, the most perfect surviving specimen of "Opus Anglicanum" (English embroidery of the period was famous throughout Europe), though it was mutilated when it was converted from a chasuble to a cope. Once it belonged to the nuns of the Bridgettine foundation at Syon in the British county of Middlesex. The main portion of the ground is worked in large quartrefoils containing the figures of saints or scenes from the life of the Virgin. Rich heraldic borders form the orphreys

72

27. *The Syon Cope. Early 14th Century. Embroidered garment.*
Victoria and Albert Museum, London

that run along its edge, blazoned with coats of arms including those of the earls of Derby and Warwick.

The workmanship, as can be seen from the illustration, is superlative. The main groundwork of the cope is linen embroidered in colored silks and threads of silver and silver-gilt. Yet to judge it, as one must, from a photograph, is like judging the quality of a movie from an isolated " still. "

The Angers Apocalypse.   French Tapestry

A P A R T   F R O M   one isolated example in Brussels, the Apocalypse of Angers is the oldest French tapestry in existence. It was commissioned about 1375 by Louis of Anjou from the Parisian weaver Nicolas Bataille, who worked from cartoons by the Flemish painter Hennequin of Bruges. It hung in the rooms of the castle and in the chapel at Angers. It was taken to Arles in 1400 for the wedding of Louis II of Anjou. In 1474, at the command of King René, it was transferred to the cathedral, where it remained until it was discarded in the 18th Century, offered for sale but did not obtain a bid, was used as a covering for the orange trees of a local abbey, was removed to the bishop's palace and lost sight of till 1843 when, in a mutilated condition, it was bought for three hundred francs and presented once more to the cathedral.

The ill treatment and neglect of a century have not improved its appearance, yet today, though the colors have faded considerably and the   73

28. *The Apocalypse. Late 14th Century. Tapestry.*
Angers Cathedral, France

original ninety designs have been reduced to seventy-two, it is still one of the major treasures of French tapestry, less ornate than those of a century later but more imaginative and varied in its imagery.

Originally it consisted of seven huge hangings measuring 472 feet in length and 18 in height, the scenes being divided horizontally in two tiers. On each of the separate panels St. John himself appears, watching the fantastic happenings that unfold themselves before him against a background of varied floral or decorative patterns. Hennequin of Bruges, relying partly on a conscientious determination to interpret the extravagant imagery of the Apocalypse as faithfully as possible, has risen surprisingly to the demands of a text that would have baffled most of the artists of his time.

The scene in Plate 28 illustrates chapter thirteen of the Book of Revelation. The beast with seven heads, ten horns and ten crowns, with the body of a leopard and the feet of a bear, stands in the center opposite a group of 74 "them that dwell on earth." Behind is the creature who appears in verse XI,

"And I beheld another beast coming up out of the earth, and he had two horns like a lamb and he spake as a dragon... and he doeth great wonders so that he maketh fire come down from heaven upon the earth." Formalized Gothic clouds radiating flames are the best that the artist can do with this difficult passage. Moreover, he seems to have been a little careless about the number of horns on the beast.

Dürer's Apocalypse (see Plate 62) was published almost exactly a century after the Angers tapestries were woven. Dürer's vision is certainly more powerful but not more strange.

The Wild Men. Swiss Tapestry

THE CREATURES that were known to mediaeval Europe as "wild men" have always formed an important part of civilized man's conception of himself. Man, since the beginning of history, has regarded himself as having a lower, or animal, and a higher, or spiritual, nature. From the hairy beast-man of Babylonian mythology and the satyr of the Greeks to Kipling's Mowgli or the Tarzan of the movie world of today, such creatures have been envisaged and have found their way into art and literature in different forms. Shakespeare's Caliban is certainly one of their number. Even the "noble savage" of Rousseau is a version of the same conception inverted by the romanticism of a later century.

Mediaeval Europe created a prolific race of such mythological men and women. They lived in forests. They either grew fur on their bodies or dressed in furs. The men brandished clubs. They were enemies of society. They lived in caves or forests. They sometimes mingled with wild or mythological beasts or were sometimes at war with them. They were passionate creatures, emotion-

29. *Wild Men. 14th Century. Swiss tapestry.*
Victoria and Albert Museum, London

ally uncontrolled and physically immensely strong, for hairiness and strength are naturally connected. Hercules wore a lion's skin; Samson could only be subdued by robbing him of his hair.

In the 14th Century, especially in the districts of the upper Rhine and in Switzerland, wild men appear frequently in tapestry; sometimes at war with civilized man, sometimes living their own separate lives in forests, sometimes, as here, in conjunction with animals. The tapestry shown in Plate 29 was woven in Switzerland—probably near Lucerne. It is typical of its kind, though the creatures subdued by the bearded man crowned with leaves and the woman to his right are more fantastic than usual.

Later—in the late 15th and 16th Centuries—the legend of the wild men lost some of its sinister qualities, and it even became fashionable to dress as wild men at masques and on other occasions when fancy dress was permitted. It is thought that the patched costume of Harlequin is a formalized version of an earlier garment in which loose rags were stitched onto a foundation to represent fur or hair. Harlequin was eventually permitted to mix with normal men and women but he still retained his mischievous and unruly nature.

The Reawakening of Humanism

SCHOLARS and historians have agreed to call the period that immediately followed the Middle Ages in Europe the Renaissance, thus placing the emphasis on the rebirth of much that the Greeks and the Romans had known but which mediaevalism had forgotten or ignored. But "rebirth" is too simple a word to describe a movement that discovered ways of living, seeing and thinking that Greek and Roman civilization had never envisaged.

What happened, though it was of massive importance, happened gradually. The slow emergence, first of all in Italy, later spreading northward across the Alps and westward to Southern France and Spain, of a new attitude to the art of living manifested itself in all the arts, but in none more strikingly than in painting and sculpture.

It is, of course, impossible to fix a point at which the Renaissance began in Italy. I have arbitrarily placed this essay between a Swiss tapestry of the Wild Men—a thoroughly mediaeval concept—and a fresco by Giotto, who is perhaps the first painter who seems to prophesy the dawn of a new spirit. It is the spirit of an observant, enquiring, intelligent man, deeply concerned with the behavior and sensations of other men and women and with the appearance of the material world in which they live.

Giotto, even as early as the beginning of the 14th Century, sowed the seeds of what was to come. And what did come was the result of a gradually increasing sense of the importance of the individual, a gradually mounting curiosity about his physical environment, a desire to come to grips with it and to exploit its beauty. And while this new spirit of intellectual curiosity and this re-establishment of man as a noble animal was increasing in intensity, the mediaeval human soul was not forgotten. Both Pheidias and Michelangelo saw man as a noble animal, but only Michelangelo could understand that his body was inhabited and agitated by his soul.

I have taken Giotto as a starting point for a series of more than fifty plates and have hesitatingly decided on Tintoretto as bringing this extraordinary period to an end. Those fifty-odd plates must tell their own story, and the reader must draw his own conclusions from them as to what was

77

the most important contribution of the Renaissance to the cultural history of mankind. Some of those plates, especially those that illustrate what was happening outside Italy, still retain strong echoes of mediaevalism. The four tapestries, for example, woven in France at the end of the 15th or beginning of the 16th Century, lovely though they are, are products of keen observation but not of intellectual curiosity. The spirit of the Middle Ages still clings about them, as it still does in the paintings of that master of playful fantasy, Hieronymus Bosch.

But, in general, it should be possible for the reader to follow, from Giotto's Betrayal (1306) to Tintoretto's Three Graces (1577) the crescendo of discovery and excitement that marks the progress of the Renaissance, the different forms it took in Florence, Venice, Germany and Flanders, until finally it reached the climax of what is known as the "High Renaissance."

Giotto. Frescoes at Padua

WHEN AT THE beginning of the 14th Century, Enrico Scrovegni, a prominent citizen of Padua, built a chapel there, on the site of the Roman Arena from which it takes its name, and commissioned Giotto to fill its interior walls with frescoed illustration from the New Testament, he took one of the most decisive steps in the history of Italian Renaissance patronage. Perhaps not until Pope Julius II handed over the Sistine Chapel ceiling to Michelangelo three centuries later, or the committee of the Scuola of San Rocco appointed Tintoretto as its official artist with orders to fill the walls and ceilings of their buildings, half a century later still, was an artist given so magnificent an opportunity to prove his genius.

Those three experiments in patronage mark the beginning and the end of the most creative period in European art. But a beginning makes more demands on genius than an end. What Giotto did in Padua was to rouse the people of his generation from their mediaeval dream and make them conscious of a new world—the world of men and women, taken from the life around him, seen with an abnormally acute eye, understood in terms of weight and structure, with solid, convincing limbs moving under their draperies.

That in itself would have been a sufficiently important contribution to the history of European painting. But Giotto was more than the first realist. He was also the first dramatist. His understanding of human motives and human behavior, his instinct for the dramatic relationship between the characters in his narrative, and his power to invent the precise gesture that would explain their part in the drama is sometimes positively Shakespearian.

Consider, for example, this detail (Plate 30) from the fresco illustrating the Betrayal of Jesus. It is perhaps the most dramatic though not the most

30. *Giotto (? 1266-1336). The Betrayal (detail). c. 1304-06. Fresco. Arena Chapel, Padua*

poignant in the series of Christ's Passion. Like every good theatrical director, Giotto has grouped his actors in such a way that they will give the situation its maximum clarity and its maximum power. In the center of the stage the two protagonists confront each other—the decisive confrontation of good and evil. The eye is arrested not so much by the two heads and the steady gaze of Jesus as he submits to the kiss of betrayal, as by the immense sweep of the cloak of Judas, tightly drawn over his body to make a smooth area in the picture's center, and by the sequence of vigorous folds drawn up by Judas' left arm as he flings it round Jesus' shoulder. As though to underline this central section to which everything converges, two anonymous hands, grasping spears, rise up out of the crowd behind the figures of Jesus and Judas, and the forest of agitated spears that breaks the plain blue of the sky radiates inward threateningly.

The rest of the crowd is disposed in such a way as to add to this dense concentration on the central group. Each figure has his allotted place as a minor contributor to the action. None of them weakens the central theme. The solid back view of the man on the left (a favorite device of stage directors); the raised arm of Peter who cuts off the ear of Malchus, balancing the arm of Judas; the accusing arm and hand of the high priest on the right; the packed pattern of heads behind Jesus that forms a background and cuts him off from the world.

The fresco is an essay in claustrophobia. Jesus is hemmed in. His enemies close on him from all sides. One cannot imagine a painter of any later age—not even Rembrandt—telling a tragic story more clearly.

When Giotto began his work in Padua his reputation was already established. He had already completed a cycle of frescoes in the Church of St. Francis at Assisi. But at Padua he is more mature in his dramatic imagination, more confident in his handling of the fresco medium and more acute in his notation of human behavior.

It is true that in his discovery of solid, weighty form he made a gigantic stride forward in the history of style, which his successors could not fail to note and were quick to imitate. But his dramatic imagination and his instinct for significant gesture could *not* be imitated. A century passed—and a by no means barren century if we judge it by the amount of art it produced—before another artist of comparable calibre was born. Not until Masaccio started to paint his series of frescoes in the Carmine Church in Florence, in the early years of the 15th Century, did it become clear that Giotto had laid the foundations of the Tuscan tradition.

31. *Jacopo della Quercia*
    (1367-1438).
    Creation of Adam. c. 1430.
    Istrian stone.
    S. Petronio, Bologna

Jacopo della Quercia. The Creation of Adam

JACOPO DELLA QUERCIA, the greatest of the Sienese sculptors, was a contemporary of Lorenzo Ghiberti, who made the two famous pairs of bronze doors for the Baptistry in Florence. Perhaps because Ghiberti's doors have been described and praised by so many artists and art historians from Michelangelo onwards, and perhaps because any great work of art attracts more attention in Florence than in Bologna, Ghiberti's name is more familiar to us than that of Jacopo della Quercia. Yet Quercia's masterpiece, the carved reliefs around the main west doorway of the Church of San Petronio in Bologna, which occupied him during the last thirteen years of his life, is in many ways a more original work than Ghiberti's second set of bronze doors. The comparison is almost inevitable since both were commissioned in the same year, 1425, though Ghiberti's doors were not completed till after della Quercia's death in 1438.

81

Low reliefs of subjects from the Book of Genesis fill the faces of the pilasters on either side of the main door to the church. Each pilaster is divided into five squarish panels, each measuring roughly two and a half feet in width and three feet in height—approximately the same size as the ten panels in Ghiberti's door. Since they are carved in white Istrian stone, brought from Venice for the purpose, they are inevitably broader in treatment than Ghiberti's which take full advantage of the process of bronze casting, which is never dismayed by detail.

The *Creation of Adam* is the top panel of the left-hand pilaster. Like Michelangelo, Jacopo della Quercia was obsessed by the rhythms of the human figure and almost completely uninterested in its environment. Hence, in this panel, a simplified tree and a sketchy indication of a smooth rock have to do duty for the Garden of Eden. Everything depends on the two figures and their relationship to each other. The Creator's gesture of blessing and the expressive hand that grasps the heavy folds of the cloak foreshadow the prophets of the Sistine Chapel. Adam's muscular adolescence, the relaxed pose of his body, the eager lift of his head as he receives the blessing of the Almighty are far more Michelangelesque than anything in the corresponding panel in the Baptistry doors.

Jacopo della Quercia's mastery of low relief almost rivals that of Donatello. With a depth of hardly more than two inches at his disposal to suggest the full volume of the human body, he explains the cupped palm of Adam's right hand, the grip of his left on the rock, the weight of the torso, the muscular construction of the arms.

Novgorod School of Ikon Painters.   The Nativity

THE SPIRIT of Byzantium—or at least the basic elements of the Byzantine style—penetrated into Russia in the 11th Century, where local artists, at first in Kiev, later in many centers, converted it to their own purposes and produced a national school of ikon painting that has no exact parallel elsewhere. For eight centuries the tradition of ikon painting persisted in Russia, each center contributing its own slight variations of style, the whole forming, cumulatively, a movement whose finest products combine deep religious intensity with purity of form and eloquence of color. The focus of "classic" ikon painting eventually centered on Moscow where, among a sequence of anonymous painters, one or two names emerge. The most famous of them is that of Rublev, who lived in the early 15th Century

Ikons of the Moscow school were characterized by a refinement and a delicacy of color. The more popular School of Novgorod produced ikons of greater strength and vigor and a more direct appeal. But in general the

82

32. *Novgorod School. The Nativity. c. 1400. Ikon painting. George R. Hann Collection, Pittsburgh*

Russian conception of an ikon as an object sacred in its own right (sometimes even capable of working miracles) made it very different in character from a Western religious painting which was an artist's interpretation of a sacred scene. The Russian ikon was, itself, as sacred as a scriptural writing and was therefore incapable of iconographical variations or of stylistic development. It could and did become decadent as standards of craftsmanship decayed, but since it could never change its essential nature as an object of veneration, it could equally never be a vehicle for genuis or the expression of personality.

This Nativity, a typical product of the Novgorod School, and probably painted at the beginning of the 15th Century by a contemporary of Jan Van Eyck and Masaccio, is one of the series which was placed in the screen (ikonastasis) dividing the nave from the chancel in every Greek Orthodox church. This series shows the twelve annual festivals of the Church. In the Nativity are included certain apocryphal symbols, unfamiliar in Western iconography. The shepherd playing the pipe is a reference to a legend that the angels' message " interrupted the sound of the shepherds' flutes. " The handmaidens preparing the bath for the newborn Christ Child is commonly found in Western Nativities, but the figure of the devil, disguised as the shepherd Thyrsus, tempting St. Joseph as he sits brooding on the left, is part of the Russo-Byzantine tradition.

What strikes us at once is the boldness of the stylization and the grand simplicity of the color. The orange-red of the rocks makes a daring background to the garnet and green figures. Particularly moving are the silhouettes of the three angels against the cold expanse of the sky at the top of the panel.

The picture is no more than seventeen inches in width, but there is no sense of constriction and the fourteen figures and the animals have plenty of room to move round the graceful, recumbent form of the Virgin Mary.

Duccio di Buoninsegna.   The Annunciation

IT WAS characteristic of a country that had never enjoyed political unity, that each of the major cities of Italy should follow its own artistic destiny according to its own civic temperament. Siena and Florence are even to-day, architecturally, monuments celebrating the ambitions of the days of their greatness. Outwardly, Siena is still a mediaeval, Florence still a Renaissance city. Florentine art is an adventurous journey : Sienese art a wonderful event.

Duccio di Buoninsegna, the earliest of the Sienese painters, was a contemporary of Giotto. Less observant, less intellectual, incapable of Florentine breadth or robustness, his best work has a lyrical charm and a small-scale intensity that was seldom matched in Florence. When Duccio undertook the great *Maiestà*—the elaborate double-sided reredos painted between 1308 and

33. *Duccio di Buoninsegna (Op. c. 1278-1319). The Annunciation. 1308-1311.*
Tempera on wood. National Gallery, London

1311 for the place of honor behind the High Altar of Siena Cathedral, he
produced a masterpiece which had little of the human drama of Giotto's
Paduan frescoes, but which was, none the less, a landmark in the history of
Italian painting.

Its central feature was a great enthroned Virgin and Child supported
by angels, still Byzantine in spirit but richer in detail and more poetic in
sentiment than any Byzantine panel. Surrounding this central feature, in a
series of small, squarish panels, were New Testament narratives, each based
on a Byzantine prototype, yet each taking the old Byzantine formula further,
refining on it and making it more emotionally expressive.

85

Those panels are now, alas, scattered. *The Annunciation* is one of three that now belong to the National Gallery in London, and must have formed a part of the series that once adorned the front of the *Maiestà*.

The angel Gabriel approaches, with all the confidence of a messenger with an important commission to fulfil, yet with an innate reverence, as though knowing that the message he delivers is the first announcement that God's only-begotten Son is soon to appear on this earth. The Virgin Mary stands, in an attitude of hesitant humility: on the open page of the book in her left hand is the prophecy of Isaiah, "Behold a virgin shall conceive, and bear a son..." Between the two is the symbolic vase of white lilies. A row of arched windows whose semicircular tops echo the circles of the two haloes carries the rhythm of curvature across the picture. Through them can be seen a plain gold background, an indication that the Renaissance has not yet fixed the attention of mankind on the earth's surface, its skies, its meadows and its trees. Gold is the symbol of idealized space. Another indication that Duccio still clung to the Byzantine formula is the treatment of the Virgin's red robe. Her blue cloak has been painted in shaded folds, but the robe is a formalized pattern of gold on a flat background of vermilion.

The panel is only seventeen inches square, yet Duccio achieves a massive dignity that suggests a larger picture. The forward movement and raised arm of the archangel and the bowed head and bent arm of the Virgin are quiet but unforgettable gestures. The slender column that separates them is no barrier yet it acts as a dividing line between the world of God and the world of mankind. Even the color—the transition from pink to gray—reinforces this tension.

Sassetta. Temptation of St. Anthony

SASSETTA was the last important painter in the line of truly Sienese artists that began with Duccio. In him we find the same lyrical intensity, the same refinement, the same impression of having been brought up in the atmosphere of a mediaeval city as in his precedessors; and the same incapacity to work on a broad monumental scale. Nevertheless he belongs stylistically to the 15th rather than the 14th Century.

At some date between 1432 and 1436 he probably painted a full-length, life-sized figure of St. Anthony the Abbot and placed on either side of it, one above the other, a set of small pictures illustrating incidents from his life, from his renunciation of worldliness, through his temptations in the desert, to his death. There may have been ten in all. Only seven survive, of which this panel, representing St. Anthony meeting on his way to his cell with the devil disguised as a fair maiden, is one. The panels are dispersed, as are so many attractive little pictures of the 15th Century, and there is no

34. *Sassetta (1392-1450). The Temptation of St. Anthony.*
1432-1436. Tempera panel.
Yale University Art Gallery

trace of the large figure of the saint, if it ever existed. But, as in the case
of Domenico Veneziano (see Plate 44), we can assume that his smaller works
are more vivid than his larger altarpiece and tell us more about his personality.

The old hermit, wandering back to his cell along the stony path that
leads through a typical little valley among the hills that surround Siena,
stops suddenly at the sight of the young girl who has just materialized at
his side. The two confront each other with a mysterious mutual antagonism
though the saint cannot see the little bat's wings that betray her identity. 87

ELONGAVI FVGIENS Z MANSI INSOLITVDINE . PS . XXXXXV . C

SVRGE ACCIPE PVERVM Z MATREM EP Z FVGE INEGIPTVM . MACEI. II . C .

35. *Fra Angelico (1387-1455). The Flight into Egypt. c. 1450.*
Tempera panel. San Marco Museum, Florence

The colors are those of a dream—the pale red hut on the left, the pale
pink dress of the girl on the right, the gray-green hills, the black-green trees,
the sinister orange sky. The light catches the saint's outstretched left hand and
the gnarled staff he holds in his right, as though to emphasize the sudden
pause in his progress down the hill. The effect is of deepening twilight,
entirely appropriate to the mood of a clash of wills between an elderly saint
88   and the little temptress who so suddenly accosts him.

Fra Angelico.   Flight into Egypt

A T   S O M E   M O M E N T   near the middle of the 15th Century Cosimo
de Medici, the first member of the Medici family to practice art patronage
on a grand scale in Florence, ordered a great wooden treasury chest for the
Church of the Santissima Annunziata. The chest no longer exists; its painted
doors, divided into thirty-five separate scenes, each about three feet square,
are now in the Museum of San Marco in Florence.

Art historians, relying on their sense of style rather than on documentary
evidence, have wrangled considerably about the authorship of these panels.
There is no doubt that almost all of them show the influence of Fra Angelico,
and in some of them there are direct "quotations" from the frescoes he
painted in the Convent of San Marco while he was resident there as one of
the Dominican novices. The arguments need not be summarized here, but
certain of these panels are so close to Fra Angelico in style, and one, at
least, "The Flight into Egypt," seems to me so masterly an instance of his
essence as a painter that I cannot bring myself to disbelieve in his authorship.

The seated Madonna on the donkey is one of the tenderest and most
graceful Madonna and Child images in Italian art: the landscape through
which they move is typical of the master, the color has Fra Angelico's luminous
purity—always pale and bright but never crude. If the artist who painted
this was not Fra Angelico, he was a pasticheur of genius, an almost unknown
phenomenon. This is surely a case where one must trust one's instinct. The
panels, if my guess is right, must be late works painted within a few years
of Fra Angelico's death in 1455.

He was, in many ways, a link between the mediaeval world and the
awakening spirit of the Florentine Renaissance. This little panel is more
mediaeval in composition than most of his later works, but a set of small
furniture panels demands a decorative, formalized treatment.

Each of the panels, all of which are scenes from the New Testament,
bears two inscriptions to emphasize the correspondence between the Old and
the New Testaments. In this case the upper quotation is from the Psalms,
the lower from St. Matthew's Gospel.

Illuminations from Books of Hours

B E F O R E   T H E   I N V E N T I O N   of printing, the distinction between
the written word, the decorative addition to the page and the pictorial
illustration to narrative or moral precept was less sharp than it was to become   89

36. *The Murder of St. Thomas à Becket. From the Ramsey Abbey Psalter. Late 13th Century. Illumination. Morgan Library, New York*

later. One can easily imagine the monastic scribes in the years before the 12th Century, or the professional scribes of the centuries that followed, passing from text to decoration and back again without much consciousness of the difference between the two. And when the need for added vividness arose, it must have been a positive relief for the illuminators to enlarge a capital letter and turn it into a frame for a pictorial illumination. From that device to allowing the illumination to enlarge itself still further and become what we now think of as an illustration was an easy step.

With mediaeval illuminated books the marriage between text and decoration and between decoration and picture is far closer than is generally possible in the days of printing. The artist's hand is responsible throughout. Richness of effect is more important than legibility. In the Book of Kells (Plate 14) the great initial *Chi* and the letters that follow it are almost too beautiful to be legible.

The two illuminations in Plates 36 and 37 approach the problem of fusing text with illustration in a less extreme way. The first is a formalized representation of St. Thomas à Becket's murder, from the Ramsey Abbey Psalter (an English work of the late 13th Century); the second shows an initial letter *D* from a Table of Christian Faith (produced in the Low Countries at the beginning of the 15th).

Something, of course, has been lost by isolating them. They have been divorced from the page; the carefully planned fusion between painting and writing has been destroyed, to the detriment of both. The third example, in which a full page from a Spanish Book of Hours of the end of the 15th Century asserts itself as a picture in its own right, surrounded by its own elaborately painted frame, is the first step in the decline of the manuscript book. Printing has by this time been invented, and the cleavage between the pictorial and the literary language is clearly felt.

St. Thomas à Becket, murdered in Canterbury Cathedral in 1170 by four knights anxious to please Henry II of England, was an early victim of the struggle between Church and State. From being a rebel against the king,

37. *A Chess Game. From a Table of Christian Faith. Early 15th Century. Illumination. Morgan Library, New York*

he became, almost immediately, a martyr to a cause. The illuminator's description of the scene, painted just over a century after the event, includes the standing figures of St. Oswald—a founder of Ramsey Abbey—on the left, and St. Paul on the right. As narrative the little illumination, just over four inches in height, is clear enough, but the artist, familiar with the organization of color in heraldry and also with the art of the stained-glass window, has been unusually inventive in the use of counterchanged patterns of pink and blue and in the distribution of his accents of red to balance the tunic of the blue and red knight in the center.

The same heraldic convention can be seen in the Netherlandish initial letter—the chessboard would have lost not only its significance as a chessboard but its value as decoration had it been shown in true perspective. A tree behind the players, a meadow at their feet in which their four coroneted companions sit at ease in conversation establishes the mood of the outdoor scene, just as the foliated arcading in the Ramsey Psalter stands for the interior of a cathedral. The game of chess, so Dirk van Delft's text tells us, and as his artist underlines the lesson, is an appropriate one for the Christian aristocrat.

The Spanish Book of Hours, more realistic, less diagrammatic, has a different purpose and makes a different impact. The Renaissance has arrived, and though we are still meant to be alarmed by the arrival of Death on the White Horse shooting down a pope, a cardinal, an abbot and a monk with his bow and arrow, the sense of the supernatural and the unknown has departed. Even Dürer (see Plate 62) retains more of the mediaeval spirit than this Spanish illuminator, working between 1465 and 1475.

Illuminations from the "Très Riches Heures"

JEAN, DUC DE BERRY, uncle of Charles VI of France, commissioned Pol de Limbourg, his *valet de chambre,* together with his two brothers, Hennequin and Hermant, to paint the illuminated pages of a calendar showing the months of the year. At the duke's death in 1416 the manuscript was incomplete, and it was not until seventy years later that the illuminations were resumed and the book finished by another artist, Jean Colombe of Bourges.

The earlier series of illuminations is incomparably the finer. Not only are they the most distinguished examples of French illumination of the early 15th Century, but as de Limbourg was a member of the duke's household in his residence outside Paris and had a close personal knowledge of his castles at Lusignan, Dourdan and Melun-sur-Yevre, he thoroughly understood the activities of the countryside. The earlier series provides invaluable documentary   93

38. *Death Rides Abroad. From a Spanish Book of Hours. Late 15 Century. Illumination. Morgan Library, New York*

39. *Limbourg Brothers. The Haymakers from* Très Riches Heures.
Early 15th Century. Illumination. Condé Museum, Chantilly

evidence of the architecture and the manners, customs and dress of the time.

Plate 39 shows the month of June. In the foreground two girls are haymaking, in the middle distance three men are mowing the grass with scythes on a sloping hillside that is now in the heart of Paris on the left bank of the Seine, where the duke's house stood. Behind the haymakers runs the river, fringed with pollarded trees, and on its far bank is the Ile de la Cité, surrounded by a battlemented wall. Had the illumination been extended to the right we should be shown the Cathedral of Notre Dame as it appeared about the year 1410. The church on the right is the Sainte Chapelle; farther left are the gables of the royal palace. A postern gate with steps leading down into the river occupies the space now called the Vert Galant, where the Pont Neuf spans the river at the tip of the island. Topographically, the artist must be entirely reliable, yet the page has the air of a fairy tale.

Above the rectangular picture on each of the calendar pages, is a semi-circle in blue monochrome picked out with gold showing the chariot of the sun drawn by winged horses and the zodiacal signs of the month.

During the duke's lifetime the book was one of his most treasured possessions and at his death it was described in his inventory as "*Plusieurs cayers d'une très riches Heures que faisoyent Pol et ses frères*" ("Many pages from a Book of Hours executed by Paul and his brothers").

Masaccio. *Detail from the Brancacci Chapel*

A CENTURY PASSED before Florence produced an artist of the same stature and with the same feeling for human drama as Giotto. Masaccio, in his tragically short life of twenty-eight years, left little behind him, but that little marked him out as a genius of a very high order—monumental in the breadth of his design, exceptional in his power to note and describe expressive behavior and gesture, a realist long before realism as understood by Velasquez and Rembrandt had been established.

Only in one series of frescoes in the Brancacci Chapel in the Church of Santa Maria del Carmine in Florence can his full range be grasped, and death overtook him before he had completed the work. Yet the Brancacci frescoes pointed the way to almost everything that Florentine art was to achieve during the rest of the 15th Century; they set a standard for his successors. Michelangelo himself studied them and made drawings of isolated figures in them. Giotto had struggled mightily to free himself from the fetters of Byzantine tradition. In Masaccio there is no indication of such a struggle. He is the first undoubted master of Italian Renaissance painting. His Adam and Eve Expelled from the Garden of Eden is the first Italian painting in which the unclothed human body was seen as inherently noble. *95*

Adam and Eve are embodiments of shame, but Masaccio makes it clear that their tragedy lies in their disobedience and not in their nakedness.

Among the frescoed panels in the chapel is one showing St. Peter distributing alms. Plate 40 shows a detail of this story: a peasant girl with her baby, taking money from the saint. It reveals clearly how Masaccio's observant eye and creative mind worked. One feels at once the weight of the child supported on the crook of her arm, the quick impulsive gesture of the clumsily outstretched arm, the need to shift her position and hold the child in a firmer grasp as she does so, and the inevitable readjustment of balance that will occur once she has done so. It is one of those gestures, like those in a painting by Degas of women ironing shirts or trying on hats at the milliner's, which can only be understood and communicated by the closest and the most sensitive observation.

In his humanity and his grasp of form Masaccio was a true Florentine, but in his untroubled realism and his assurance that it was not necessary to idealize human beings in order to make them acceptable in painting, he was two centuries in advance of his time. The true realist accepts life as it presents itself to him, attempting neither to emotionalize it, as does the romantic, nor to reorganize it, as does the classic artist.

Campin (?). The Mérode Altarpiece

THE MÉRODE ALTARPIECE (so called because it was in the possession of the Mérode family in France for two generations during the mid-19th Century) is now the most cherished possession of The Cloisters museum in New York. It consists of a central panel showing the Annunciation flanked by two side panels, of which the panel on the left depicts the kneeling figure of the donor and his wife in an open courtyard and that on the right, St. Joseph, working in his carpenter's shop and engaged in making an object which has considerably puzzled students of iconography.

Indeed the whole of the triptych abounds in questions, some of which have been answered by art historians; others remain unanswered, including the most puzzling of all—who painted this undoubted masterpiece?

Even to list the tentative answers to this and other problems would overload this book of brief notes. There is no difficulty in enjoying the picture for its own inherent merits; it is astonishing for so many reasons— the affection lavished by the artist on its innumerable details, the tender domesticity of the central panel, the combination of materialistic realism with a sense of spiritual mystery, and the wealth of symbolism underlying the whole conception. Those who are anxious to read a full discussion of these 97

40. *Masaccio (1401-c. 1428). Mother and Child (detail). c. 1425. Fresco. Brancacci Chapel, Florence*

41. *Campin? (d. 1444). The Mérode Altarpiece (center panel).*
Early 15th Century. Oil on oak. The Cloisters, New York

and other problems are referred to the Metropolitan Museum's *Bulletin* for December, 1957.

Meanwhile it can be said with some confidence that the Mérode altarpiece was probably painted by the Flemish artist called Campin, who worked in Tournai and was active there at the end of the first quarter and the beginning of the second of the 15th Century. He was therefore a contemporary and a compatriot of Jan Van Eyck in Flanders; Fra Angelico in Italy was working at the same time but following an entirely different set of artistic traditions.

In her quiet room (surely this is one of the most charmingly intimate of all painted interiors) the Virgin Mary is seated on the floor, her left arm leaning against a cushion on the settle. She is reading a precious book whose cover is protected by a napkin. She is unaware of the arrival of the Angel Gabriel and his message, or of the symbolic Christ Child, bearing a tiny cross, descending along the seven slanting rays of light that announce the presence of the Holy Ghost. On the table in a jug are her lilies, and a candle whose flame has just been extinguished and from which a delicate whirl of smoke ascends. Behind her the little window is filled, partly with clear glass through which one sees the sky and white clouds (these are later additions; the space was originally filled with gold) and partly by stained glass showing the coats of arms of the donor and his wife. The drapery of her cloak falls in the angular folds that are typical of Flemish painting of the period. The picture's strange secret lies in the fact that everything in the room, from the angel to the polished bronze laver in a niche in the wall and the towel hanging on its rack, has been described in photographic detail, yet photography is the last thing we think of as we examine the panel, either piecemeal or as a whole. It has both the vividness and the unreality of a dream. What it suggests, above all, is the silence of holiness. A miracle is taking place and none of the furniture of daily life, on whose prosaic solidity Campin insists in every square inch of the surface, can detract from the impression of a supernatural occurrence.

Perhaps if we could fathom the mystery of the extinguished candle, the open book on the table, or the carved lions on the settle, the picture would lose some of its fascination.

Jan Van Eyck. The Marriage of Arnolfini

I N A rectangular space (two feet eight inches in height and two feet wide) Jan Van Eyck has created a quiet interior within which two personages face us hand in hand. Neither Giovanni Arnolfini nor his wife (or perhaps she is his betrothed), Giovanna Cenami, have any claim to physical distinction, nor are their faces lit up by even the slightest gleam of expression. Outwardly it is one of the most prosaic and one of the least dramatic masterpieces ever painted. Yet for some reason that can hardly be analyzed it is immediately interesting. Slowly, as we submit ourselves to its spell, it begins to reveal its secret. In fact Jan Van Eyck himself gives us a clue to its magic in the inscription he has placed on the wall below the metal candelabra, with its single lighted candle, and above the circular convex mirror which reflects, in miniature, the whole room. The inscription, *Johannes de Eyck fuit hic: 1434* 99

("Jan Van Eyck was here") has a startling abruptness and simplicity that echoes the simplicity of the painting.

"I, Jan Van Eyck," he seems to say, "was an eye witness of this unremarkable happening. Thus, to a hairsbreadth, was their room furnished; thus were they dressed; thus did he leave his wooden pattens carelessly on the floor; this was her dog; the oranges on the table under the window were there; so was the rosary on the wall and the little brush hanging near the bed." There is something almost alarming in such objective honesty of eye. And when one remembers that Van Eyck was an exact contemporary of Fra Angelico, for whom objective honesty hardly mattered (Plate 35) one realizes at once the difference in spirit between Northern and Southern Europe. Both artists painted with reverence, but Van Eyck's reverence was for the material world, Fra Angelico's for the spiritual.

Van Eyck's meticulous powers of observation are backed up by a mastery of sheer craftsmanship that no Italian would even have wished to possess. There is no fussiness in the picture, yet no painting could be more precise. No detail has been omitted, yet no detail is allowed to interfere with the quiet dignity of the design. It is with surprise that we note that the frame of the circular mirror contains ten little medallions, each containing a scene from Christ's Passion, each no larger than a small coin.

Little is known about Arnolfini and his wife. Both were Italian settlers in the Netherlands. Arnolfini was a merchant from Lucca, though one is astonished to learn it. His face, like the interior decoration of the room, looks Flemish; the stiff movement of his raised right hand is not the gesture of an Italian. But perhaps for so unemphatic a painter as Van Eyck any Italian gesture would have seemed needlessly violent and melodramatic.

Portraiture was no monopoly of the Netherlands. It became common enough a little later in Italy. Yet there is a vast difference between Flemish and Italian portraiture in the 15th Century. The Italian portrait painter underlines the dignity of man, the Flemish his humanity. And in this double portrait, one of the earliest in the history of Flemish painting, humanity, at its least impressive, achieves a curious pathos.

Pisanello. The Vision of St. Eustace

"GOTHIC" is not a word with a precise meaning except when applied to architecture, but if any Italian painting ever deserved to be called "Gothic" it is surely this little panel by Pisanello. No less than eleven quadrupeds and innumerable birds inhabit this dark, romantic landscape; and though only two of them are necessary to the story of the huntsman-saint to whom a vision appears of a stag bearing a crucifix between its antlers,

100

42. *Jan Van Eyck* (? 1385-1441). *The Marriage of Arnolfini. 1434. Oil and tempera on panel. National Gallery, London*

43. *Pisanello (1397/99-1455). Vision of St. Eustace.*
Early 15th Century. Tempera. National Gallery, London

Pisanello makes it clear that he has been more interested in birds and animals
than in the saint himself.

This intense preoccupation with animal life (the illustrated bestiaries of
the time also reflect it), coupled with a wealth of pattern and rich ornament,
is typical of the spirit of late Gothic art; it found its way southward across
the Alps in the early 15th Century, became particularly apparent in Verona,
where Pisanello spent many of his formative years and where his approach
crystallized into the elaborate style known as International Gothic.

Pisanello has left few finished paintings but a mass of exquisite drawings
of whatever caught his alert eye. Women with the huge hats, the shaven
foreheads and the elaborately decorated cloaks of the time became, in his
sketchbooks, predecessors of the modern fashion plate. In all of them there
is that hint of exaggerated fantasy, that preference for charm of detail rather

than breadth of design that betrays the mediaeval spirit. He was also a medallist of distinction, and it is from his medals and profile portraits and drawings that we know the characters and features of his patrons and their friends—Lionello d'Este, Alphonso of Aragon, Filippo Maria Visconti and the Emperor John Palaeologus.

Domenico Veneziano. *St. John in the Desert*

HARDLY ANYTHING is known about Domenico Veneziano. He is first heard of in 1438, begging for an introduction to the great Cosimo de Medici whose patronage all ambitious Florentine artists hoped for. He was on a committee of judges that included Fra Angelico and Lippo Lippi in 1454. He died in Florence in 1461. His principal surviving work is the St. Lucy altarpiece in the Uffizi Gallery, below which he painted five small "predella" panels, including incidents in the lives of the four saints who appear in the altarpiece—St. Francis, St. Zenobius, St. Lucy and St. John the Baptist. It is from these, now scattered among the collections of Europe and America, that we can guess at his quality.

The little St. John in the Desert, no more than twelve inches square, is the most remarkable of them. Despite its small size it carries across the room in which it hangs in the National Gallery in Washington, and at once arrests the eye. The lonely naked figure of a young man unexpectedly wearing a halo, standing in a little valley hemmed in by pale precipitous mountains that suggest a landscape on the moon, strikes us at once as furiously romantic; and when we come to analyze the reasons for this romantic atmosphere we find them in the dreamlike contradiction between the figure and the landscape. The former is a descendant of the pagan Apollos of pre-Christian Greece, the latter an echo of the fantastic Byzantine formula for landscape, based on nothing that the human eye had ever seen in nature.

Domenico Veneziano was evidently one of the first artists of the Italian Renaissance to break away from the mediaeval sense of shame in respect to the naked human body. This little panel contains one of the earliest "noble" nudes since Apollo and Venus had ceased to set a visual standard for physical beauty. Domenico would never have dared to introduce such a figure into the altarpiece for which this is a pendant, but small predella panels often tempted artists to make bolder statements than the formal altarpieces to which they belonged. It is certainly odd that Domenico should have chosen the ascetic St. John the Baptist to be the Christian equivalent of a Greek Apollo; he selected the moment when the saint rejected his clothing in favor of a suit of camel skin as a pretext for painting the male nude. This delightful picture reveals the expanding spirit of the early Renaissance when Italy was beginning

103

44. *Domenico Veneziano (active 1438-1461). St. John in the Desert.*
    c. 1450. Tempera. Kress Collection, National Gallery, Washington, D.C.

to understand that physical beauty did not cancel out spiritual meanings, but
had not yet realized that nature was as deserving of study as man.

Donatello. David

THE EARLY YEARS of the 15th Century produced, in Florence,
a group of famous sculptors of whom the most painstaking was Ghiberti,
the most charming Lucca della Robbia, and the most original and daring
Donatello, whose range was so wide that no sculptural problem seemed to
frighten him, from the frieze of dancing children in the Singing Gallery of

104

the cathedral to the bald-headed "Zuc-cone" of the Campanile. Equally wide was his range of narrative, as can be seen in his series of low relief panels at Padua. One thinks of him, in fact, not as the re-discoverer of Greek ca-nons of physical beauty, but as the student of human character and emo-tion who discovered the secret of com-bining "expressionist" content with "classic" form.

It would be tempting, therefore, to choose from his work an example that showed him at his most dramatic. Yet to do so would be to deprive this book of one of the most casually elegant statues ever modeled.

Donatello's David in the Bargello in Florence has almost the air of an answer to a challenge—perhaps a self-imposed one. It is as though he has, for once, attempted to give us a figure in which perfect ease and serenity had found their abode in a young body of flawless physique.

That, of course, is precisely what one expects to find in Golden Age Greek carving. Yet only a glance at Donatello's David is needed to realize that neither Pheidias nor Praxiteles could have envisaged anything so con-ventionally beautiful that was also so strange and provocative. It contains so many hints of insouciance, of jaunty swagger, of youth's defiance against authority, even of gentle undergra-duate mockery; Donatello shows us how the young man, who in his ma-turity was to write the Psalms, allows himself subtly to burlesque the perfec-tion of Greek sculpture as he treads carelessly on the severed head of Goliath.

45. *Donatello (1386-1466). David. c. 1443. Bronze. The Bargello, Florence*

Nothing could more clearly reveal the difference between the Greek and the Renaissance spirit—the former striving after physical perfection, the latter charged with the tremor of nervous movement; the former serene, the latter restless. Yet no Renaissance statue ever paid more sincere homage to its Hellenic prototypes.

Andrea del Castagno.   David

THE YOUTHFUL FIGURE OF David must have had a strong appeal for the Italian, and especially the Florentine, artists of the early 15th Century. What interested them was not David the elderly king, praising

46. *Castagno (? 1410-1457).*
The Youthful David. c. *1450.*
Tempera on leather.
Widener Collection,
National Gallery ,Washington, D.C.

God to the sonorous rhythm of the Psalms and listening to the music of his harp, but David the young man, pressing forward, sling in hand, astonishing his generation by slaying giants singlehanded. Donatello (see Plate 45) shows him casually placing his foot on the gigantic head of his enemy, in a moment of rest, but inwardly prepared for further adventures. For Andrea del Castagno, a little later, David is filled with energetic determination. The bleeding head of Goliath lies at his feet, but he has recharged his sling and he is ready for new enterprises, his wine-colored cloak flying behind him. When Michelangelo carved David at the end of the same century, the youthful fire of the early Renaissance was already losing its intensity. Michelangelo is concerned with the muscular athlete, demanding our admiration for his physique rather than his conquests.

Andrea del Castagno was one of those intensely serious artists who would always prefer nervous energy to grace or gaiety. His paintings are extremely rare and this painted "parade shield" is unique. Such shields were made for use on ceremonial occasions or at jousts and tournaments, but this is the only surviving example painted by a great artist. It is made of stiff leather, about four feet in height, and is painted with a high finish. The only other considerable Florentines who could have conceived so forceful a figure were the Pollaiuolo brothers (see Plate 54). They too were students of virility in action and it is not by accident that Pollaiuolo's Tobias, setting out on his journey, does so in just the same spirit as the youthful David. But Andrea del Castagno's picture must have been painted at least a decade earlier than Pollaiuolo's.

Uccello.   *The Rout of San Romano*

IN THE YEAR 1432 a skirmish occurred between the hired mercenaries of Siena and the hired mercenaries of Florence under the leadership of the *condottiere*, Niccolo da Tolentino. The Florentines won, more by accident than by intelligent tactics, but the battle was of little consequence to the subsequent history of either city. The Rout of San Romano would have been heard of only by a handful of historians if Cosimo de Medici had not commissioned Paolo Uccello, twenty years later, to paint three large pictures of the battle for the Medici palace in Florence.

These pictures, now distributed between the Louvre in Paris, the Uffizi in Florence and the National Gallery in London, are as famous as the event they commemorate is obscure. Plate 47 is a detail from the center of the National Gallery picture, once the left-hand member of the trio. Tolentino himself fills the center of the stage (one can only think of the battle as taking place, decoratively, on a stage), his head surmounted by a huge turban, *107*

47. Uccello (1397-1475). Rout of San Romano (detail). c. 1455.
Tempera on wood. National Gallery, London

on a prancing white horse, waving a baton, followed by his young, fair-haired page who carries his helmet. Above him floats his white banner bearing his device of "Solomon's Knots."

Nothing could be gayer, more heraldic, less fraught with the sinister implications of warfare. One calls to mind Machiavelli's cynical remark that wars between cities were "waged without danger and concluded without loss." Yet Uccello has responded magnificently, if innocently, to his theme. Spears, banners and horses (generically halfway between chargers and rocking horses), seen against the dark hills of Tuscany and the darker sky above them, combine to make a composition of wonderful richness and animation.

Vasari tells us that Uccello was obsessed by the problem of perspective and the remark has hardened into a legend, so that we look for confirmation at the spears, so carefully arranged on the ground to lead the eye to a vanishing point. But Uccello's preoccupation with perspective can have been hardly more than a schoolboyish hobby. What really matters is that he was a magnificent colorist and a masterly designer. In this picture one seems to feel that the Italian Renaissance is getting into its stride. The world of tapestry is becoming the world of fact. This picture is a remarkable halfway house between the make-believe tournaments of the mediaeval world and the great picture, Las Lanzas, that Velasquez was to paint two centuries later.

Agostino di Duccio. Musician Angels

THE LONG LIST of 15th-Century Italian sculptors includes a few men of great inventive power, such as Donatello and Jacopo della Quercia, and others of unusual grace and sweetness, like Ghiberti and Lucca della Robbia, but none of them have the rhythmic charm of Agostino di Duccio, whose best work was done in the little "Tempio," a chapel designed by Alberti for the Malatesta family in Rimini. Nothing that Agostino did was impressive but all of it has a freshness and an innocence that is rare in Italian Renaissance sculpture. Carving "in the round" never attracted him, but his low-relief panels with their restless flowing line are the work of a skilled draftsman turned sculptor, but far more interested in line than in mass. Agostino's line reminds us of the similar dancing line in Botticelli's drawing. Like Botticelli he is a master of sinuous rhythm rather than of mass.

48. *Agostino di Duccio.*
   (b. 1418).
   Musician Angels.
   c. *1452. Marble.*
   Rimini

49. Piero della Francesca
(? 1416-1492).
Legend of the
True Cross (detail).
c. 1455. Fresco.
Arezzo

Piero della Francesca.   Legend of the True Cross

OF ALL THE Italian artists of the 15th Century it is Piero della Francesca who has most firmly captured the responses of our own generation, almost exactly five centuries later. And of all Piero's major works it is the great series of frescoes in the Church of San Francesco in Arezzo that seems to us to exhibit his quiet authority most completely. Yet, impressive though they are, no reproduction can do them justice. The spell they cast over the mind of the spectator seems to be uttered in so unemphatic and yet such a confident tone of voice that one has to contemplate the whole of this extremely elaborate conception in order to understand its full meaning.

This is obviously beyond the power of any reproduction, however ambitious; one is forced to select a detail, and although any detail, however small, is bound to carry with it the imprint of Piero's personality (that of the "noneloquent" artist as Mr. Berenson has called him), no isolated fragment can speak for the whole. In despair one selects a single head from among a multitude of figures in the hope that, like a phrase from a symphony, it may suggest the flavor of the whole: so that the reader may exclaim "This tells me nothing of the structure of the symphony, yet even the isolated phrase could only have been composed by Piero."

The Golden Legend is Piero's subject in the Arezzo cycle of frescoes. It is the mediaeval story of the tree whose fruit was eaten by Adam and Eve, a branch of which was planted on the grave of Adam. It grew and endured until the time of King Solomon, who cut it down and used its wood for a bridge over the river Siloam. The Queen of Sheba, visiting Solomon, recognizes the sacred wood and falls on her knees before it. Ultimately it is made into the Cross on which Jesus was crucified. After the Crucifixion it was lost and later rediscovered by St. Helena.

The detail shown is that of the head of the Queen of Sheba as she kneels, surrounded by her retinue on the threshold of King Solomon's palace. What stamps the fragment as undoubtedly Piero's is its stark, almost geometrical simplicity. But behind the geometry is a sensitivity. The outline is as steady as though it were that of the carved figurehead of a ship. Yet it is the very reverse of wooden. The Queen of Sheba is impassive, monumental and full of dignity—but she is human.

It is worth comparing the qualities of Piero's contours with those of Botticelli (Plate 53). Botticelli's are quivering and nervous: Piero's are imperturbable and steady. Yet, no less than Botticelli's, they obey the slightest inflections of a hypersensitive hand and eye.

School of Avignon. Pietà

THERE IS nothing in the art of any European country that prepares us for this wonderful masterpiece. We know that it was painted by an anonymous master of the School of Avignon in Provence about the year 1460. Having said that, we have done nothing to explain its sudden, unheralded appearance or its isolation; for just as nothing like it had been painted before, so nothing resembling it has been painted since. It is either the work of a *111*

50. School of Avignon. Pietà. c. 1460. Tempera on panel. Louvre

genius whose other works have vanished, or of some artist in a moment of
inspiration which enabled him once, and only once, to create a timeless and
almost regionless work of art.

Its mood is of austere and intense tragedy, but tragedy expressed without
the aid of agonized facial expressions or gestures of despair. It is stark and
quiet and saturated with silent grief. None of the four figures of the living
communicates with the others over the body of the dead Christ. And, on
analysis, one realizes that what makes the painting's impact so strong is a
highly sophisticated process of elimination. Nothing could have been omitted,
nothing added, without impoverishing it or diluting its impact.

The three majestic silhouettes of St. John, the Virgin and the Magdalen
break across the low, distant horizon. Behind them is an expanse of plain
gold that, even for provincial painting, was archaistic after the middle of
the 15th Century. Yet here, for once, a naturalistic sky would have been
intolerable. What painters call the negative shapes—the intervals left between
the figures—would have lost their meaning. And when the eye drops to the
112   pale, stiff figure of the dead Christ, the negative shapes become even more

significant. The helpless right arm of the Christ, the lower line of the torso, the line of the loin cloth form the edges of an angular shape that thrusts itself upward from below.

The edges are hard, almost metallic. Features and folds of drapery are described like the drawing of a map. The line never hesitates. The artist is utterly confident about the placing of every contour. The delicate line, for example, that establishes the lower edge of the Virgin's cloak, is necessary to the composition, keeping all the downward-thrusting forms above the cloak in their place. If the picture were not so passionately intense one would describe such a line as a painter's "device." But to speak of devices in connection with the Pietà of Avignon is inappropriate.

The unknown donor who kneels at the side ought to upset the balance of the picture's uneven symmetry. Oddly enough he does no such thing. He relieves the tension by forming a link between ourselves and the stricken mourners. And his head—an unusually finely drawn and sympathetic portrait —acts as a foil to the timeless silhouettes against the gold background. He is a tough Provençal, yet he is caught up into the mood of the picture. He is not entitled to wear the halo that they wear, yet he has the right to be present and share their grief; and he, like them, is self-contained. He makes no attempt by glance or gesture to communicate either with them or with us.

Art historians have been immensely puzzled by the picture. Iconographic-ally it certainly has prototypes, but stylistically it stands alone—or almost alone. There are hints in it of Spanish or Portuguese influence (there are none of Italian) but there is no known Spanish or Portuguese artist who had the refinement of this painter.

Cossa. Frescoes in the Schifanoia Palace

SUCCESSIVE HEADS of the family of Este had ruled the city of Ferrara for centuries, enriching it both materially and artistically, when in 1450 Lionello, thirteenth marquis of the city and himself a distinguished patron of the arts, died and was succeeded by his brother, Borso.

It was Borso who gathered round himself and his court the group of artists whom we think of as forming the Ferrarese School: Cosimo Tura, Ercole de' Roberti and Francesco del Cossa. None of them had the gravity or the intellectual stamina of their best Florentine contemporaries but all of them had original minds, and Borso, the first Duke of Ferrara, was determined to make good use of them. It is to Borso that we owe the elaborate frescoes of the Schifanoia Palace in Ferrara and the fact that the great hall on the first floor of the palace is one of the most charming of the courtly interiors left behind by the Italian Renaissance. Cossa was responsible for most of its *113*

51. *Cossa (1435-1477). April from frescoes in the Schifanoia Palace.*
c. 1467. Ferrara

frescoes, but it was Borso, a typical specimen of the sport-loving squire, more interested in classical legend than in Christian iconography, who set the mood for them.

The frescoes combine a love of the outdoor life with a frankly pagan outlook. The subjects are the months of the year, and the quality of Cossa's imagination can be fairly judged from this detail from the section descriptive of April. For Cossa, April is the month of aristocratic leisure and pleasure. Winter is over, the earth pregnant, the gardens are gay with flowers, young men and maidens discreetly make love under the blue sky, rabbits (symbols of fertility) run in and out of their burrows, harnessed swans swim toward the shore. The mood is gay and pastoral—very different from that of Botticelli's Allegory of Spring, which is wistful, thoughtful and charged with a more poetic kind of symbolism.

Love in Idleness is Cossa's theme. Apart from the young man who plants a kiss on the cheek of a girl (who holds a lute), the rest of the company is engaged in conversation, though surely they are not discussing philosophy. Nothing could be a more appropriate illustration of one of Boccaccio's stories in *The Decameron*. And nothing could more completely sum up the atmosphere of Borso's court at Ferrara. At almost exactly the same moment (in the late 1460's), Mantegna was celebrating in wall paintings, in the Camera degli Sposi in the palace at Mantua, the daily life of the Gonzaga family. The Gonzagas, one feels, comparing the two frescoed rooms that are so similar in intention, were a good deal more solemn than the Estes. Worthier perhaps, but less lovable. Both families got the artists they deserved and both artists gave their princely patrons exactly what they wanted.

Mantegna. *Agony in the Garden*

THERE IS something frightening in Mantegna's relentless, noble austerity, especially in his earlier work when he was serving as court painter to the Gonzaga family in Mantua, and particularly during his early years in Padua when he was the leading artist in Squarcione's academy. He was a precocious artist and, even in his early youth, his impeccable draftsmanship and the complexity of his composition laid the foundations of the Paduan school of painting.

But Mantegna was more than the leader of the Paduan school. He was an artist of great personal intensity. In his earlier pictures the air is always preternaturally clear; the rocks are carved out of granite by some landscape gardener turned sculptor; the clouds, too, are carved out of some slightly less resistant substance. Trees and shrubs struggle to fix their roots in the arid rock, and when they manage to put forth foliage, Mantegna seems to resent   *115*

52. *Mantegna (1431-1506). The Agony in the Garden. c. 1466. Tempera. Museum of Tours*

its attempts at luxuriance. Leaves are stamped out of tin, flowers cut out of paper. Even the marble limbs of his human figures are clothed in pliable sheet metal.

Only a mind charged with immensely serious purpose could have achieved such grandeur at the expense of so much mystery. Such a man was bound to influence those with whom he came into contact. The artists whom Mantegna most influenced—the painters of Ferrara, notably Cosima Tura—could accept his material world of granite and sheet metal, but out of it they built a tortured, restless world, never a noble one.

The subject of the Agony in the Garden must have appealed to his temperament. He painted it twice and his pupil and brother-in-law, Giovanni Bellini, was inspired to tackle it during his years with Mantegna in Padua. Bellini's picture, together with one of Mantegna's versions, is now in the National Gallery in London, where the two paintings offer the student of style a fascinating glimpse of Bellini's attempt to escape from the domination of his master into a more sensuous mood—the mood of Venice. Mantegna's other version which is illustrated here is in the Museum of Tours.

Some authorities have doubted its authenticity. I cannot share their doubts. This picture, more complex and a little more diffuse than the London version, is designed with immense conviction. The rockbound landscape, with its two sinister peaks whose summits are cut off by the frame, dwarf the four foreground figures even more completely than that in the National Gallery, giving them an even more pathetic meaning. There is a greater poignancy in the Christ of Tours; and the three disciples are even more deeply sunk in the oblivion of sleep. The road from the city to Gethsemane is more closely defined and the procession that approaches, led by Judas who is about to betray Christ, is more formidable. The Tours version contains more of the essence of inner tragedy. In the London version a group of child angels, each one bearing a symbol of the passion, appears to the praying Jesus. In this picture a single angel (more iconographically conventional) descends through layers of little clouds with the chalice. The effect is of greater intimacy.

Mantegna's paintings (and none more so than this one) often have the strange effect of foreshadowing 20th-Century Surrealism. They have the same atmospheric clarity and insistence on detail. And both Mantegna and the Surrealists have the same obsession with distance. The two hillsides, which intersect where the sky line dips down to a mountain pass, curve away from us in a perspective that draws the eye back, beyond the sleeping disciples, beyond the winding road and the city to the brightening sky. The day of the Betrayal is dawning.

Botticelli. *Allegory of Spring*

NO ARTIST, with the possible exception of certain Chinese drafts-men, has ever had a finer command of rhythmically modulated line than Botticelli. His winding linear arabesques seem to have a life of their own that is quite independent of the arm, the strand of hair or the fold of drapery they describe. That is one reason why a detail from one of his major pictures can do him fuller justice than the picture itself. An additional reason is, of course, that the main groupings and the romantic content of the Primavera have become so familiar to us through constant reproduction that there is a risk of failing to respond immediately to the whole, whereas the isolation of a part can surprise us and open our eyes afresh to the well-known Botticelli rhythms.

Yet the picture as a whole is important for the light it sheds on that distinguished group of painters, poets and philosophers that gathered in the third quarter of the 15th Century round the central, catalyst figure of Lorenzo the Magnificent in Florence. The Primavera was painted for one of the Medicean country houses and its subject was taken straight from a poem by Lorenzo's favorite poet, Poliziano. The pregnant figure of Spring stands, as everyone knows, static yet lithe in the center of the picture. On the right, Flora and a nymph pursued by the wind move inward and forward through the thicket; on the left, the Three Graces (from which our detail is taken) dance in a close circle. Mercury turns his back on them. Overhead a flying Eros discharges an arrow.

The theme is a satisfying fusion of allegory and classic mythology—a fusion particularly acceptable to the Renaissance mind and particularly to the Florentine Renaissance mind. But the treatment of it is by no means classic, for although Botticelli was an intimate member of the Medicean circle with its craze for dabbling in classical literature and its attempts to discover reconciliations between Christianity and paganism, he was a mediaevalist at heart. There are distinct traces of the "International Gothic" style in the figure of Flora—angular, heavily patterned with brocaded flowers, her dress decorated at the edges with scalloped serrations.

A peculiarly elaborate mediaeval miniature has come to life and has been endowed with a new kind of fluent grace. Paganism and Christianity *have* met and fused, but not through Medicean philosophy. It is Botticelli's own genius that has cast a spell over both.

It was not easy to choose which section of the picture would most completely illustrate Botticelli's mixture of wistfulness, sinuous grace and decorative mediaevalism. In the end it seemed reasonable to sacrifice Flora's unearthly beauty to the semitransparent counterpoint of moving arms, rippling draperies and flowing hair that constitutes the upper half of the Three Graces. The pattern of the arms alone is like the rhythm of a mildly agitated sea, with one wave that reaches a climax in the raised arms and intertwined fingers above the three heads.

What is, perhaps, most remarkable is that, though the artist seems to have exerted his full powers on the invention of this ultrarefined linear arabesque so that all the *meaning* of the figures resides in their contours, the figures are still solid and resistant to the touch. The shadows whereby they are "modeled" are reduced to a minimum, yet they are by no means cut from cardboard. They have weight, their muscles are tense and their limbs have enough volume to make their transparent draperies *enfold* them instead of being skillfully laid across them. Perhaps the expressiveness of his line is so complete that it carries with it a conviction about the nature of the surfaces enclosed by it.

118

53. *Botticelli* (1444-1510). *Allegory of Spring.* c. 1475. *Tempera. Uffizi, Florence*

54. *Pollaiuolo*
(1432-1498).
Tobias and the
Archangel Raphael.
c. 1475.
Regia Pinacoteca,
Turin

Pollaiuolo. Tobias and the Angel

SCHOLARS have tried in vain to discover some stylistic difference between the two Pollaiuolo brothers, Antonio and Piero, so that undocumented pictures could be firmly ascribed to one or the other. All that can be said with certainty is that all the "Pollaiuolo" pictures whose authorship is known are by Piero.

Such problems belong to the "detective" side of art history. What really matters is that between them the two brothers painted certain pictures and produced certain engravings which bear the unmistakable stamp of the "Pollaiuolo style." In all they did is a restless energy, a thrusting movement that one sees at once in the figures. Then one notices that the same restlessness has infected the whole picture and that the landscapes in which the two brothers place their figures share this restlessness. Behind the angel and the young man, the river winds away tortuously into the distance.

Something of that same nervous youthful energy runs through much of the art of the Florentine 15th Century. Ten years earlier (see Plate 46) Andrea del Castagno had painted the young David setting out to slay another Goliath, and earlier still, Donatello's David (Plate 45), even more youthful, paused in a moment of suspended energy, with his foot carelessly resting on his victim's severed head. About 1475 Pollaiuolo painted Tobias in much the same spirit, but he had neither the grave monumentality of Castagno nor the power of Donatello. Life by this time is more assured and more scholarly. Pollaiuolo's Tobias is the eternal sophisticated student setting out on life's journey with his tutor. He is a young dandy, in search not of giants but of knowledge. He is a rich young man dressed in expensive clothes, but also an athlete.

Pollaiuolo specialized in the male body in action. The great altarpiece of St. Sebastian's martyrdom in the National Gallery in London is little more than an excuse to display the flexed muscles of archers at target practice. The central obsession of the Florentine painter or sculptor was the study of the human body, but no previous Florentine had regarded it so exclusively as a machine for violent movement. It was on Pollaiuolo's studies that Michelangelo based the nobler and more harmonious behavior of his figures in action at the end of the century.

Carpaccio. Two Venetian Women

THE HISTORY of Venetian painting in the second half of the 15th Century is crowded with the names of artists of the second rank. They painted charming pictures; they were excellent craftsmen, good and, in one or two instances, noble colorists; they were conservatives, dwarfed by the steadily increasing power of their great contemporary, Giovanni Bellini. With him, ultimately, lay the responsibility of establishing the grand Venetian tradition which he passed on to his two brilliant young pupils, Giorgione and Titian.

Yet among the minor contemporaries of Bellini there were one or two who painted lovable, intimate, glowing pictures of a kind that had never been   *121*

55. *Carpaccio (1450-1522). Two Venetian Women. 1495.*
Oil. Museo Civico, Venice.

painted before. There was Cima born in Conegliano, in the foothills of the chain of mountains that guard Venice from the north, whose landscape backgrounds to his Sacred Conversations are among the first paintings in which the structure of hilly country and the clear mountain light of the distant ranges has been truly observed. And there was Vittore Carpaccio, a devoted citizen of Venice, who was so fascinated by its daily life and its pageantry that he became one of the earliest *genre* painters.

It is from Carpaccio and not from Bellini that we know the look of a Venetian girl's bedroom (even though he pretends it is the bedroom of St. Ursula) and how the young gallants of the time were dressed and how the courtesans of Venice idled away the summer afternoon on the balcony. Not until the mid-17th Century, and then only in Holland, are such everyday scenes painted with the same affectionate understanding.

Whenever Carpaccio tried his hand at something more exalted his imagination could hardly rise to the occasion (though his Meditation on the Passion in the Metropolitan Museum, New York, is a notable exception). The final triumph of St. Ursula, in which he attempts a grand climax to his story of the saint's adventures, is a complete failure, just where Bellini would have succeeded. But this intimate little slice of life that describes two rather unattractive and slightly overdressed women, playing with their pets and obviously a little bored with their occupation, is a startling success, just where Bellini would have failed.

It is in this kind of picture, one that was never intended to be a masterpiece, that we find Carpaccio so lovable. He is both emotionally detached and visually fascinated. One finds the same refusal to glamorize and the same obsession with occupational gesture in Degas three centuries later.

The effect, of course, is different. Carpaccio belongs to a school of artists who had been slowly building up a way of seeing life in terms of glowing patches of wonderfully harmonized color. He was always one of the most sensitive of Venetian colorists. Among later Venetians only Veronese could surpass him in color orchestration. Both painters had an almost oriental instinct for color that was both rich and infinitely subtle. But there the resemblance ceases. For Veronese had no humor, no sense of the oddity of human behavior, no delight in the unexpected. This little picture is packed with all three qualities.

In a century when every great artist in Italy was striving for grace or grandeur or nobility, this delight in the commonplace is refreshing. Carpaccio's avid eye for the detail of the scene—the rather ridiculous dogs, the two pigeons that have settled on the balustrade, the two absurdly high Venetian pattens that one of the girls has shuffled off to ease her tired feet—mark him as a "Social Realist" of his time. The rather merciless insight into the character of the two women, their florid taste in dress, their decorous boredom, are certainly not Gothic. They belong to a later, more democratic and more disillusioned age.

Pintoricchio. Return of Ulysses

HIGH UP in his palace in Siena, the Palazzo del Magnifico, Pandolfo Petrucci commissioned the decorations for a room with eight frescoes, each about four feet square. All of them depicted scenes from Greek or Roman legend or history. Two of them are said to be still there, buried under coats of whitewash; two of them are now in the gallery at Siena; one is lost and the remaining three, two of which are by Signorelli and the third, illustrated here, by Pintoricchio, are in the National Gallery in London. The decorations of the room were completed in 1509.

One could wish that the room had remained intact, for it must have been a gem of early 16th-Century interior decoration. But we can make a rough guess at its general effect if we remember the charm of the suite of apartments that Pintoricchio decorated for Cesare Borgia in the Vatican. The Borgia apartments are light and fanciful but never trivial, for Pintoricchio, though not a profound artist, was always tasteful and occasionally gay. He was, in fact, a typical product of the Umbrian school of the 15th Century, the school that produced Signorelli, Perugino and the young Raphael.

There is a childish innocence in most of Pintoricchio's work. Serious themes, with him, develop a "told to the children" air. This is how a nursery should be decorated, though the children would learn from it a rather inaccurate version of Homer's story. Penelope sits at her loom weaving the shroud for her father-in-law, which she unwove each night (though Homer tells us that her trick had been discovered before the return of her husband, Ulysses). Behind her, on the wall, is the famous bow which none of her suitors was able to draw. Her son, Telemachus, dressed in the height of fashion of 1509, runs in to tell her that he has still no news of his father. One of the suitors stands dreamily on the right with a hawk on his wrist (Umbrian painting was never robust). The identity of the man wearing a turban and of the youth who gazes at the ceiling cannot be established. They could be the soothsayer, Theoclymenus, and the swineherd, Eumaeus. Ulysses himself appears through the door disguised as a beggar; it is his first entry into his own home after an absence of twenty years and Pintoricchio certainly follows Homer in establishing that the hero's return was unnoticed by his family.

Through the window, Pintoricchio has given us, like a miniature in an illuminated manuscript, two of the adventures of Ulysses during his voyage—his encounter with the Sirens and his meeting with the enchantress, Circe. Pintoricchio's attitude to the task of narrative painting is indicated by the fact that the ship in which Ulysses had made his long journey is decorated

56. *Pintoricchio (1454-1513). The Return of Ulysses. c. 1509. Fresco.
National Gallery, London*

with the arms of the Petrucci family, and Circe's castle is flying the Petrucci
flag. The artist was more anxious to please his Sienese patron than to follow
the Greek story.

Giovanni Bellini. St. Jerome in a Rocky Landscape

IF ONE WERE to attempt to sum up in a phrase the basic difference
between Florentine and Venetian painting in the late 15th Century when the
artistic creeds of the two cities were crystallizing, one would say that in
Florentine art man dominates nature, whereas in Venetian art he is contained
by her.

That, of course, is by no means the whole truth but it explains a good deal. We can hardly remember what kind of a landscape is behind Raphael's Madonnas; Michelangelo's Adam, created in the Garden of Eden, lies on a bare slab of formless rock; whereas Titian's figures (see Plate 74) cannot be thought of without the blue skies, the mountainous distances and the lush meadows in which and against which they move.

It was Giovanni Bellini who first developed this Venetian passion for trees and flowers, hills and open skies. And it was he who during his long life developed more and more intensely the idea that the landscape contains the figures. It was Bellini who infected his two great pupils, Titian and Giorgione, with this nostalgia for the open air, so that their landscapes, like his, never seem to have been painted in the studio, though we know, of course, that they must have been.

With the awakening Venetian interest in the countryside that lay to the north of Venice and the foothills of the Dolomites came a less reverent, more cavalier attitude to the human figure. What Florentine would have squeezed St. Jerome into one corner of his canvas, or allowed him to concentrate his gaze intently on a lizard, or allowed two rabbits to occupy the center of the stage? Florence was the center of humanism. Bellini, one could say, turned Venice into a city of pantheism and in doing so laid the foundations for the landscape painting of later centuries.

This was only one side of Bellini's immensely rich temperament. In his formal altarpieces he could be as noble as any Florentine, and in his lyrical or allegorical paintings he moved into a world that lies beyond logic and out of reach of the physical eye. But this little panel (eighteen inches by fifteen) is typical of the Bellini who, rebelling against the claustrophobia of a Venetian studio, crossed the lagoon to the mainland on a bright spring morning and lost himself in an affectionate contemplation of rocks and flowers and trees, lizards and rabbits, open skies and villages on the distant hillside. Having set his stage so delightfully, one would almost think that he had introduced St. Jerome and his lion as an afterthought. Nothing in the old man's appearance suggests the saint. Rather does he suggest some aged satyr left behind and forgotten in his rockbound cave when the gods of Greece and Rome were finally banished by Christianity.

The picture was probably painted fairly late in Bellini's life—about 1510 —but it retains the crispness and freshness of vision that characterized him throughout his career.

57. *Giovanni Bellini* (c. *1430-1516*). *St. Jerome Reading. 1510. Wood.*
Kress Collection, National Gallery, Washington, D.C.

58. *Winemaking (detail). Late 15th Century. Tapestry.*
Cluny Museum, Paris

Tapestries from Flanders and France

O F   A L L   F O R M S of art, it is tapestry that brings to life for us most vividly the spirit of the late Middle Ages, especially the tapestries of Flanders and France. Kings and knights do battle in front of fantastic castles, allegorical figures surround man in his journey through life, laborers work in the fields and the vineyards, courtiers hunt the stag and the boar. And after the struggle is over, death intervenes. Life, one feels, is beset by dangers and difficulties, yet behind it all is a restless, exuberant gaiety. Nothing could be more elaborate than the brocaded and embroidered dresses worn by the men and women; they live in an eternal garden of patterned flowers and fruit-bearing trees, among which small animals and birds live in delicious contentment. The great tapestry weavers of Brussels and Tournai created a world of make-believe in which danger was tempered by romance and even the arduous labors of sowing and reaping and viniculture were transformed into a colorful decorative pattern.

It is easy to explain this transformation of difficulty into delight by saying that the medium of tapestry tempted the designer to fill the great spaces he had to cover with a wealth of variegated detail. Weaving is a slow process as compared with painting, and the man at the loom was almost forced to invent a pattern of flowers and animals to fill the areas which a painter would normally have covered with an unbroken surface of color. But the art of every age produces not only an image of the world it longs to live in, but chooses the medium most appropriate for that image. At the very moment when Italy was solving the problem of material reality in terms of paint, Northwestern Europe was producing a wealth of fantasy in terms of tapestry. We cannot be certain of the dates when Brussels and Tournai were weaving their grandest designs. It may well be that some of them were produced in the very years in which Michelangelo was working on the ceiling of the Sistine Chapel (see Plate 72). Yet the former belongs to the mediaeval world, the latter marks the climax of the High Renaissance.

The three tapestries here are utterly different in their subject matter, though they are so similar in effect. One can reconstruct every detail of the pressing of the grapes, the pouring out of the grape juice into vats and its transfer into barrels. We know at a glance the social difference between the toiling laborers and the courtiers who watched them at work. Yet, in an almost similar garden, we see Man in his symbolic journey through life, reclining in the lap of Luxury—or rather of Luxuria, a lady far more closely connected with carnal desire—attacked by Justice with her avenging sword and defended by Mercy who intervenes on her behalf. It is the visual equivalent of the journeys of Everyman or Bunyan's Christian.

59. *Man in the Toils of Luxury (detail). 16th Century. Tapestry. Metropolitan Museum, New York*

60. *The Sense of Taste (panel from La Dame à la Licorne). 16th Century. Tapestry. Cluny Museum, Paris*

Undoubtedly the most touching and the most beautiful of the three tapestries is the panel from the series called La Dame à la Licorne which occupies an unforgettable room to itself in the Cluny Museum in Paris. Here is the distilled romanticism of the Middle Ages. It consists of six panels, in five of which the Lady, whose name was probably Claude le Viste, always accompanied in her enclosed garden by a lion and a snow-white unicorn, each carrying a banner, enjoys the delights of the five senses. Plate 60, The Sense of Taste, shows her taking a sweet from the bowl offered to her by her handmaiden. In the sixth (not illustrated) she stands in the entrance to a tent of blue cloth sprinkled with golden flames, with the inscription *"A Mon Seul Désir"* over her head.

The tapestries were probably a gift to her from her betrothed, Jean de Chabannes-Vandenesse. The unicorn—emblem of virginity—is her protective companion; the lion, which occurs on his coat of arms, is the mark of his protective devotion. The device on the banners (gules, on a bend azure, three crescents argent) is that of the Le Viste family.

Mediaeval romance can go no further than this. Human love has found its ultimate expression in a visible ritual, as it found it in words in Dante's *Vita Nuova*. The tapestries are a melody without words—but for the invention of the loom such a melody could never have been invented. No painter, not even Veronese, that master of aristocratic hedonism, could have achieved it.

L'Homme. *Tapestry by Jean Lurçat*

W H A T M I G H T be called the "decorative" media—stained glass, mosaic, champlevé enamel and tapestry—popular in mediaeval Europe, was rendered obsolete by the desire for a realistic presentation of the material world which began with the Italian Renaissance, spread to the rest of Europe in the mid-16th Century and continued until the end of the 19th Century. During that period the decorative media became obsolescent. For Velasquez and Rembrandt, for Courbet and Degas, nothing would serve but oil paint. It was not till the end of the first decade of our own century that a formalized treatment of the visible world again became acceptable. Realism, quite suddenly, became not only unnecessary but unacceptable. No sooner had Picasso and Braque begun to evolve a new language in the painting of easel pictures than the mediaeval media began to be revived. Not only did "modern" vision replace the vision of the last century, but oil paint suddenly ceased to be the only means of expressing that vision.

Our own century, therefore, has seen a vivid revival of the crafts of stained glass, mosaic and tapestry. And in the design of tapestry the French, *131*

61. Lurçat (b. 1892). L'Homme. 1946. Tapestry.
Jansen Collection, Paris

with their tradition of weaving, have led the rest of the world. Outstanding among contemporary designers is Lurçat.

Comparing Lurçat's tapestry, L'Homme, with its mediaeval prototypes, it is obvious at once that a great tradition has been revived and revitalized. The same sparkle, the same formalization of plant forms, the same inventiveness of texture can be seen in this 20th-Century French tapestry as in the tapestries of Tournai. Even the same attitude to the world. Lurçat's L'Homme is not *a* man, an individual, but Man, a symbol. And the world he moves in is not the world of phenomena but the world of creative imagination. Prose has been replaced by poetry, space by pattern, realistic photographic color by emotive color.

Dürer. *Four Horsemen of the Apocalypse*

IT WAS in 1498 that Dürer published the great Book of the Revelation of St. John on Patmos, in which text and woodcut illustrations combined to bring home to the reader the full force of an apocalyptic vision. Such a vision was peculiarly appropriate to the troubled times through which Germany was passing at the end of the 15th Century. The horsemen of Death, Famine, War and Plague were riding destructively through the land. What Dürer did in this famous woodcut was to invent an imagery for them that would be as vivid as St. John's written words.

The Apocalypse of 1498 (it was published in two editions, Latin and German) is, historically, one of the most important books ever published for it at once established Dürer as a major artist with a European rather than a German reputation, and it turned the woodcut, as such, into a powerful medium for the communication of ideas. Prolific though Dürer was as a painter, draftsman and engraver, it could be convincingly argued that his Apocalypse is his most important work—the most daring, the most visionary and the most aesthetically satisfying in his whole output. It could also be argued, though with less confidence, that out of the Book's total of fifteen prints, the Four Horsemen is the most monumental and the most truly inspired.

The book was not commissioned. Dürer alone was responsible for its inception and for its unusually large format. Like Hogarth, he intended his prints not for the portfolios of connoisseurs but for wide distribution among burghers and artisans. The imagination that fired him when he designed the plates was peculiarly his own, but their vigor and enthusiasm were doubtless the result of his determination to make them, in the most literal sense, popular. The combination of riotous symbolism, mystery and allegory in the text would, one might have thought, be impossible to translate into visual terms, yet Dürer seems to manage it with ease. The whore of Babylon seated on her many-headed monster; the dragon whose thrashing tail draws a third part of the stars from heaven; even the devouring by St. John of the book, impressive as a literary idea but inevitably embarrassing for a descriptive draftsman, are made to seem possible and convincing in these magnificent prints.

Dürer did not actually cut the blocks himself but, true craftsman that he was, he adapted his drawings to the needs of the medium, simplifying the design, strengthening and stiffening the line, finding a convention for drapery, hair, landscape, trees, clouds that has now become accepted as inevitable but which, in Dürer's lifetime, required both imagination and intelligence. In the print of the Four Horsemen nothing could be more expressive

133

62. *Dürer (1471-1528). The Four Horsemen of the Apocalypse.*
1498. Woodcut

than the massed cumulus clouds, the flying drapery, the manes of the horses, yet they have been forged out of one of the most stubborn of media.

The design itself, with its strong upward surge that tramples beggars and bishops underfoot as it passes furiously across the page, needs no description. Its inherent energy is triumphant. The noble urgency of the central figure holding the scales is a conception worthy of Michelangelo, whose grandest inventions, be it remembered, did not yet exist when Dürer designed these woodcuts.

63. Dürer (1471-1528).
Portrait of his Mother.
1514. Charcoal drawing.
Albertina, Vienna

Dürer.   Portrait of His Mother

THE ENERGY of Dürer's draftsmanship can be best seen in his woodcuts for the Apocalypse, but it is in his portrait drawings that he most clearly reveals his profound and sympathetic insight into human character. In his painted portraits—which are many and the best of them are memorable —something of the incisiveness and the intimacy of the drawings is lost. In this respect he is unlike Holbein, whose portrait drawings may be wonderfully accurate but rarely probe into the character of the sitter.

Of all Dürer's portrait drawings that of his mother, done when he was forty-three and she had only two months to live, is one of the most searching. Dürer himself has described in words the woman who married his father at the age of fifteen and bore him eighteen children. "She had often suffered from the pestilence, had suffered poverty, derision, insults, mocking words, terrors and great afflictions, yet she never became vindictive."

Dürer took her into his house on his father's death in 1504, and there she sat patiently in her room, in lonely, unthinking piety, her face furrowed with past suffering. Such a face could have lent itself to the kind of semi-caricature that Leonardo often indulged in when he recorded "types" of human beings. But in this drawing there is no hint of anything but affection for the old woman who had given him so much, but who now could give him nothing but the daily, almost mechanical greeting "May Christ be with you." Surely, among portrait painters, only Rembrandt could be so searching and yet so compassionate to a sitter who had been buffeted rather than enriched by a hard life.

Grünewald. The Crucifixion

FEW GREAT ARTISTS have set themselves to describe the full intensity of physical pain or mental anguish with as little reserve as Grüne-wald; and among those who have, it is rare to find any who are not either German or Spanish.

Spain, with its grim, realistic insistence on the necessity of human suffering, had produced many a powerful symbol of pain, especially in those sculptured Crucifixions that, oddly enough, fill us with awe rather than with horror. Goya's etchings, The Disasters of the War, and his unforgettable account of the executions of the Third of May, are appeals to human compassion rather than descriptions of human tragedy.

Germany, less objective, more determined to underline the details of horror rather than to elucidate their meaning, has left behind a plentiful crop of painted martyrdoms, usually resorting to what amounts to caricature in order to make the narrative vivid. From most of these attempts to tackle a harrowing theme we turn away in slight disgust. The artist, we feel, has gone too far. One might almost think that he took a positive pleasure in these sadistic attempts to horrify.

Grünewald alone moves us deeply but never makes us feel that he has gone too ·far. There is no attempt at caricature behind the horrible symbol. Rather, there is an imperturbable acceptance. Nothing is avoided that will add to its intensity, but the inevitable exaggerations that always accompany height-

ened emotion are not forced. Grünewald neither wishes to lacerate our

64. *Grünewald* (c. 1475-1530). *The Crucifixion. 1523. Painting on wood. Kunsthalle Museum, Karlsruhe*

emotions, nor does he spare us. Behind Goya's Disasters of the War is the thought "This was unnecessary; it must never happen again." Behind Grünewald's Crucifixion is the unspoken comment: "This happened; it was inevitable."

Unlike his contemporary, Albrecht Dürer, Grünewald had never felt the magic touch of Italian gentleness and Italian serenity. He was untouchable. Had he accompanied Dürer on his journey to Venice in 1505, I doubt if he would have been affected by the bright loveliness of the city or the serene lyricism of the aging Giovanni Bellini whom Dürer admired. Dürer was strengthened by the contact. Grünewald, if it had affected him at all, could only have been weakened by it. His gigantic single-mindedness was incapable of compromise. What he sought were the extremes of tragedy, of ecstasy or of the sinister and the macabre. The serenity of classicism was positively distasteful to him.

By far his most ambitious work is, of course, the great polyptych at Colmar originally painted for the altar at Isenheim. There, too, a Crucifixion is the central theme, though it is surrounded by a multiplicity of side panels and enfolded by hinged doors on whose surfaces are painted scenes of grotesque fantasy or uneasy, radiant ecstasy.

The Karlsruhe Crucifixion, on the other hand, is a single unit, simple in mood and composition. Partly for that reason and partly because it plumbs even profounder depths than that at Colmar, its impact is more decisive. It leaves behind an even more unforgettable impression. As a symbol it is more potent. Hanging as a centerpiece on the wall of the gallery it dominates, it carries further and hits harder.

All the frightening distortions and emphases are subordinated to a single theme—the feet that writhe and grip like the roots of a tree, the lacerated body, the cruel complexity of the crown of thorns, the utter refusal to compromise with Hellenic or Raphaelesque ideas of beauty, the anguish expressed in the figures of the Virgin and St. John, the noble resignation, despite distortions, of the Christ.

Grünewald alone held the strange secret of pushing expression to its ultimate limit without making us shrink. This is tragedy purged of sensationalism. It is, perhaps, shocking, just as the plucking out of Gloucester's eyes in Shakespeare's *King Lear* is shocking. But it is redeemed by Grünewald's Shakespearian sense of the real meaning of Christ's Death on the Cross.

Veit Stoss. The Virgin and Child

V E I T   S T O S S was probably born in Nuremberg. Certainly most of his long life was passed there, though his masterpiece is the famous Marienaltar in Cracow, where he spent an active ten years executing some of the most vigorous and elaborate carvings which were produced in the last quarter of the 15th Century. The Cracow altarpiece is a highly complex construction in carved and painted wood, to which no single photograph can do justice; more than fifty figures are included in the central triptych alone.

But the same boldness and the same implicit movement can be found even in his smaller isolated figures, of which this Madonna and Child in boxwood is a superb example. Despite its diminutive size—it is less than nine inches high—it has a monumental vitality. The Madonna's head is that of an amiable Nuremberg *hausfrau* with the shaved forehead fashionable at the end of the 15th and beginning of the 16th Centuries. But the slight backward curve of her body, natural as a balance to the weight of the Child on her arm, was probably derived from the ivory figures whose rhythms were dictated by the curve of the tusk. That curve gives the figure a supple elegance. The serpentine fall of crumpled drapery, as her cloak descends from the shoulder to the crescent moon at her feet, adds a delightful agitation, as though a gust of wind were lifting her through the air.

65. *Veit Stoss (d. 1533).*
The Virgin and Child.
c. 1477-1489. Boxwood.
The Virgin Mary's Altar,
Victoria and Albert Museum,
London

It is a tour de force by a master craftsman. Even the fluent curves of the Virgin's hair, and the rather gauche gesture of the Christ Child, and the slight tilt of His head as she proudly offers Him to our gaze add to the effect of harnessed movement. The little statue is a typical example of that fusion of the homely and the spiritual of which Germanic art of the time held the secret.

Bosch.   Le Jardin des Délices

THE DATE of Jerome (or Hieronymus) Bosch's birth is unknown.
His life is not documented. He is first heard of as a painter in the little
town of Bois-le-Duc in the Netherlands in 1480; he died in 1516. He must,
therefore, have been an exact contemporary of Leonardo da Vinci and
Giovanni Bellini. Yet, judged by his paintings, Bosch seems hardly to belong
to any identifiable period and might almost have lived on another planet.
The fantastic imagery that recurs in almost all his pictures had never appeared
in serious painting before. His very style is an invention of his own. He
raises problems of interpretation that have never been fully solved, though
art historians have recently begun to realize that the solution to them must
lie not in a study of other artists but in a more profound knowledge than
we yet possess of mediaeval alchemy and symbolism.

Le Jardin des Délices, or The Garden of Delights, though no translation into English will convey the combination of pleasure and folly implied
by the word, is a work of his later maturity. Into it he has poured, with an
inexhaustible fantasy and an almost unbelievable resourcefulness in creating
images of the grotesque and the diabolic (though rarely of the horrible or
the tragic), the whole of his imaginative power. It takes the form of a
triptych, of which the left panel is a Paradise, the right a Hell, while in
the central panel he shows us in symbolic form the dreams, the follies, the
disorders of the life of the senses. Taken together the three panels could
almost be regarded as a 16th-Century version of Dante's *Divina Commedia*
in visual terms.

It is a commonplace that the devil has all the best tunes and that
sermonizers are apt to find a richer field for inventive eloquence in evil than
in good. Hogarth is at his best when he satirizes the sins and stupidities of
mankind, and as one examines, square inch by square inch, the symbolic
world that Bosch has created—from the peaceful serenity of the Garden of
Eden to the fires and torments of Hell—one's interest inevitably centers on
those passages in which fantasy, at once humorous and grotesque, is predominant. For no 20th-Century Surrealist has been able to devise imagery as
riotous or as surprising as that of Bosch. The whole of the animal and
vegetable worlds seem to have contributed to produce a landscape in which
men, women and monsters mingle to perform antics that must have a meaning,
though they could only take place in the world of imaginative fantasy.

It is, of course, possible to accept such a world unquestioningly, as one
accepts the world of dreams, without asking what each detail "means." Yet
Bosch's symbolism is evidently full of specific "meanings," some of which

66. *Bosch (Op. 1480-1516). Le Jardin des Délices (detail).*
Early 16th Century. Oil. Prado, Madrid

have been fully unravelled by recent research into mediaeval writings. Even
to refer briefly to such meanings as have been discovered in The Garden of
Delights would lead us away from Bosch as an artist into the half-understood
mazes of alchemy and symbolic morality. These brief notes can make no
such attempt. *141*

Bosch's dream world often achieves a strange and innocent lyrical beauty side by side with its macabre and grotesque elements, and in this detail, which is to be found in the right-hand bottom corner of The Garden of Delights, this lyrical note is predominant. The slender figures of the naked young men and women have an enchanting purity despite Bosch's intention to describe an orgy of the senses. In the background a procession of monsters circles round the Fountain of Youth. Nearer, strange symbols of man's desires —transparent eggs that imprison the victims of folly, or gargantuan fruits— seem to us quaint rather than alarming. In the center is a pair of lovers, one of whom has exchanged his own head for one of these fruits.

Surrealism has enabled us to accept and enjoy imagery of this illogical kind. But to Bosch's contemporaries there must have been a rather frightening lesson to be read into what seem to us the spoils of a journey into the subconscious mind of man.

Drawings by Leonardo da Vinci

B O T H Leonardo and Rembrandt were superlative draftsmen. Rembrandt could be described as a painter who poured forth an unbroken spate of drawings; Leonardo was essentially a draftsman who at intervals produced a rare but unforgettable painted masterpiece. The Mona Lisa, The Last Supper and The Virgin of the Rocks are too familiar to need inclusion in an anthology that does not aim to be a collection of the world's most famous works of art. But Leonardo's drawings cannot be excluded. In style they are among the most delicately sensitive ever made, in subject matter they reflect every aspect of Leonardo's enquiring and inventive mind. For most artists the world they live in is a stimulus to creation; their first task is to interpret their experience. For Leonardo the world was primarily a stimulus to a nagging intellectual curiosity that gave rise to drawings of the anatomical structure of men and animals, designs for machinery and engines of war (including prototypes of modern tanks and heavier-than-air flying machines), studies of the movement of water, botanical and geological structure, town planning and architecture.

Such drawings, fascinating as they are to the student of the history of scientific development, are works of art only in the sense that they are the productions of a superlative draftsman as well as reflections of a restless, questioning mind. But among them are drawings of other kinds in which Leonardo momentarily forgets the attempt to unravel the mysteries of nature and becomes an artist of a very unusual kind. These are indeed works of art. Some of them are highly finished drawings of the fall of drapery, or portrait heads and hands. Some are experiments in composition connected with known

67. Leonardo (1452-1519). Darius. 1480. Drawing. British Museum

pictures or planned statues. The remainder, in many ways the most precious of all, reveal a romantic mind obsessed by fantasies of various kinds— monsters unknown to man, allegories whose meaning cannot be resolved, intricate modes of hairdressing, costumes (doubtless connected with court pageants in Milan) and, most mysterious of all, a series of drawings that seem to represent progressive stages in some apocalyptic upheaval of the

143

68. and 69. Leonardo.
   Left: *Star of Bethlehem.*
   c. *1505-08.*
   Red chalk drawing.
   Below: *The Deluge. 1514.*
   Drawing.
   Royal Collection, Windsor

earth. Here and there one comes across exquisite drawings that can only be described as doodles—the uneasy expression of subconscious impulses. Some of these are merely ingenious, sometimes they are fantastically beautiful in their rhythms, sometimes obsessional as though some constantly recurring image (often a head of monstrous ugliness or epicene beauty) haunted him and demanded an outlet.

It is difficult to choose, out of this medley of drawings, three which will give an idea of Leonardo's range, especially as one of his most notable characteristics is his reluctance, whenever an image haunted him, to regard any single statement of it as final. He is one of those artists who can never reach a decision because he perpetually hesitates between the claims of a host of possible alternatives. For him, more than for any other great artist, the journey is more attractive than the destination.

The so-called Darius drawing is, in essence, an inspired and elaborately finished doodle. No such head, no such helmet ever existed—yet Leonardo had to draw it. Every curve has the same flowing vitality that always fascinated him in his studies of the movement of running water. Darius is an early drawing in which one can trace the influence of Leonardo's master, Verrocchio.

The Star of Bethlehem drawing (done in the first decade of the 16th Century) is freer in style and manifestly drawn from nature. Yet here again we find the same rhythmic flow of line, as though the plant had been selected because of its wonderful intersections of contrasting curves and Leonardo had discovered in the rhythm of its leaves an affinity with all he hoped to find in the world of hydrodynamics.

The third drawing, done later still and now in the library at Windsor Castle, which contains so many of his most exquisite drawings, is at once more mysterious and more charged with meaning. It is one of the series, already referred to, which seems to trace the successive stages of some vast upheaval. It is as though volcanic forces had been let loose and Leonardo was discovering the secret of their power and finding a notation for them by translating them into terms of chalk line. One can profitably compare this strange drawing with the Chinese Dragon Scroll reproduced on Plate 166. But the intention is rather different. Both drawings are based on a wonderful intuitive sense of vital curvature, but Leonardo's comes from a deeper level of experience. The pent-up forces of nature are no longer beautiful. They are positively alarming. They collide and are bent back on themselves. They are uncomfortable reminders of the forces released by modern physicists.

Raphael and Michelangelo

NO DECADE in the history of painting was more decisive than the first ten years of the 16th Century in Rome. These years, in which Michelangelo conceived and completed the whole spread of the Sistine Chapel Ceiling and Raphael was at work on the rooms in the Vatican that now bear his name, are a climax for which everything done in the previous fifty years seems to be a preparation and everything that followed in the next fifty, an anticlimax. It was a predestined moment of complete maturity, and one cannot help feeling that providence, using Pope Julius II as its instrument, had a hand in providing the ideal opportunity for both artists at the moment when both were at the height of their powers.

Both the Sistine Chapel Ceiling and the Stanze of Raphael have been photographed and reproduced until, through sheer familiarity, they have almost ceased to surprise or astonish us. Moreover, no reproduction can do justice to either as an ensemble. Here two details must serve as tokens for both. In Michelangelo's case the loss is less damaging than in Raphael's, for despite its architectural cohesion the Sistine Ceiling remains in our memories as a series of detachable, isolated figures, each one memorable in its own right, whereas each of the great lunettes of the Raphael Stanza is a complex, organized whole. Each is an object lesson in composition—the interweaving of mutually dependent forms, any portion of which suffers by being divorced from its context yet any portion of which still retains its own character and nobility despite the divorce.

There is, I think, a general agreement that no artist but Raphael has been able to achieve so expressive a unity in the grouping together of so many figures. When we count the individual figures in any one of the Stanze lunettes, we are surprised at their number. Yet there is nowhere an effect of crowding. And in each case the problem seems to have been solved effortlessly and inevitably. There are no repetitions, no "devices" of composition. Nowhere does Raphael produce a cliché or follow a formula. Yet the lunette form, with, in some cases, an intrusive doorframe breaking into it from below, is by no means an easy one to fill.

Out of the group of four frescoes that fill the first of the large rooms in the Vatican, the Stanza della Segnatura, the Parnassus is, appropriately enough, the most lyrical and the least formal. Apollo, seated on the mountain top, dominates, with the nine Muses grouped on either side of him in such an unobtrusive and subtly varied symmetry that one hardly notices the underlying mathematics. Lower down, and again grouped with an infinite resource

70. *Raphael (1483-1520).*
Parnassus (detail). 1507.
Fresco. Vatican, Rome

in disguising the basic symmetry, are the great poets, compositionally inter-dependent, dramatically separate, each with his own character and gesture, each an indivisible part of a larger whole.

This is a feat that would have been inappropriate on the ceiling of the Sistine Chapel. Its area is too great and it has its own inherent unity of structure which any superimposed pictorial unity could have weakened. But when, thirty years later, Michelangelo painted the Last Judgment on the end wall of the same chapel, he achieved a titanic failure. What was needed was a grasp of pictorial organization even firmer than that of Raphael. It was something that Michelangelo had never possessed. Beside Raphael's suave and effortless power, the Last Judgment had a forced and restless grandeur.

As an isolated token of that effortless suavity, the figure of Apollo in the Parnassus is as typical an example of the Raphaelesque as can be found   *147* in any of his major works. Raphael's gift for discovering the underlying rhythm in a human gesture was as remarkable as Michelangelo's, though his portrayal of physical power was rarely extended, as with Michelangelo, into physical *effort*. There is no hint of the well-known Michelangelesque *terribilità* or tension in the marvelously relaxed pose of the god as he listens to his own music. Yet there is no excess of sweetness. The act of playing a musical instrument, the description of correlated movement of every limb, together with the realization that the gesture is an outward expression of an inward melody, has never been more completely understood and portrayed. Raphael's Apollo is a symbol of an inner impulse that has discovered its precise outward equivalent. Whereas Michelangelo's most memorable single figures too often suggest a deliberate self-dramatization, a conscious determination to be forceful and impressive, brooding or threatening.

When one searches the Sistine Ceiling for a single figure to set beside the Apollo and to point the familiar contrast between sublimity and beauty, the task becomes almost impossible. Like Shakespeare's *Hamlet,* the ceiling is

71. *Raphael (1483-1520).
Woman Kneeling
(Drawing for the Mass
of Bolsena). c. 1517.
Chatsworth House,
Duke of Devonshire*

72. *Michelangelo (1475-1564). Creation of the Sun and Moon. 1507. Fresco. Sistine Ceiling, Vatican, Rome*

altogether too rich in tempting quotations. At least a dozen out of the total of twenty-four young athletes and every one of the alternating sequence of prophets and sibyls is worthy of inclusion—the brooding weight of the Jeremiah; the inspired, swinging movement of the Libyan; the ponderous weight of the Cumaean sibyl, lost in her own thoughts; the abandon of Jonah; the enthusiasm of Daniel.

Each one of these titanic creatures, so typically charged with Michelangelo's energy, could conceivably have been carved in marble. What has finally guided me in my choice has been the desire to select a section of the ceiling which could only have been executed in fresco, and in the end it seemed inevitable that the choice should fall on one of those unforgettable panels in which the artist described the Almighty engaged in the task of creating the world.

Anyone who has studied the ceiling carefully will have noted that somewhere about the middle of the vast area to be covered the style changes, the scale of the figures becomes larger and their gestures more emphatic. The change may have been partly the result of a growing confidence as the work proceeded, but it was also the direct consequence of his decision to remove the scaffolding on which he was working in order to obtain an unbroken view from the floor of the chapel fifty feet below, of what he had already done. After this momentary pause the prophets and sibyls become more monumental, and one has only to compare the Zachariah, the first of the prophets to be painted, with the Jonah, the last, to note not only a change of style and scale but a change of heart—an increase both of weight and passion. As he worked along the ceiling toward the altar he must also

149

have felt the need to respond to the final challenge, the invention of an image that would do justice to God's own act of creation.

It is from among these images, the last to be finished in the vast expanse of the ceiling, that one must choose a detail to represent the Michelangelo of the year 1511. Any one of the four, the Separation of the Firmament from the Ocean, the Creation of the Sun and Moon, the Creation of Vegetable Life or the Separation of Light from Darkness, would serve. The last is the most visionary, the first gives the most vivid impression of power, the second and third are images of limitless energy. All of them have the kind of planetary movement that could never have found expression in marble.

The Creation of the Sun and Moon—the heavenly bodies come automatically into existence, as the result of a far-flung gesture of two powerful arms as the Creator whirls through space—is the boldest of the four in its daring use of light and shade and the most dynamic in its command of swinging rhythms.

The aestheticians of the 18th Century delighted in their discovery of two categories of beauty, the suave and the sublime. Neither they nor we can easily imagine the first taken further than it was by Raphael or the second more profoundly explored than it was by Michelangelo.

Both artists were among the greatest of European draftsmen and both made studies in pen or chalk in preparation for the great frescoes in the Vatican. Forced by the exigencies of space to choose between them, it is Raphael who must be represented here as a draftsman, Michelangelo as a sculptor.

It is not known when the marvelous study of a kneeling woman in red chalk was made or with which of Raphael's frescoes it is connected. It hardly matters for it is completely self-contained. Michelangelo seems to be searching, while he draws, for the significant turn of the wrist or the muscular tension that is to be the essence of his study. Raphael has already discovered these things before he begins to draw. Hence the unforced ease of the girl as she holds some unspecified object in her right hand and reaches upward with her left. The outline of her body never hesitates (except in one passage, the upper curve of the right thigh), yet it is never hard, never suggests an "edge" rather than a disappearing contour.

That "searching" quality referred to above which one often finds in Michelangelo's drawings is the very essence of his sculpture, and especially in the four famous recumbent statues that lie on either side of the two seated figures of the Medici dukes in the New Sacristy of San Lorenzo in Florence. Here, as in some of the "unfinished" slaves for the tomb of Julius II, he gives us that uncanny feeling that he is working downward through the marble to a predestined surface hidden from every eye but his own. The

detail shown in Plate 73 is taken from the figure of Day, the most massive

of the four and the most eloquent of Herculean strength slowly rousing itself to some task that awaits it. That great shoulder and the hidden arm ready to swing across the body, the mountainous knee preparing to hoist the left leg free are memorable. It is a giant preparing himself for action. The head has been left with the predestined surface not quite revealed, as though Michelangelo felt that to do so would be to turn a natural force into a personality, a symbol into a portrait, thereby weakening the central meaning of his statue.

Titian. Bacchus and Ariadne

WHEN ALFONSO D'ESTE, Duke of Ferrara, decided to decorate his newly furnished suite of apartments in the palace with four paintings of pagan mythological subjects, he turned to Venice for his artists. His first choice was the aged Giovanni Bellini; and Giovanni lived long enough to paint his last great picture, The Feast of the Gods, now in the National Gallery in Washington, for Alfonso. When Bellini died, Alfonso placed his order for the remaining three canvases with Titian, giving him full instructions as to subject matter and treatment. Titian was a natural choice for he had been trained in Giovanni's studio.

The subject was to be a scene from the story of the love of Bacchus for Ariadne, who had been deserted by Theseus on the island of Naxos. There was plenty of literary material for Titian—or his iconographical   *151* advisers—to draw on. Ovid had described their meeting: how Ariadne, lamenting her sad fate on the shore, was overtaken by Bacchus who leapt from his chariot to the ground to console her. Catullus, too, had described in detail the wild procession of dancing bacchantes and satyrs who followed the chariot.

The commission came at exactly the right moment for Titian. Thitherto —up to the year 1520—he had been under the influence of his friend and contemporary, Giorgione, painting dreamy idyls in the Giorgionesque manner. When Giorgione died in 1510, Titian gradually shook off the Giorgionesque mood. Now was the moment for him to assert himself with something more energetic and exuberant. Bacchus and Ariadne is his first great picture in which the fiery athletic Titian appears.

It has all the freshness of a new adventure in painting. The golden afternoon glow on limbs and draperies is there, and the equally Venetian sense of open air, blue skies, cumulus clouds, distant green meadows and blue mountains. All this was appropriate to the theme, but Venetian artists, including Titian himself, had done it before. What was new was a vigorous exultation, a release of energy. Bacchus leaps impulsively from his leopard-drawn chariot and Ariadne, with a marvelously invented gesture, half flees from him and half turns toward him. Behind him the little band of girls and satyrs sweeps forward and onward out of the forest, clashing cymbals and carrying the dismembered limbs of goats.

The whole picture is a hymn to Dionysus. But what gives it its irresistible movement is a compositional trick of which, perhaps, Titian himself was unaware, for he is not one of the world's masters of composition. The isolated figure of Ariadne becomes a kind of magnet to the weight of moving forms on the right, and by the daring corkscrew twist of her body as she looks back over her shoulder, seems to act as a pivot for the movement of the rest. Bacchus himself twists round to follow her direction as he leaps, and the crowd behind him seems to change direction as it moves.

The remaining two paintings for Alfonso were delivered later. They are both worthy of a great master but neither of them has the vitality of this. When Titian delivered the picture in Ferrara in 1522, he took the opportunity to make certain alterations in Bellini's Feast of the Gods. His own version of the pagan theme, so much more energetic and fluent than Bellini's, must have made the Feast of the Gods look a little stiff and harsh. Titian repainted the landscape background in a more swinging set of rhythms. Bellini's picture was only eight years old, but so quickly was the Venetian style developing in the second decade of the 15th Century that it had already begun to look a little out of date.

74. *Titian (1480-1576). Bacchus and Ariadne. 1523. Oil.*
National Gallery, London

75. *Altdorfer* (c. 1480-1538). *St. George. c. 1511. Painting on wood.*
Alte Pinakothek, Munich

Altdorfer.   St. George

ASKED TO NAME the most German of all artists, one would reject Dürer, for though he may be the greatest, he had come into contact with classical influences in Italy; and though he could not absorb them, they had softened some of his hard Northern European romanticism. But one would certainly hesitate between Grünewald (see Plate 64) and Altdorfer, and in the end one would probably choose Altdorfer, if only because Nature plays so large a part in his painting. In Grünewald, though Nature is often present as a threatening influence in his backgrounds, man occupies the foreground.

For Altdorfer, Nature dwarfs and even seems to swallow up mankind. The gnarled and tangled forest towers above the little figure of St. George. He seems to be entrapped by it and to be looking desperately for an outlet by which to escape into the valley below him.

Only in Germany does one feel this sinister and almost hostile power of natural forces. Altdorfer's picture (it was painted early in his life, about 1511) might be an illustration to Wagner's Siegfried as he makes his way to the Rhine and listens to the song of the birds. But Altdorfer's forest is less friendly than Wagner's. Its luxuriance is claustrophobic, and wherever a trunk detaches itself from the mass of oppressive foliage one becomes aware of its upward-thrusting strength. This, surely, is the sinister undercurrent that explains one side of Gothic architecture—its dominant verticals and the spreading ribs and vaults that expand into dark tunnels high above one's head.

Cranach, Dürer, Grünewald and Altdorfer were contemporaries. Each reflected one aspect of the Teutonic, but of the four it is Altdorfer who gives us the most typical symbols of the German romantic spirit.

Cranach.   The Judgment of Paris

IT IS WITH something of a shock that one compares Cranach's version of a famous mythological event with that of Rubens, painted 108 years later (see Plate 89). At first one would guess that the difference could be accounted for by a "progress," which had taken place in the interval, in the mastery with which artists could tackle the problems of landscape and space and the even more difficult problems presented by the nude. But something more than a stylistic development is involved. Even if Rubens had been a contemporary of Cranach (and that involves him also in being a contemporary of Raphael and Michelangelo) the contrast would have been startling. It is a contrast of temperament. Rubens, in any generation, would have striven for nobility, opulence and amplitude. In Cranach there is always something impish, perverse and affected.

He is, of course, German, but that only partly explains him; no other German artist has ever wanted to be so chic or succeeded in being so provocative. Perhaps it is his perverseness that links him most closely with his German contemporaries. Everyone knows the story of how the young Paris, serving as a shepherd on Mount Ida, was permitted by Zeus to judge which of the three goddesses, Hera, Aphrodite and Athene, was the most beautiful by presenting a golden apple to the winning contestant. The siege of Troy was the ultimate result, and Cranach must have been as familiar with the story as Rubens. But Cranach has perversely turned Paris into a middle-aged and rather pompous warrior, Hermes into a bearded and aged prophet with none of the god's attributes, the apple into a globe of crystal and the goddesses into something more closely resembling the Three Graces—certainly they are more interested in each other than they are in the verdict of their judge.

Iconographers trace Cranach's picture (painted in 1530 and the first of several versions) to a mediaeval romance entitled *The History of the Destruction of Troy*. But such literary derivations need not disturb us; Cranach's interpretations of feminine beauty are stranger and more personal than his distortions of Greek mythology. They have no counterparts in German or any other painting. They are both restless and haunting; their slender, almost boneless, bodies, hardly able to support the weight of the huge hats and heavy necklaces which are often their only attire, seem to shine with a pale phosphorescence. Rubens' goddesses belong by right to the Golden Age in which nudity is normal. Cranach's, delicately fashioned and rather frivolous, appeal to the erotic, and their vulnerability is heightened by contrast to the ornate and ponderous armor of Paris.

Hans Holbein the Younger.   Portrait of Georg Gisze

THE PORTRAITS of Hans Holbein the Younger are familiar enough. Each one of them, whether painted in Basle or in England where he spent the last eleven years of his life, is a document whose honesty and truthfulness no one could possibly doubt. With the exception of Velasquez, no artist has ever succeeded in being so emotionally detached from his sitter and at the same time so dedicated to his task of recording, as a conscientious historian, the facts as he saw them. To this task he brought an equipment that every artist must envy. His steady, expressive, economical line (which can be best studied in his portrait drawings of the personalities that gathered

156

76. *Cranach (1472-1553). The Judgment of Paris. 1530. Oil. Karlsr*

77. Holbein the Younger
(1497-1543).
Portrait of Georg Gisze.
1532. Oil.

in London round King Henry VIII) is as masterly as Velasquez' equally steady, economical brushwork.

In most of his portraits the sitter is seen in isolation, without a spatial environment to contain him. But on two occasions he added to the portrait a setting crowded with a complexity of objects on which he lavished the whole of his amazingly patient skill in the delineation of still life. This portrait of Georg Gisze and the even more ambitious double portrait of The Ambassadors in the National Gallery in London are, as it were, "trial pieces" specially designed to attract further commissions. The Ambassadors was Holbein's passport to the circles of diplomacy and the Court: Georg Gisze was painted to prove his skill to the rich Hanseatic merchants of the London Steelyard, among whom Gisze was a leading figure.

The portrait was painted soon after Holbein's return to England in 1532 and bears that date, together with an inscription on the wall giving Gisze's age as thirty-four and his motto in Latin "No joy without sorrow." He is in his London office, seen in the act (action even of the mildest kind is rare in Holbein's portraits) of opening a letter addressed to him which has evidently just arrived from his brother Thadman, Bishop of Danzig. On the table, which is covered with an oriental rug similar to that in The Ambassadors, are his writing materials—a box of seal wafers, a cylinder for scattering sand, pens and a heavy seal. Other letters and sealed tapes are tucked behind the wooden bars attached to the wall. Books, keys, a balance and a spherical container for a ball of string form part of the minutely described office furniture. On the table is his signet ring.

Evidently this elaborate portrait did exactly what was intended. During the next year or two he painted a series of portraits of Hanseatic merchants in London, though none of them seems to have demanded such a multitude of still-life accessories.

Pieter Brueghel. Netherlandish Proverbs

It is rare for great art to be based on an acute sense of the follies and humors of everyday life, yet no one could deny that Pieter Brueghel the Elder was a humorist and his greatness as an artist is beyond doubt. Only in a few of his more serious paintings does he abandon the attempt to make us laugh with him at the stupidities of mankind. Occasionally (as in the Massacre of the Innocents) he strikes a deeper note of pathos, but for the most part his crowded canvases are packed with incident of a Rabelaisian kind. His comments on human absurdity—almost invariably the absurdity of the villager and the peasant—are never malicious. What strikes us at once is the sympathetic gusto, the uninhibited enjoyment with which he describes each incident. His pictures may be sermons but they are delivered with good humor and an occasional outburst of unrestrained laughter.

The similarity between Brueghel and Bosch (Plate 66) is obvious. Both artists crowd their canvases with imagery, and both are compelled by the riotous quality of their visual imagination to invent a vast expanse of landscape filled with small figures. But whereas Bosch's world is the world of dreams inhabited by monsters, Brueghel's is the world of everyday life twisted by his temperament into a pattern of absurdity. Occasionally Brueghel was tempted to stray into the nightmare land of Bosch, but it was not the land that suited him best.

No subject could have been more congenial to him than that of proverbial philosophy. In the Netherlandish Proverbs, dated 1559, and painted, therefore, at some time in his early thirties, he includes almost a hundred references to the proverbs of the Low Countries. To reproduce the whole picture on a reduced scale would be to make it "unreadable"—and like Hogarth, who was equally fascinated by human folly, Brueghel must be "read" if we are to enjoy him to the full.

Even in the small detail shown here there are at least a dozen illustrations of proverbial phrases—the man who bangs his head against a   *159*

78. *Brueghel* (c. *1528-1569*). *Netherlandish Proverbs* (*detail*). *1559. Oil.*

brick wall; the man who attempts to shear a pig, in emulation of his neighbor
who shears a sheep; above him, the man who bells the cat; to his right, the
two gossips, one of whom holds the distaff while the other spins; above
them, a man carrying baskets of light out into the sunshine.

Brueghel's is not the first attempt to turn proverbs into pictures but it is certainly the most convincing presentation of a world dominated by proverbs. The robust "earthiness" of the Flemish temperament has never found a more complete expression than in Brueghel's paintings.

Tintoretto. The Three Graces

IN THE YEAR 1577 a disastrous fire broke out in the Venetian Doge's Palace. The loss in works of art alone was immense, but looking back on what followed it is possible that the gain was even greater. In the scheme of reconstruction that was undertaken immediately by the Venetian senate, some of the richest examples of 16th-Century interior decoration in the world —a series of masterpieces by Veronese and four of Tintoretto's most perfect pictures, the four Allegories of Venice—came into being.

What the Venetian senate required from Tintoretto was by no means what he was famous for in the Venice of that unusually productive decade. He was approaching the end of that long series of wall and ceiling paintings on which he had been engaged for so many years for the Scuola of San Rocco, where they are still to be found—one of the greatest monuments to an artist's genius ever assembled under one roof. The paintings deal with stories from the Old and New Testament and they are conceived in a spirit of dark and often tragic seriousness. The Ducal Palace, on the other hand, wanted a set of blithe optimistic mythologies, radiant and colorful—the kind of pictures, in fact, that Titian would certainly have been commissioned to paint had the fire occurred twenty years earlier.

Tintoretto, always an opportunist, assumed the mantle of Titian for the occasion and proved, not for the first time in his career but more decisively than ever before, that he could wear it with ease. The four Allegories are the most Titianesque of all Tintoretto's paintings. Yet only Tintoretto could have painted them. Taken together, they sum up the complex qualities of Venetian power and pride. The Forge of Vulcan symbolizes Venice preparing for war; The Marriage of Bacchus and Ariadne refers to the annual ceremony whereby the doge celebrated the union of Venice and the Adriatic by throwing a ring into the waters of the lagoon; Minerva Repelling Mars and The Three Graces (reproduced here) are self-explanatory.

Allegory on this elementary level doubtless pleased the Venetian senators. What pleases us is not the self-satisfied subject matter of the paintings, but Tintoretto's extraordinary power, when he wished to do so, to transport himself into a mythical world inhabited by nude figures of unusual grace and beauty, a world in which physical health and spiritual optimism are stated in their most radiant terms, and bathed in warm sunshine.

79. *Tintoretto (1518-1594). Three Graces. 1577. Oil.*
Palace of Doges, Venice

The composition is simple but it announces, half a century before Rubens finally set his seal on it, the dominant baroque diagonal. The central figure establishes it fearlessly, her two companions enclose her, as it were, between brackets. The sunshine that dapples their limbs cuts across this diagonal, making a counterpoint of light cutting across the form and creating a new kind of pattern—one that Titian had never thought of.

It is not difficult to analyze Tintoretto's system of composition in this picture. It is, for him, unusually simple but also unusually dense and closely woven. It is more difficult to discover how Tintoretto has managed to use the Venetian formula of sensuous lyricism and the Venetian motive (developed in the long sequence of Titian's nudes) of idealized womanhood, and yet to

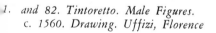

80. *Tintoretto (1518-1594).*
Archer. c. 1560. Charcoal drawing.
Uffizi, Florence

81. *and 82. Tintoretto. Male Figures.*
    c. 1560. Drawing. Uffizi, Florence

avoid all those erotic overtones that are almost always present in Titian's mythologies.

Of all nudes Tintoretto's are the least conscious of being naked. It is impossible to imagine them clothed. Dressed in the fashionable silks and satins of the 1570's, they would lose their meaning. They do not ask for admiration or kindle our desire. They have the healthy, careless innocence and the uninhibited movements of race horses. The only caresses they invite are those of the sunshine that falls on them. Renoir, at his best, could achieve that interplay between light and the surface of flesh; but Renoir was incapable of Tintoretto's dynamism. The Three Graces have, behind their movements, an effortless reserve of power that makes Renoir's *baigneuses* look static by comparison.

Drawings by Tintoretto

DRAWINGS BY Venetian artists of the 16th Century are plentiful but few of them are of the highest quality, for the Venetians were essentially painters and they reserved their creative energies for working direct on to their canvases. The great Italian drawings of the early part of the century are by Florentines—Raphael and, above all, Michelangelo.

But there was one Venetian—Tintoretto—who used drawing for a new purpose. For him, drawings of the human figure in action resembled the shorthand notes of a secretary taking down rapid dictation. These drawings, once made, were either squared up immediately and handed to studio assistants for enlargement on the canvas, or they were filed for future reference, added to the studio stock and consulted when a new picture was being planned.

A great many of them survive and most of the best of them are vigorous works in which some violent action or unusual foreshortening has been caught and fixed onto paper with extreme rapidity. The emphasis is always on muscular stress and strain, and their meaning is contained not in the outline or the contour of the individual limb but in the draftsman's convention, invented by Tintoretto, to indicate the muscular force implicit in a gesture or the sculptural structure of the body.

Some of these drawings are evidently from models waiting in the studio for the master to indicate a required pose, others are from the small wax figures which he modeled himself when he was planning some unusually energetic or complex motive. But all of them are alike in that they are, as it were, diagrams reduced to a minimum of detail and a maximum of explicitness.

No one had ever drawn like that before (each drawing can have occupied him for hardly more than five minutes) and rarely has any artist attempted such swift elimination since; Tintoretto's nature urged him to a furious

164

83. *Milanese Goblet. Late 16th Century. Crystal. Metropolitan Museum, New York*

84. *Venetian Dragon-stem Goblet. Late 16th Century. Glass. Corning Museum of Glass*

impatience. One or two of Rodin's drawings (Plate 115) have the same intention of distilling the essence of an action into a few lines. They are equally fluent, but they lack the reckless force of Tintoretto's.

Goblets from Milan and Venice

THESE GOBLETS are two superlative examples of the art of the worker in a transparent medium: similar in form, almost contemporaneous in date (for both are probably products of late 16th-Century Italy), but quite different in their approach to the medium. The Milanese artist has used the translucent material of crystal as a surface on which to practise the art of engraving. The Venetian craftsman has exploited the inherent nature of glass itself. The contrast is striking. There is something dead and mechanical about the precision of the Milanese goblet, as though the material had not been allowed to speak for itself, so anxious were the Sarachi brothers, who practised the art of gem cutting in Milan, to allow nothing to distract the eye from their skill and fantasy as engravers. The Venetian glass blower, on the other hand, has permitted the molten glass to dictate terms to him. While it was still pliable he knew how to produce the spiral ribbing of the base and the fluting of the pear-shaped support above, to twist the double curve of a sea monster into a figure 8, to add a goblet whose shape was settled by the pressure of the air blown into the glass while still red hot, and to surmount the whole with another fantastically twisted figure 8. Consequently every curve and every shape has its own vitality. Only the best glass blower knows how far to let his medium's behavior contribute to the final result and yet to control it at every stage. What amazes one is that an object so alarmingly fragile should have remained intact for four centuries.

The Milanese goblet is a more spectacular tour de force. Its delicately engraved surface could be magnified ten times without looking coarse or revealing any hesitation of the engraver's hand. In style it is a good example of North Italian Mannerism, that rather tortured, sophisticated complexity that swept across the country in the mid-16th Century, when the dignity of the High Renaissance was decaying but the exuberance of the Baroque style had not yet been developed. It was an ideal style for the craftsman who engraved this goblet. It contains a whole world of restless fancy. Winged monsters, birds, fishes, tritons, even a seal, play about in the undulating waves. Swags and festoons of fruit and flowers and ribbons hang above. In paint such overworked fantasy would have been intolerably heavy. In crystal, with the light shining through it, it becomes insubstantial and therefore delightful.

The Baroque and the Worldly

BY THE END of the 16th Century the spirit of the Renaissance had spread from its birthplace, Italy, to the whole of Europe. And it had communicated its discoveries—the discoveries of line, structure, volume, color, space, light, movement—to every cultural center that could understand them and make use of them. At that moment there was a pause, as the creative current became less swift; yet at that moment it became wider. A new language had been forged, or to be more accurate, a new family of languages, each capable of serving a new set of causes.

The next group of plates covers, roughly, the 17th and 18th Centuries. And whereas the art of the Renaissance, though complex, has a certain homogeneity in that it intensified and ennobled everything it touched, the period that followed has no such homogeneity. In Holland it becomes domestic—a vehicle for the expression of a Protestant community, utterly contented with the surface of everyday life. It is true that Rembrandt's genius managed to penetrate below that surface, but even he based all his statements on his study of the life around him. The Dutch artists of the 17th Century were realists.

But the Flemish genius was different. Rubens, who had learned so much from Italy, used his exuberant and dynamic brush to create a world far removed from everyday life. When we use the word baroque to describe the rhetorical power of the 17th Century, we think of Rubens in Antwerp and Bernini in Rome—leaders and creators of that militant style which never shunned theatrical gesture or heightened drama.

Caravaggio, in Italy, somehow combined the two, using the almost photographic realism that was later to develop in Holland, in the service of dramatic or, at least, impressive subject matter. In Spain El Greco used the language invented by the Renaissance for a purpose diametrically opposed to that of Rubens. Where Rubens was earthy, El Greco was mystical. The same *167* flowing, baroque rhythms served both, but where Rubens danced, El Greco soared. Rubens' native elements were earth and water; El Greco's air and fire.

One other giant of the 17th Century, Velasquez, was the greatest of all masters of realism. Yet his realism had little in common with that of his Dutch contemporaries. They were intimate; he was monumental.

As the 17th Century came to an end, the sweeping baroque rhythms began to lose their power. Rococo succeeded baroque; charm followed grandeur; the banqueting hall gave way to the boudoir. Only one great artist of the 18th Century remained to fill the vast wall and ceiling spaces of churches and palaces—Tiepolo. The rest, a group of painters attached to the French court of whom the earliest, Watteau, was also the only one who deserved to be called a genius, painted pictures in which frivolity, elegance and immense painterly skill are combined.

The 17th Century began with exuberance and developed into worldliness. The 18th Century ended with a set of delightful but trivial small-scale gestures.

El Greco.   The Agony in the Garden

WHEN ONE COMPARES this picture by El Greco of what is probably the most tragic theme in the story of Christ's Passion with the version by Mantegna (see Plate 52), one finds oneself transported to another world. Mantegna's world is hard, clean-cut, metallic, materialistic; El Greco's is full of mystery. Nothing in it is quite tangible. Clouds take on the nature of icebergs, rocks and the sparse vegetation which grows among them heave themselves up into the air as though made of some flexible material; it is a world governed by no fixed laws of perspective. The sleeping disciples are enclosed in a cocoon-like hollow created, as it were, out of their own dreams, spatially unrelated to the rest of the picture. The angel, kneeling on a cloud and offering Christ the Chalice of Suffering, is equally free of the laws of perspective and gravity. The moon, half hidden by transparent veils of cloud, sheds a lurid light on the distant landscape, and the tiny group led by Judas, on its way to the betrayal and the arrest, is outlined in phosphorescent light.

Equally mysterious and illogical is the color. Everything is ice-blue or earthy brown against the black night sky. In the center, unprepared by any echo of warmth, the kneeling Christ is clad in a robe of brilliant wine-colored crimson, melodramatically lit by a diagonal shaft of light from above.

The picture was probably painted soon after El Greco's arrival in Spain. His childhood was spent in Crete, where he absorbed the mediaeval Byzantine traditions of the Eastern Mediterranean. As a youth he came to Venice where he familiarized himself with the sensuous, painterly qualities of Titian and Tintoretto; a brief visit to Rome brought him into contact with the grandeur and vigor of Michelangelo. Finally he left Italy for Spain and there, in Toledo,

85. *El Greco (1545-1614). Agony in the Garden.* c. *1580. Oil.*
National Gallery, London

he evolved that intensely personal style which is a synthesis of Byzantine
forms, Venetian coloring and Roman grandeur.

This fusion of opposites was made possible in the crucible of El Greco's
passionate imagination. His figures, as he developed, became more and more
creatures of air: weightless, ecstatic, made up of the flamelike forms which
permeated all his compositions once he had left Italy behind and settled
in Spain.

There are several versions of this theme by his hand, for El Greco was
in the habit of repeating the main outline of his important pictures or
entrusting his studio assistants in Toledo with the production of variations on
them. It has been suggested that this version (one of three in the inventory
of his possessions drawn up at his death in 1614 by his son) may be a
"studio" product. I doubt it. It is unlikely that even the most gifted of his
assistants could have achieved this degree of visionary intensity. All one can
say with confidence is that it must have been painted between 1580 and 1590.   *169*

Caravaggio. St. Matthew and the Angel

THERE ARE three paintings by Caravaggio in the Contarelli Chapel of the Church of San Luigi dei Francesi in Rome, of which this—St. Matthew inspired by an angel in his writing of the Gospel—is the central panel. But it is not the first version of the theme painted by him for the same chapel. Baglione, in 1642, and Belloni, in 1672, both tell the story of how Caravaggio, anxious to impress his patrons with his first important public commission, painted a picture of St. Matthew, with bare legs and a wrinkled brow, struggling with the difficult task of writing the life of the Saviour, while an angel guides his hand as he spells out the Hebrew letters.

The picture was instantly criticized for its lack of dignity and reverence and for the implication that so great a saint could have been so nearly illiterate. The picture was removed from above the altar and passed into the possession of the Marchese Vincenzo Giustiniani, an enthusiastic admirer of Caravaggio, and was eventually transferred to the national collection in Berlin. It was destroyed by fire in 1945.

Plate 86 shows the more conventional version painted by Caravaggio in an attempt to please his critics and patrons. The saint is no longer a slow-witted peasant and the angel no longer needs to guide the hand that holds the pen. It is the attempt of a temperamental realist to reconcile his natural vision with the idealism imposed on him from without. It could have been painted by no one but him, yet one knows that he has been trying to adapt himself to the official taste of the time.

It was probably painted in 1600. The Mannerism of the late 16th Century was coming to an end. The baroque style that was to succeed it a few years later had not yet established itself. Caravaggio was a born rebel and his startling realism, which not only presented saints as peasants, with the faces and gestures of peasants, but portrayed them in the harsh cold light that we loosely call "photographic," at once shocked the conventional but soon delighted the adventurous.

Once his innovations were understood they spread like wildfire both to Holland, where a group of painters centered on Utrecht imitated his choice of types and his system of dramatic lighting, and to Spain, where the young Velasquez even outdid him in realistic intensity. There was a brief period during which it almost looked as though the new realism might become the accepted style of painting throughout Europe. But in the end the photographic vision of Caravaggio was superseded by the exuberance of Rubens and the profundity of Rembrandt. Velasquez, himself, eventually abandoned the harsh cold shadows of Caravaggio and worked out a new system. In his portrait of Queen Mariana (Plate 91), it is evident that the influence of Caravaggio has at last been shaken off.

170

86. *Caravaggio (1569-1609). St. Matthew and the Angel. c. 1600. Oil. San Luigi dei Francesi, Rome*

Hilliard.
Portrait of a Young Man

WHEN THIS enchanting miniature was painted, about the year 1588, the great climax of the High Renaissance in Italy was past. Raphael had died in 1520, Leonardo in 1519, Michelangelo in 1564, Titian in 1576. In 1588 Veronese had died and Tintoretto was an old man. Yet, as far as Nicholas Hilliard was concerned, they might never have been born. He is still, at heart, a mediaevalist, rejoicing in the crisp, Gothic pattern of rose gardens, and the only master he acknowledges is Holbein who, himself, had died forty years earlier. Sixteenth-Century England, so creative and adventurous in literature, was isolationist and incredibly conservative in the field of the visual arts. At the moment when Shakespeare was making his most astonishing experiments in the mastery of words, Hilliard, almost the only original artist England possessed, was painting in a style that had been obsolete elsewhere for almost a century.

87. *Hilliard (1537-1619).*
Portrait of a Young Man.
c. 1588. Watercolor miniature.
Victoria and Albert Museum, London

Yet despite his conservatism Hilliard is an endearing artist, elegant and sophisticated, and his exquisite tastefulness puts him into the category of the great masters of stylishness—Watteau, for example, or Braque. In addition, this little oval (no more than 6 inches in height) is full of a romantic ardor that is characteristically British and quite beyond the range of Holbein.

This fashionably melancholy young dandy, painted at a moment when England led the rest of Europe as arbiter of taste in male attire, leans in an attitude of calculated boredom against the trunk of a tree, evidently composing epigrams to his lady's eyebrow. He is a character from one of Shakespeare's early comedies—say, *Love's Labour's Lost*—come to life. Stylistically he is an anachronism; psychologically he is the last word in highbrow

172

self-confidence. He scorns the Michelangelesque worship of muscular nobility. To find his prototype it is necessary to turn the clock back nearly 150 years, to the period of International Gothic and the spiky elegances of those proud, birdlike creatures we find in the drawings of Pisanello. This unknown Elizabethan is more languid than they, but equally stylish and self-confident.

Hilliard may have studied and learned a good deal from the firmness and precision of Holbein's draftsmanship, but it was probably Queen Elizabeth herself—whom he had painted more than once—who urged him to trust to expressiveness of outline and to mistrust shadows. He had looked attentively at the portraits of the great German and listened respectfully to the advice of his queen. But what we value in this little portrait is something he owed to neither of them. It is his own Englishness, which he shared with the young writer William Shakespeare.

Georges de la Tour.   La Madeleine

C A R A V A G G I O was one of the first artists to exploit the possibilities of dramatic lighting. Once the discovery had been made, it was bound to spread. As already mentioned, it was picked up by painters working as far apart as Utrecht and Madrid. With Honthorst it became almost a trademark and from him it spread into France, where Georges de la Tour became its most single-minded exponent.

Such a device could be turned, among superficial artists, into an excuse for a mere tour de force. With others, more serious, it served as a revelation of something they had always been looking for. That, surely, is the secret of de la Tour's curiously haunting art. It was not merely that he was fascinated by the phenomenon of artificial light. What he always searched for was an ultimate simplification of form—the true sign of the classical painter. Raphael and Ingres arrived at the "grande généralisation" by sheer imagination. Georges de la Tour found it ready-made in the kind of scene he paints here. Everything—outline, volume, the broad pattern of light against dark— is automatically reduced by the light itself to its simplest and therefore its most effective forms. And at the same time there is no lack of realism. De la Tour is in the happy position of painting the kind of picture nearest to his heart's desire, and yet he can innocently explain that he did so because Nature obligingly presented it to him, optically, in just those terms.

A second glance at this simple study of a girl seated at a table and gazing into the flame of a nightlight—the only source of illumination—is enough to show that it is far more than a study of light—far more than a Caravaggio at third hand. It is an essay in pure form, as calculated and as deliberate as anything by Poussin or Seurat. Like them, Georges de la Tour

88. *Georges de la Tour (1590-1652). La Madeleine à la Veilleuse.*
c. *1630-35. Oil. Louvre*

is a "manufacturer" of design, and like them, there is something a little wooden but profoundly satisfying in the result. The picture has the formal solidity of well-constructed furniture. The cylinder of the Magdalen's left arm, the sphere of the skull on which she rests her right hand, the line of light on her lower leg, the steady cone-shaped flame, the equally steady horizontals of the books on the table, the unbroken dark square that fills the bottom left-hand quarter of the canvas—all these formal elements combine to turn the picture into a near-abstract design, far more so than in any painting by Caravaggio.

Such a basic feeling for form is congenial to the aesthetic appetite of today and for that reason Georges de la Tour has emerged, during the last decade, from comparative obscurity into an almost fashionable prominence.

Rubens. *The Judgment of Paris*

R U B E N S painted three versions of The Judgment of Paris. It was a theme after his own heart, for it gave him full opportunity to express his three greatest passions: the drama of a story involving human conflict, the setting of a landscape full of space, light and the springing curves of growth, and the idealization of feminine physical beauty.

Ever since his first journey from Antwerp to Italy, when he was a young man of twenty, he had set himself to weld these three elements of painting into a pictorial unity which he was perhaps the first to achieve. In doing so, he perfected the formula for the baroque style. Often one feels that he was on the verge of becoming the victim of the formula, but as he grew older, as his style broadened and matured, his stature increased until in the last years there was no complexity of detail that he could not combine into a single controlling rhythm. The splendor of his landscapes became richer still, the nobility of his nudes more commanding.

The Judgment of Paris was painted in 1639 for Philip IV of Spain, who had been his patron ever since his first contact with the artist and who now urged Rubens to produce even larger and more ambitious works than ever before. Canvases came pouring in from Antwerp, and Rubens quaintly assured the king that, in order to increase the speed of his output, he was executing this one with his own hand. For the Rubens "factory system," while it enabled the master to work simultaneously on several paintings, actually slowed down the process of work on a given canvas. It is well known that when Rubens was at the height of his powers and inundated with more commissions from his many patrons than could be executed by an artist singlehandedly, he organized his studio on what would now be called "factory lines." His many assistants (including Van Dyck himself) enlarged his drawings and sketches while the master supervised the work, making corrections as it proceeded and adding finishing touches when they could carry it no further. Rubens made no secret of his method, and often informed his patrons when his pictures had been painted by his own hand from start to finish.

As usual, sumptuousness is the keynote of the work. The glowing beauty of the nude goddesses, each keeping its own undulating movement,

89. *Rubens (1577-1640). The Judgment of Paris. 1639. Oil.
Prado, Madrid*

yet each contributing to the larger design that holds all three together; the glitter of Minerva's armor; the satin cloaks of Venus and Juno; the iridescent tail of her peacock—all these elements and more besides contribute to a cumulative effect that, in the work of any other artist, would have produced a sense of overcrowding.

The central goddess, the Venus to whom the apple is being offered and who is being crowned by a flying cupid, is Rubens' second wife, Helen Fourment, whom he married when she was sixteen and he was fifty-three. When he painted this Judgment of Paris he was sixty and she was twenty-four. It is one of his last tributes to her beauty. Doubtless it shows Helen as she was in 1639. Yet she has been transformed by that curious trick, which Rubens had known since his youth, of accepting a Flemish ideal and then linking it up with a tradition that stretched back through Titian, through Raphael, to the Aphrodites of Golden-Age Greece. Helen is almost the last of the line to pay homage to her Greek and Italian ancestresses and yet to remain a buxom Flemish girl.

In writing of Cranach's version of the same story I suggested that the reader should turn the pages forward and compare Cranach (Plate 76) with Rubens. If the pages are now turned back it does little harm to Cranach—his affectations become ever more piquant—but it enlarges Rubens, to whom the word affectation could never be applied.

Bernini. *Vision of St. Theresa*

BAROQUE IS one of those words used by art historians to describe a style that can never be exactly defined, yet which is instantly recognizable when it appears in an extreme form. Among painters no artist has ever been more baroque than Rubens; among sculptors no one has pushed the possibilities of the baroque style to more extreme lengths than Bernini. It was he who designed the curved colonnade which defines the axis of the immense open space in front of St. Peter's in Rome, and it was he who imagined the great baldacchino (an immense architectural canopy) over the high altar inside the church, which arrests and focuses the eye of every visitor who enters so that it becomes the central feature of that vast interior. It was Bernini who designed and executed the famous carving of The Vision of St. Theresa in the Church of Santa Maria della Vittoria in Rome.

One of the most baffling characteristics of baroque sculpture is that no photograph can give a complete idea of its dramatic impact on the eye. The Vision of St. Theresa, like the well-known soliloquies from *Hamlet,* is magnificent even when divorced from its context, yet only when it is considered as part of a larger artistic unit does its real meaning become apparent. And so much of that meaning is concentrated into the head of the saint that I have ventured, in this plate, to isolate it.

As one enters the church the eye has to search for it, but once found it produces an unfailing thrill of surprise. Composed of two figures set back in the recess of a scooped-out niche high in the wall of the dark nave, the saint and the angel appear like apparitions in the mysterious light that filters down onto them from an opening in the ceiling above. The lighting alone, like that of a tableau in a theater, would make the two figures memorable. The angel, with a strangely peaceful gesture in which violence and tenderness are somehow mingled, stands poised on a marble cloud that seems to have no inherent weight, brandishing an arrow and looking down with a faint, inward smile at the saint who swoons backward with closed eyes and parted lips in an ecstasy that is half-sensual, half-spiritual. Quite apart from this ambiguity in which the religious and the physical meet, one would have thought that such a tremulous, unstable grouping would be impossible in so ponderous a medium. Yet, despite the virtuosity that gives to white marble the texture of feathers (in the angel's wings), drapery, flesh and cloud, the effect is of lightness, as though neither angel nor saint were tangible creatures.

Nor is this all. A few feet farther along the nave where the wall changes its angle, Bernini has carved what amounts to a box in the theater that contains, again in carved marble, a group of donors, members of the *177*

90. *Bernini (1599-1680).*
The Vision of St. Theresa.
c. 1645-52. *Marble.*
Santa Maria della Vittoria,
Rome

Cornaro family, who gaze at the illuminated tableau in grave astonishment. Not until the whole of this complex design of stage and audience has been grasped does Bernini's daringly melodramatic intention become clear. And even then it can only be "read" in relation to the spacious interior of the church itself.

Admittedly, this is a triumph of dramatic invention that breaks all the accepted rules by which we are accustomed to test the validity of a work of art, including the generally acknowledged rules of "good taste." But the baroque style so often depends on this kind of violation of accepted law that in extreme instances of it we must either succumb to it unquestioningly or else reject it utterly. And in presenting it in this anthology of masterworks of art we must despair of seeing it as a whole and hope that a detail—the thrown-back head of the swooning saint—will give some faint impression of Bernini's quality of vision as well as his virtuosity as a carver.

The later phases of Greek sculpture (one thinks of the agonized thrown-back head of the central figure of the Laocoön group) had attempted something of the sort, but in sheer subtlety Bernini far outstrips the Greek sculptor. In the presence of such works it is useless to complain that marble should not be allowed to lose its identity in an imitation of flesh or drapery. If, by doing so, Bernini can achieve an effect never achieved before, and if that effect can communicate the intended tremor, Bernini can snap his fingers at the purists.

Velasquez. *Mariana of Austria*

VELASQUEZ was born in 1599—seven years before Rembrandt— and died in 1660—nine years before him. They were, therefore, almost exact contemporaries, working in opposite corners of Europe practically unknown to each other and without influencing each other. Certainly there was no similarity between life in Rembrandt's Amsterdam and Velasquez's Madrid. Yet the two great painters of the 17th Century have this at least in common : both were realists, fascinated by the spectacle life offered to them and reluctant to distort or idealize it, though each interpreted it in his own way. And both made some of their most memorable statements in the realm of portraiture. Nonetheless it strikes us at once, when we compare them, that Rembrandt seems to penetrate below the surface while Velasquez dwells affectionately on it, obsessed by it, never attempting to search for deeper meanings. And while Rembrandt's great portraits are of obscure Dutch citizens, Velasquez, as court painter to Philip IV of Spain, was largely concerned with the pomp and glitter of the Spanish court.

It is surprising, therefore, that in the presence of these alarmingly aloof and magnificently dressed—or overdressed—creatures he could still present them to us as human beings and not as puppets. The secret lies in his imperturbability. He is never overawed by ceremony. Whatever lies before his eyes is good material for his impartial eye and the wizardry of his brush. Among the great artists of the world—and there is no questioning his greatness—he is the least poetical, the least imaginative and the least visionary. He raises only one question in our minds : how could an artist whose vision is essentially prosaic produce pictures that have so powerful an impact?

Here stands the queen of Spain, Philip IV's second wife, who had been betrothed to his son, Don Balthasar Carlos, but whom the king married after his son's early death, while she was still in her teens. Velasquez was over fifty when he painted this magnificent portrait in 1652. Many replicas of it exist, studio versions and none of them negligible, but the picture in the Prado in Madrid is certainly the original.

She stands, stiff and sulky, in an enormous farthingale dress of black silk, trimmed with rows of silver braid, red bows at her wrists and in her fantastically elaborate hair, scarlet splashes on the ostrich feather on her head, gold jewelry and a gold medallion at her throat. There could be no greater contrast than that between her pale expressionless face and the dramatic clothes she wears—the dress of the Spanish court.

To make such a portrait acceptable, indeed even to avoid turning it into an absurd caricature, required a virtuosity that no painter of the time and few of any other period possessed. The simplicity of that expanse of black

91. *Velasquez (1599-1660). Portrait of Mariana of Austria,*
Queen of Spain. 1652. Oil. Prado, Madrid

and the subtlety with which Velasquez has handled the bands of silver, the exactness with which he has established the tonal relationships between the queen and the curtain above her head and the table behind her are proofs of Velasquez's genius both as an observer and as a technician. More remarkable still, despite the distracting pattern of black and silver with accents of red, is that lackluster face and those uninterested eyes which dominate the picture. It could have been a decorative costume piece. It is, in fact, an unusually satisfying portrait.

Rembrandt's Drawings

IF ALL OF Rembrandt's paintings (of which nearly a thousand are still extant) were to be destroyed, we would still regard him as a giant on the evidence of his drawings. From the beginning of his career to the end of it he used drawing not as most painters do, as a means of preparing the way for the more serious task of painting or of resolving problems of detail or composition, but as an end in itself. For Rembrandt, drawing was a means of recording his impressions of the outer world, or of realizing aspects of his own imaginative processes that could never have found their way onto canvas. His drawings can, in fact, be roughly divided into two types: those in which he swiftly noted the seen object, the observed incident, and those that came to him as a result of brooding on a theme. Naturally the two categories cannot be divided sharply from each other, for Rembrandt was a realist, and the difference between the Madonna and Child and a sketch of his wife nursing her baby is a subtle one. But they have this in common: behind them both—behind almost everything that he drew—is a kind of desperate urgency, as though he felt that if the speed of the pen or brush racing across the paper were to slacken some of the immediacy would be lost.

That, at least, is our impression after glancing through a hundred typical drawings. They are pulsating with the very essence of the life that they record. But—and this is the secret of his gigantic stature as an artist—white-hot though they are, they are never restless. His hand is always under the strictest control. The lift of a little finger, the raising of an eyebrow could not be more exactly registered, yet the hand that draws them never loses its urgency. It moves at the bidding of his eye and his mind, both of which work at the same incredible pitch of intensity and penetration. Nothing essential is missed; nothing superfluous is allowed to act as a brake on these simple yet unbelievably subtle statements.

The three drawings reproduced here have been chosen in order to show him in three different moods. The Naughty Boy (done about 1635 in his twenty-ninth year) is a product of the eagle eye which grasps all the implica- 181

92. *Rembrandt*
(1606-1669).
The Naughty Boy.
1635. Drawing.
Kupferstich Kabinett,
Berlin

tions of an incident that can have lasted for not more than two seconds. The solicitous gaze of the grandmother, who hurriedly opens the door because the mother is fully occupied in trying to grapple with a struggling, screaming child; the child who kicks off his shoe in a violent attempt to wrench himself free from the arms that so awkwardly clutch him; the two elder children watching the scene from within the house; the few furiously rapid strokes that indicate the wall, the shadow on the wall and the door (Rembrandt hardly ever omits describing the stage on which his actors perform)—all this has been seen in a flash and described at lightning speed. It is only when one begins to note details that one becomes aware of the precision that accompanies the speed: the impotently clutching left hand of the child whose eyes are swollen with hysterical weeping, the clenched jaw of 182 the mother, the "I told you so" expression on the grandmother's face. And

93. *Rembrandt. Sleeping Girl.*
    1655. Drawing.
    British Museum

94. *Rembrandt. Seated Man.*
    1645. Drawing.
    Gemeenta Musea,
    Amsterdam

by the side of these tiny areas packed with meaning, other areas that contain a minimum of what lines are needed to explain the gesture or the tension.

The Sleeping Girl, drawn with a brush about twenty years later, is deservedly one of Rembrandt's most famous; although the problem of drawing the motionless girl is a less exacting one, the solution of it is little short of miraculous. The swiftness of hand is still there. To it has been added a set of variations of pressure that outdo even the best of Japanese brushwork: the loaded, liquid areas that describe her hair; the light on it and the ribbon that binds it; the shadow which conceals the tucked-in hand; the lightly brushed lines indicating the folds of drapery that skim across the grain of the paper; the structure of the head in which two dark splashes conceal the closed eyes; and two small areas of a medium tone that model the curve of the forehead and cheeks. As an impression of repose it is masterly, as calligraphy it is astonishing, as a fusion of the two it is unique.

The subject of the third example, Esau, is halfway between repose and movement—an impulsive handshake between two men, a profound study of facial expression (a postage stamp would easily cover the whole of the head and hat), a rapid indication of the two upper halves of the seated men, an even swifter suggestion of a doorway behind them and a table between them. Nothing needs adding and nothing can be subtracted. Yet not only expression and gesture are there but also space and the play of light. This drawing was probably done in 1645—halfway in time between the other two. Of the three it is the most concentrated and the most remarkable as a demonstration of economy of means. Perhaps that is because it belongs to the category of the "imagined" rather than the "seen."

Rembrandt. Family Group

ALMOST ALL PAINTERS and a majority of connoisseurs of painting agree that Rembrandt is the world's greatest painter. It is a judgment that deserves careful consideration, for the greatest painter is not necessarily the greatest artist. We know from his drawings that his environment—the little corner of 17th-Century Holland that he knew so well and with which he was so content that he never wished to leave it—provided him with everything he needed. Out of its citizens, their relationship to each other, its undramatic countryside and its modest buildings he constructed a world that has never been equalled in profundity of human understanding or in the mastery of paint. Only one thing limited him—his reverent acceptance of that world. Of him alone it can be said that though he was a poet, he was also a realist. He refused to make what he saw more physically perfect, like Praxiteles, or more graceful, like Raphael, or more noble, like Michel-

95. *Rembrandt. Family Group. 1669. Oil.*
Herzog Anton Ulrich Museum, Brunswick

angelo, or more exuberant, like Rubens, or more cruel, like Grünewald. He
had no wish to remake the world nearer to his heart's desire as so many of
the greatest artists have done, for to Rembrandt the world as it existed *was*
the world of his heart's desire. If realism is Rembrandt's only limitation it is
also the secret of his power.

His portraits are numbered in hundreds. Almost all of them are of
undistinguished people, unremarkable in most respects, certainly not noticeable for their physical beauty, and almost all of them amaze us by the depth
of his human penetration, which increased as he grew older.

The Family Group from the Brunswick Museum is a typical specimen
of his portraiture at the end of his life. Reproduction can hardly do justice
to the handling of the paint, so free is it, yet so controlled. But some notion
can be conveyed of his insight into human character. It is a quality that every
serious adult can appreciate for himself, and Rembrandt is essentially a painter
for the serious adult. It is surely not necessary for the critic to dwell on a   *185*

96. *Vermeer (1632-1675). The Artist in his Studio.* c. 1670.
Oil. Kunsthistorisches Museum, Vienna

quality that has so much to do with everyday experience and so little to do with aesthetics.

In understanding the genius of Botticelli or Tintoretto or Cézanne (the names are chosen almost at random) a critical commentary can be of considerable assistance. Rembrandt needs no such assistance. Here is a family of five ordinary people: a father, mother and three children, united by the ties of family affection. Animated, each of them, in their own way; each quietly reacting to the others. A moment in time has been caught and described and yet the description is timeless. The year happens to be 1669, yet we hardly notice the local characteristics or the dresses they wear. They are samples of the universal civilized average human being, valid as such in any century since civilization began.

Vermeer. *The Artist in his Studio*

THE ASTONISHING OUTBURST of painting in 17th-Century Holland, which lasted for so comparatively short a time, covered such a wide range of subjects and expressed so narrow a range of feeling, is one of the minor wonders of art history. In the first quarter of the century it could hardly have been predicted; before the century was over little remained of it but echoes. It included one outstanding genius, Rembrandt. It also included a hundred minor masters who operated with wonderful skill and consistency on an altogether lower plane. Each of them had his chosen field—portraiture, landscape, still life, shipping, townscapes, tavern scenes with peasants, drawing room scenes with middle-class burghers. So specialized were the minor masters of Holland that they seem to us almost ludicrous in their narrowness. We can hardly project ourselves into the frame of mind that could gravitate naturally to moonlight or skating or the interiors of churches, or even half-peeled lemons.

It is only when we consider what they did not and could not paint that the school begins to cohere. Gods were beyond them and man's attitude to his gods. Miracles never occur, nor does fantasy or whimsy. They cannot be exuberant; tragedy and exultation are beyond them; so is everything that is mystical and supernatural. What they achieved was a complete documentary account of almost every conceivable aspect of daily life in Holland during that enormously productive period of sixty-odd years.

That being so, it might be thought that there were no artists among them who could consistently produce poetry in paint. If they could not see beyond and behind the material surface of the church, the boat, the drawing room, the sitter's features, what could they express beyond a generalized affectionate contentment with their own environment?

187

It is a reasonable question, and for the most part the honest answer is "nothing." They were realists and masters of good, though rarely elegant, prose. But there were one or two exceptions, and among those exceptions Vermeer of Delft is, in our eyes, pre-eminent.

"In our eyes" is a necessary qualifying phrase. It is the 20th Century, with its fine adjustment to shades of feeling and differences of style, that sees Vermeer as a poet, while his nearest counterpart, Pieter de Hooch, is no more than a sensitive master of well-ordered prose. Vermeer took de Hooch's subject matter—the unimportant social interchange of the drawing room—and raised it to a higher power, so that it no longer mattered what the love letter contained, what kind of people were sipping their wine, what dish the cook was preparing. Vermeer's pictures (alas, how few they are!) use the same furniture, the same pots and pans as those of his Dutch contemporaries, but with an entirely different effect. So exquisite is his placing of the main masses, so delicately does the light illuminate the floor and wall, so precisely does he establish the spatial relationships that his pictures begin to remind us of modern abstract painting. Form seems to be everything; content is unimportant. His figures are rarely in action or, if they are, the action is deliberate and undramatic. They have no character and no expression. Vermeer, in a century of realism, is a classical painter, uninterested in reality but forced, by the convention of his time, to accept the doctrines of realism.

Though this painting is not quite typical of him, in the sense that something is "happening," it is characteristic. The artist turns his back to us. He is not a character but a shape—and a remarkable one. His model is the silliest of lay figures, her trumpet a mere aid to the composition. So are the easel and the canvas. The great looped up curtain is no more than the first incident in a diagonal journey through space which takes in the artist's stool and easel and ends with the chair against the far wall. The huge map is there partly to establish an abstract rectangle and partly to explain, by its creased surface, the impact of raking light on the wall.

As with the form, so with the color. It is cool and impersonal, like the color of Piero della Francesca. And the texture of the paint, as always with Vermeer, hardly betrays the fact that a human hand applied it to the canvas. It, too, is impersonal.

Vermeer is the least human, the most calculating, the most aloof from life in a generation of artists whose main concern was to come to the closest possible quarters with life as they knew it. One of the secrets of his fascination for us is that he is a paradox; the other is that he is a perfectionist.

97. *Hispano-Mauresque Dish.*
Early 17th Century.
Gold luster pottery.
Metropolitan Museum,
New York

Hispano-Mauresque Dish

MOORISH CRAFTSMEN working under European masters produced the great tradition in Spain of gold luster pottery. The best specimens of it, produced in the kilns of Manisco in Valencia (its most productive and best period was during the 16th Century) are among the world's most daring examples of freedom and vigor in painted pottery. The massing of the heraldic motives—bulls, gryphons, eagles with wings fiercely spread, lions rampant—on backgrounds of controlled but spontaneously growing floral ornament combine Gothic decorative traditions with Islamic idioms and craftsmanship. And the rich luster gives these designs a depth and quality that makes them precious as well as bold.

The bull on this great dish, who fills the bowl and overflows recklessly on to its outer margins, is a comparatively late product of the Manisco kilns—toward the end of the 16th or beginning of the 17th Century. The freedom of its movement; the delicacy of the linear stems that spiral across the background; the two fish that swirl over its back and keep the circular form of the dish "spinning" counterclockwise; even the two casual rosettes that break the heavy mass of its body; the two innocent circles that mark   *189*

98. *Toft. Charles II in the Oak Tree. Late 17th Century. Staffordshire ware. Metropolitan Museum, New York*

its eyes and the Y-shaped line between them that defines its nose—all this is the mark of a fearless, confident craftsman who has grown up in an old tradition but has never been afraid to invent fanciful variations on it. This is the apotheosis of folk art.

Dish by Thomas Toft.   Charles II in the Oak Tree

AFTER THE EXECUTION of Charles I in 1649, his son, who afterward became Charles II, made his escape to France and history relates how he hid in an oak tree and so escaped from Cromwell's soldiers.

The adventure is charmingly depicted on many of the Staffordshire ware plates turned out by Thomas Toft, the potter, in the last quarter of the 17th Century. Toft ware is distinguished by its bold decorative simplicity. It has all the vigor of folk art and the best specimens of it have even a magnificent, naïve self-confidence. They follow the formula invented by Toft himself. It is usually a light buff or red clay, washed with a white slip wherever a light ground was required. Onto this the design was traced in bold dark brown

190

outlines and filled in with a dark orange. The outlines were afterward enriched with white dots. A yellowish lead glaze over the whole gave the surface a mellow glow.

Such items of everyday manufacture came very near to the borderline of decorative commercial art, and as such they would hardly deserve a place in an anthology of masterpieces. But Toft himself, judging from the boldness of his signature and the date often incorporated into the design, must have been proud of his work. And certainly it is rare to find manufacture that amounts to peasant ware approaching so near to the monumental and using heraldic devices, or, at least, the formalized conventions of heraldic design, so confidently that they achieve a life of their own.

Watteau. Fêtes Venitiennes

WITH WATTEAU the pedantic academicism and the austere nobility that had characterized the French 17th Century come to an end; the frivolity and the gaiety that were to be typical of the 18th Century begin to appear. Art transfers itself from the formalities of the palace to the intimacies of the boudoir. Between the heavy-handed seriousness of Vernet and LeBrun and the pink-and-blue frivolities of Boucher and Fragonard there is a gap in time and an even greater gap in spirit. That gap is bridged by the exquisite art of Antoine Watteau.

Only a man with an exceptionally acute eye and an unusually sensitive hand could have constructed so tough yet so fragile a bridge. Watteau inherited from Rubens the grand principles of baroque design, and by applying them on a smaller scale and giving them a sophisticated twist he turned the baroque into rococo, substituting charm for power, tremulousness for dynamism, lyric song for dramatic orchestration.

An art that depended on such extreme refinement was inimitable. Yet Watteau had his imitators. His delicious little lyrics so exactly expressed the spirit of the age that they could not fail to please the society that revolved so uselessly and so elegantly round the Court of Versailles. And what was so acceptable was bound to be emulated. Pater and Lancret at once picked up the Watteau formula. They painted Watteauesque pictures full of Watteau's gallantries and flirtations: the guitar music under the trees, the lovers idling under the arches of the palace or stealing away into the thicket. They understood the formula but they could not capture the magic that makes Watteau so precious.

Fêtes Venitiennes is full of that magic. Only one other European artist— Giorgione—could cast the same spell or evoke the same mood, and then only in rare instances. Giorgione's Tempestà in the Venetian Accademia is one of them. Both are small pictures, trivial and elusive in subject matter but unforgettable in mood. In the two centuries which separate them, human values have changed. At the Court of Versailles no peasant mother can conceivably suckle her child in public. The social pattern has become more elaborate and artificial. No artist has ever managed to describe it as precisely as Watteau. In both pictures the figures are unexpectedly small in relation to the enclosing rectangle of the frame. They dream their lives away in an environment that dwarfs them and is an integral part of their dream.

But the two conceptions are different, though both share the same nostalgia. In Watteau's picture the nostalgia becomes all the more poignant because of its artificiality. The exquisite shy dignity of the girl in the center—her white dress is a symbol of her debutante innocence—is contrasted with the pompous authority of the dancing master to whom she listens. The fiddler who is to provide the music for the dance—with what precision does Watteau indicate by his pose and his features that he belongs to a different social stratum from the rest!—awaits his orders. The girl's friends continue their frivolously animated conversations in the background. The statue of the goddess of love looks down on the scene. The great trees in the park tower overhead, reminders that nature, unlike man, can never be drilled into a pattern of behavior. Yet behind the chatter and the laughter there are undertones of sadness. They are Watteau's personal comment. Pater and Lancret tried for them but could never achieve anything so subtle; Boucher and Fragonard, more firmly embedded in the French 18th Century, did not even try.

Two factors in Watteau's art enabled him to comment with such extraordinary precision on the small corner of human behavior which occupied him so exclusively. One is a gift of draftsmanship by which he could express the minutest inflections of gesture—the turn of a head, the pressure of fingers on the guitar strings, the exact tempo of every small movement. Each of those little sketchbook drawings, usually in sanguine crayon, are memoranda of such momentary gestures, stored up for future use in his picture. They look unforced and unhurried but they record the observation of a split second.

The other factor is his handling of the paint brush which seems to spread a film of dancing light over the satin of his dresses and the foliage of his trees. It is a caressing brushstroke, not unlike that of Renoir. Again, it seems unforced and spontaneous, yet it must have been the result of the strictest painterly discipline.

Fêtes Venitiennes is, for Watteau, an unusually formal composition. It was not often that he decided to follow the classical formula of a symmetrically balanced composition, but it is an index of his skill that the symmetry is so disguised by ingenious devices and variations that we hardly notice the centerline implied by the girl and huge urn above her and the subtle accents that give importance to the dancing master and the musician who balance each other on either side of her.

99. *Watteau (1684-1721). Fêtes Venitiennes. Early 18th Century. Oil. National Gallery, Edinburgh*

Tiepolo. Martyrdom of St. John

AT THE END of the 16th Century the long line of Venetian painters (from Giovanni Bellini to Veronese) seemed to have come to an end. The fires died down—Venetian painting throughout the 17th Century was competent, even plentiful—but suddenly, at the end of the second decade of the 18th Century, the fires blazed up again. It was the precocious young painter, Giambattista Tiepolo, who was largely responsible for this revival of a great tradition.

Tiepolo's career is a dazzling one. Considering the vast frescoed ceilings and walls covered by him in Venice, Milan, Bergamo, Würzburg in Germany and Madrid in Spain (where he died in 1770), it seems impossible that one man could have been responsible for so much, and that so little of what he did should show signs of fatigue or an exhausted imagination.

Temperamentally he harks back to the brilliance and glitter of Veronese, from whom he certainly drew much of his inspiration. The same opulent dresses, the same rhetorical gestures, radiant architectural backgrounds and glowing skies occur in both artists. But the spirit of the two centuries was different. The solemnity of the 16th Century is hardly to be found in the 18th, and, for all his opulence, a note of stylish swagger runs through the whole of Tiepolo. And with it goes a higher, more acid, key of color, an intenser light, a more airy, silvery radiance.

Tiepolo was thirty-seven when he was called to Bergamo, in 1733, to paint frescoes in the Colleoni Chapel, and during his short stay there he found time to execute a great altarpiece for the cathedral of the martyrdom of St. John, Bishop of Bergamo, who strove during the 7th Century to extirpate the heresy of Arianism from his diocese and was murdered by his enemies in A.D. 681.

The painting is done with Tiepolo's customary bravura and sense of drama. The crowded gesticulating figures in the foreground are brilliant examples of his genius. The arcading behind these figures, blazing with white light, and the balcony and the figures looking down from it are echoes of Veronese; so is the flying angel bearing the palm branch of martyrdom. But Tiepolo was a Veronese who had exchanged gold for silver, velvet for satin, grandeur for pageantry.

100. *Tiepolo (1696-1769).*
The Martyrdom of
St. John of Bergamo.
1733. Oil.
Duomo of Bergamo

101. Piranesi (c. 1720-1778). *Carceri Series.* c. 1745. *Etching*

Piranesi's Etchings

THE DECISIVE FACTOR in the life of Giovanni Battista Piranesi is that, though born in Venice, he left the city of his birth at the age of eighteen and moved to Rome. He was determined to become an architect and an engraver. In Venice he could easily have studied both arts, and having done so he would, in that most lyrical of cities, have turned himself into another Guardi, a Guardi who used line instead of color.

But Rome, instead of being lyrical, was dramatic; in moving to Rome he exchanged a city of light and fantasy for a city of weight and power. Had he not studied architecture his drawings and etchings would never have had the solidity and the logic that makes even the most oppressively romantic of his plates structurally convincing. But it was the ponderous grandeur of Roman architecture that seized on his imagination and provoked him to produce those plates of topographical views of the city, the Raccolta di Varie Vedute di Roma si Antica che Moderna, in which the weight of history is superimposed on the weight of architecture.

His most memorable plates, however, are not those that describe the temples of Rome, the ruined baths of the emperors and the baroque palaces and churches of the 17th Century, but the series of purely imaginary prisons, published in 1745. Here he could give free rein to his imagination and his sense of the sinister and the colossal. Prison scenes were not uncommon in the dramas of the time, but Piranesi went far beyond what was possible on the stage. In those awe-inspiring interiors that he invented there is no logic— except that of structural possibility which the architect in him was bound to respect. In place of logic is a fantastic *folie de grandeur*, whose only function is to terrify and oppress the human spirit. The figures that inhabit his prisons are introduced not in order to tell a story but to give scale to the architecture and to silhouette themselves on giant drawbridges or climb dizzy spiral staircases in the semi-gloom.

Everything in this etching is either minute or enormous. The pulley and the rope that hangs from it, the hanging lamp larger than a man, the great blocks of masonry that form the arch above and the bridge below are Brobdingnagian; so is the dimly adumbrated rack on the left, evidently designed for torturing giants. But their oppressive titanism is doubled by the contrast between them and the delicacy of the balustrades on the drawbridge and winding staircases. No such vision could have come to him in Venice. It would admirably serve as a décor for Beethoven's Fidelio.

102. *Angel. Mid-18th Century Austria.*
Gilded limewood.
Victoria and Albert Museum, London

Austrian Rococo Sculpture

WITH THE 18th Century the orchestral drama of the baroque style of three-quarters of a century earlier became less massive though not less dramatic. What we have learned to call the rococo style was still vigorous and, in Northern Europe at least, the effects produced by sculptors and architects working in collaboration could be breath-taking. Indeed, as in baroque, one can hardly judge rococo sculpture away from its architectural context.

But both architects and sculptors, though they still used the baroque vocabulary of form, were working in a less serious vein. Power was being replaced by elegance, movement by agitation. The passion of Rubens and Bernini was evaporating and its place was taken by a more artificial and, in general, more decorative kind of eloquence. One sees the new style at its best in the paintings of Tiepolo (Plate 100) and in the fitful light that plays on the buildings of Guardi's Venice (Plate 103). But the true rococo flutter is unmistakable in this angel, carved in limewood and gilded, one of a pair that must once have looked down from the wall on either side of an altar in an Austrian church.

It belongs to the middle of the 18th Century. Its author is unknown, and indeed his name hardly matters, for it is not the product of an individual but of a style. Such figures had become almost a cliché, but this is an exceptionally delightful example. And the skill with which the unknown carver fashioned the sprightly attitude, the lively excited gesture, the downward turn of the head, the elegant disorder of the wings is certainly remarkable. Perhaps a hundred sculptors in France, Germany and Austria possessed a similar skill and knew the secret of how to produce a similar elegance. But art does not always depend on personal genius. One could even say that the genius of rococo art resides not in the artist but in the style itself. Gravity, both in the literal and the moral sense, has no part in the rococo style, and this angel, just under life size, has discovered the secret of effortless levitation.

Guardi. Campo San Zanipolo

NO EUROPEAN CITY has captured the imagination of travelers more completely than Venice. Even over its own citizens the strangeness of its waterways, the fragility and fantasy of its architecture, the busy traffic of its gondolas, the pageantry of its daily life cast a spell; so that from the 15th Century onward its art reflects a civic pride that is not to be found in that of any other city. Gentile Bellini's great picture of the Corpus Christi procession in the Piazza of St. Mark, Carpaccio's of the rescue of a relic from the canal, reflect the artists' delight in Venetian pomp; Veronese's oval panel of the Apotheosis of Venice in the Palace of the Doges pays tribute to its social elegance and its political power. But it was not till the 18th Century that a school of painters came into being who devoted themselves almost exclusively to celebrating its purely visual aspect and recording its outward appearance with affectionate accuracy.

This outburst of "documentary" pictures was something comparatively new in the development of painting, it was certainly called into being by the demands of travelers, mainly from England, who were engaged on the Grand Tour of Europe and who, amazed that any city could be at once so strange and so beautiful, wished to take home with them a faithful record of its strangeness and beauty. That demand still persists, but today it is usually the photographer and not the painter who satisfies it.

Our vision of Venice—the image of it that we build up in our visual memory—has been largely crystallized by three artists. In the 18th Century Canaletto and Guardi painted its architecture and its canals and gondolas with untiring industry; in the 19th, Turner (see plate 111), who traveled incessantly and never ceased to paint romanticized visions of what he saw, came to Venice late in his life and responded to its magic with a series of water colors and paintings that are among the most visionary and romantic in his whole career. But of the three artists, it is to Guardi that we respond most easily. His Venice has not quite the cardboard neatness of Canaletto. The light flickers more fitfully across the glowing surfaces of his buildings. He catches some of that perpetual slight shimmer which plays over their surfaces, thrown *199*

103. *Guardi (1712-1793). Campo San Zanipolo. Late 18th Century. Oil.*
Kress Collection, National Gallery of Art, Washington, D.C.

upward from the moving surface of the water. For Guardi the city is not eaten away by light as it so often is with Turner. Guardi's Venice has a glowing patina and his nervous brushstroke is exactly what is needed to remind us of its magic.

The Venetian dialect delights in abbreviations: the Campo Zanipolo, anywhere else in Italy, would have been called the Campo dei Santi Giovanni e Paolo. It is the open space from which rises the mass of the Church of Sts. John and Paul, and in which Verrocchio's Colleoni sits proudly on his horse. Behind the church rises the elegant façade of what was then the Scuola di San Marco and is now the City Hospital, and Guardi's canvas shows it today with the addition of a flight of temporary stairs built onto it for ceremonial occasions such as the one shown in his picture.

Bewick's Woodcuts

BEWICK was a minor artist but he has a strong claim to be included in this anthology by virtue of his excellence as a craftsman. His innumerable woodcuts of birds and animals are the finest of their kind. His control, even in the smallest tailpiece, of the woodcutter's tool working on the surface of a boxwood block would be remarkable enough to make him one of the greatest masters of the medium, but he added to that an acute observation that enabled him to describe the minutest differences between one species of animal and another. His Quadrupeds and Birds (both published in Newcastle in the first half of the 19th Century) are still far more vivid from a purely descriptive point of view than anything done since. His illustrations to Aesop's *Fables* show him as a quiet humorist.

Most of his work consists of illustrative woodcuts with which no naturalist could possibly find fault. But he also amused himself by making little prints of what might be called the genre element in country life, in which he was able to catch the very mood of the weather—the fisherman in the stream, the sportsman with his dog and shotgun sheltering from the rain, the little unremarkable incident that only a true countryman would consider worth recording. And in each of them the very trees have their own specific character.

104. *Bewick* (1753-1828).
Illustration from
British Birds.
c. 1797. *Woodcut*

105. *Rowlandson (1756-1827). Soirée at the Royal Academy.*
Late 18th Century. Drawing. British Museum

Rowlandson.   Soirée at the Royal Academy

R O W L A N D S O N was a tireless and fluent draftsman; each one of his
drawings, usually in reed pen with pale washes of color, is at once recognizable
as his because of the characteristic "handwriting." It would not be quite true
to call his drawings "jottings." Rather does he resemble a diarist—a man with

a robust sense of humor that easily runs to caricature, a keen eye for the essence of the trivial event and an unfailing delight in the trivialities and absurdities of human behavior. Yet if Rowlandson is a diarist, his diary is certainly for publication. However lighthearted he may be and however absurd the characters that people his stage, his line has an elegance and his composition is often worthy of a great master. And occasionally, as one looks through a collection of these sprightly little works, the exception suddenly presents itself—a drawing that is positively inspired, so swift and vital in the pen lines, so well-invented the design that holds them together.

Such a drawing is the Soirée at the Royal Academy. It is not often that a master of gentle satire or an observer of social absurdities can discover a compositional framework so genuinely beautiful, for the sweeping spiral of the staircase and its placing within the rectangle of the drawing are faultless. And it is not often that an artist can contrive to work in a spirit of uninhibited laughter and at the same time retain his own inherent stylishness and refinement.

Blake. *The Ancient of Days*

O N E   W O N D E R S whether Blake will ultimately be most valued for his lyric poetry, his visionary "prophetic" books in which he expanded a philosophy and a religion of his own devising, or for his work as an artist-engraver who produced hundreds of engravings, drawings and small-scale water colors packed with significant imagery. There are those who find his philosophy perverse, his lyrics too naïve and his work as an artist too dependent on borrowings from artists greater than himself—in particular Michelangelo. But no one can doubt his genius. His power to discover a memorable symbol of a literary idea was inexhaustible. His illustrations to Dante, to Milton, to certain of Shakespeare's most daring phrases (for example the passage in *Macbeth* that begins "Pity like a naked new-born babe, striding the blast...") and to some of his own visionary writings are quite staggering in their appropriateness.

This water color drawing, evolved from one of his own "relief etchings" (a method evolved by himself of printing from an etching as though it were a wood block) and originally the frontispiece to his prophetic poem *Europe* published in 1794, is one of his most powerful designs. It seems to be an illustration of a passage from Milton's *Paradise Lost*:

> "He took the golden compasses, prepar'd
> In God's eternal store, to circumscribe
> This Universe and all created things."

The immense latent power in the stooping figure of the Creator, His beard and hair blowing in the wind, formless clouds surrounding Him, and *203*

106. *Blake (1757-1827).* *The Ancient of Days.*
c. 1794. *Watercolor drawing.*
Whitworth Gallery, Manchester

the abyss below Him broken only by the arms of the compasses that issue
from His hand like forked lightning—all this needs no pointing out. The
wonder is that so tremendous an image should have been compressed on to
a sheet of paper nine and a half by six and three-quarters inches in size.

Henry Fuseli. The Kiss

IT WOULD REQUIRE more than a brief appreciative note to
analyze the strange fusion of models that accounts for the art of Henry
Fuseli, who was born in Switzerland, absorbed all the grandeur of the High
Renaissance and of the Mannerist style in Italy and then settled down in
England in 1779. The mixture of German-Swiss temperament and Italian
scholarship would have been a bizarre equipment at any time, but the moment
in time of his arrival in England added to the complexity of his art. The

107. *Fuseli (1741-1825). The Kiss.*
     c. 1815. Drawing.
     Kunstmuseum, Basle

neoclassicism of the 18th Century was giving way under the growing pressure of the Romantic movement which, in literature, was beginning to express itself in Goethe's writings and Byron's poetry. Fuseli, who had "eaten, drunk and slept and waked upon Michelangelo" and had absorbed something of his titanic power, was a born romantic of the most violent kind. The visual language of his art was classic but its mood was wild and disturbing. One could perhaps describe Fuseli as an artist who dramatized, and often over-dramatized, the more obvious human emotions, but who never allowed himself to drift into bathos because of his firm expressive line. Witches, nightmares and all the lurid paraphernalia of late 18th-Century Gothicism formed the basis of his paintings and drawings. Sinister and erotic overtones are implicit in everything he drew or painted; yet they are conceived on a heroic scale that gives them power and dignity. His muscular heroes make gigantic gestures; his women, despite the strictly classical formula on which they are constructed, are exaggeratedly seductive.

In this magnificently composed drawing one sees him at his best. The arabesque of sensitive line shows what he had absorbed from Michelangelo, but it is used in a way that foreshadows the more explicitly passionate romanticism of the next century. It was at the same moment that Blake was using the classical formula for visionary ends, while Flaxman, untouched either by romanticism or mysticism, proved how sterile neoclassicism could be if it was not tinged with either passion or imagination.

Delacroix.   *Arab Rider Attacked by Lion*

DELACROIX is one of those complex artists whom it is impossible not to admire, yet each of his admirers finds a different reason for doing so During his lifetime he was thought of, in France, as the leader of the Romantic movement of the early 19th Century. The passionate but intelligent praise lavished on him by Baudelaire established him not only as a mouthpiece of Romanticism but as the official opponent of the classic faction, led by Ingres.

That is, of course, an oversimplification, for, like Baudelaire himself, Delacroix was intelligent as well as passionate, and his romanticism was based on deliberate theory rather than on uncontrolled sentiment. His copious journals are the product of hard thinking. What distinguished him from Ingres was not his defiance of tradition but his allegiance to an alternative tradition. The 17th-Century quarrel between the admirers of Poussin and the devotees of Rubens repeated itself in the early years of the 19th Century, and, as it turned out, Delacroix understood the basic principles of Rubens' art more completely than did Ingres those of Poussin.

None the less, Delacroix was consistently a romantic in his emphasis on the drama of conflict, whether it was the physical struggle of an attack by a

108. *Delacroix (1798-1863). Arab Rider Attacked by a Lion. 1849. Oil.
Potter Palmer Collection, Art Institute of Chicago*

lion on a horse and rider or the allegorical conflict of Liberty leading the People against the forces of Tyranny. All his best paintings are vehicles for this heightened tension that the classic painters of the period never attempted. Nor could they have achieved it if they had wished to do so.

Delacroix realized that these tensions must be served by a freer, more impulsive handling of paint and a heightened key of color, and as his art developed, his brush stroke gained in fluency and his palette in intensity. The first was a product of his study of Rubens, the second he admittedly owed to the first impact on him of a painting by Constable, exhibited in Paris in the Salon of 1824.

This spirited study of movement and struggle shows Delacroix at his best. In his larger and more ambitious paintings it becomes evident that he had not the stamina to emulate Rubens, but here, in the kind of subject that Rubens himself often tackled, he outpainted the great Flemish master. A tremor of excitement pervades the canvas. Delacroix seizes more surely than Rubens on the power of a sudden gesture, and he knows better than Rubens how to build up his final effect on hints rather than on positive statements.

Delacroix and his friend and contemporary, Géricault, established the plunging energy of the horse as part of the accepted vocabulary of Romanticism. More important, they led the way, by their vigorous handling of paint itself, into the techniques that were to be fully developed by the Impressionists, half a century later.

Ingres. *La Baigneuse de Valpinçon*

F O R M O S T A R T I S T S "beauty"—that indefinable abstraction we discover in the work of art though it was never consciously put there—is a by-product of the desire to communicate. For Ingres it was a quality that he pursued fanatically, for its own sake, all his life. Looking back into the past the only great painter whom he could admire unreservedly was Raphael, for Raphael, like himself, was not often tempted away from pure beauty by the itch to express power or by the desire to clarify the meaning of his narrative.

It was a dangerous program. In a lesser man it would have produced idealizations, devoid of character, lacking the elements of surprise that usually accompany greatness. Ingres himself was often led perilously near to the edge of the abyss that awaits the man who would rather his work were beautiful than interesting, and who smooths out all trace of character in order to attain the ideal. In his portraits he was saved by the character of the sitter, which could not be ignored. And occasionally, when he was searching for perfection of outline in a single nude figure, he produced a masterpiece of classic design that will endure for all time.

209

. Ingres (1780-1867). La Baigneuse de Valpinçon. 1808. Oil. Louvre

Such a painting is the Baigneuse de Valpinçon, painted in his twenty-eighth year. Like a melody in which not a single note or a single inflection could be altered without disturbing its "meaning," it has the quality of inevitability. And when one tries to discover why so simple and undramatic a conception of the human body should evoke in us the response of complete satisfaction, one finds that it is not merely because of the suave loveliness of the line and its subtle modulations but because of the sequences of the curves that never hurry, never break their continuity, always produce fresh echoes of each other. The eye is positively hypnotized by the contour that starts near the ear, leads downward without a break at the shoulder or the elbow to the wrist that supports her weight without any sense of strain. Or the invention of the drapery wrapped round the other elbow that leads *into* the picture and emphasizes the roundness of the arm. Or the turban that carries the light upward above the neck, or the simple outline of the head which is brought to life by the merest suggestion of the tip of her nose and a just discernible eyelash.

The contour has not only this inherent beauty of its own, but also the subtle gradations of light across the broad expanse of the back. Few artists could have resisted the temptation to make it more "interesting" by some indication of the spinal column.

This is one of the few cases where the deliberate pursuit of perfection has its own reward. Ingres was one of the more sensitive masters of line and one of the least interesting, because one of the least sensitive of colorists.

The Nineteenth Century

B ETWEEN the 18th and the 19th Centuries there was a sharp division, though it would be difficult to define its exact nature. All one can say with precision is that lightheartedness and frivolity ceased to be fashionable and a weighty, conscientious, though often romantic seriousness took their place. What mainly brought about the change was, perhaps, the French Revolution. In France, life ceased to be an elegant dance executed by aristocrats and became a pilgrimage undertaken by the middle classes. Hence the untiring search for an ideal undertaken by the classicists, David and Ingres. Hence also the sustained romanticism of Delacroix, followed by Courbet, the apostle of realism. Their counterparts in England were the great landscape painters Turner, the arch-romantic, and Constable, the passionate realist.

But the central contribution to 19th-Century art was entirely French. Impressionism developed early in the last quarter of the century. It shocked the critics by what seemed to them its irresponsibility of color and its disregard of classical form. By the end of the century the battle for the recognition of Impressionism as a new and serious contribution to the tradition of European painting had been fought and won. Today it is generally acknowledged that Impressionism—the study of movement, of vibrating light and prismatic color —produced the most remarkable and original works of art of the century's second half. Manet and Degas in figure painting, Monet and Pissarro in landscape and Rodin in sculpture form a group as compact and as coherent as the Dutch masters of the 17th Century or the Florentines of the 15th.

Goya. Saturn

MOST GREAT ARTISTS develop, in their old age, a kind of serenity which becomes increasingly apparent in their work—not a resignation but the reconciliation which wisdom brings between the artist's rebellious self and the demands that life imposes on him. One remembers the peace of

Titian's last picture, the Pietà, in the Venetian Accademia, or Turner's latest water colors, flooded with afternoon light (see Plate 111).

But in Goya's case the paintings of his old age are like screams of protest against suffering and injustice, suppressed to some extent during his early years when he was working as court painter in Madrid, but uttered without inhibition when he retired to the house he had bought for himself, the *Quinta del Sordo* (Deaf Man's House), and painted nightmare images on its walls.

The most terrifying of these paintings is that of Saturn devouring his children. There is no need to translate into words the indignation that Goya compels us to contemplate. Words—if they could be found—would weaken the meaning of his cruel parable. Goya had often protested, especially in his etchings, against the insane cruelties inflicted on men by their fellow men. But here he seems to fling imprecations in the face of life itself.

The picture is hardly typical of Goya, for no man could have painted, consistently, pictures of such intensity and still have retained his reason. But it could have been conceived by no other artist. Hence its inclusion in this book as an example of how far a passionate nature can go in self-expression without passing beyond the permissible limits of pictorial language.

But if one can manage to detach oneself from the impact of the dreadful message and concentrate on the language in which it is uttered, one can see Goya as perhaps the last—and the most significant—milestone on the journey to modern art. One can see how the simplification of light could lead to Daumier, how the vibrant use of the brush could give courage to the Impressionists, how the emotional and almost arbitrary use of color, especially the livid greens in the flesh, could be picked up by the Post-Impressionists and the ruthless exaggerations of form (the grip of Saturn's hands on the helpless torso of his victim, for example) could be used by Picasso or by an Expressionist such as Soutine.

Malraux, in his full-length essay on Goya which he entitled Saturn, refers to Goya's genius in "having broken with the demand for harmony and having taken horror for his province." And he ends his essay with the words "And now modern painting begins."

Turner. *The Rigi at Sunset*

TURNER'S vast output of watercolors and oil paintings (in the British Museum alone there are many thousands of his watercolors) was in essence a record of a journey in which he started, as a young man, with an assured grasp of form and a dazzling technical competence in the handling of his medium, and steadily worked his way towards a final grasp of the pheno-   *213*

). Goya (1746-1828). Saturn Devouring his Children. c. 1818. Oil. Prado, Madrid

111. *Turner (1775-1851). The Rigi at Sunset. c. 1841. Watercolor.*
Tate Gallery, London

menon of light—light which both reveals and destroys form, robs it of its
own color and bestows on it an iridescence that belongs to itself.

In the course of that journey he had been afraid of nothing. He could
tackle nature in any of her moods from the savagery of a storm in the high
Alps to the tranquility of a Mediterranean sunset.

If, therefore, one is to choose a single example out of this enormous
variety of subjects in this long progress from form to light, one must surely
settle on a comparatively late one. And since, despite his mastery of the
subtlest inflections of oil painting, it was in the medium of watercolor that
his most brilliant interpretations of light were achieved, one of those evanescent
sketches of his maturity—executed, certainly, after 1835—in which form is
still there but is almost eaten away by the light, will best serve to indicate

214 his genius.

Because of all artists he was the most sensitive to subtle inflections in the intensities and the gradations of color, no reproduction, however accurate, can quite do justice to his vision. The reader must therefore be prepared, in looking at this impression of the Rigi at sunset with the lake of Lucerne at its base, to reinforce Turner's vision with his own.

The watercolor is one of a series made by Turner during a visit to Switzerland in 1841. The scene is hardly sensational in its own right, but Turner must have felt impelled, as the sun sank behind the mountains, giving way to deepening twilight and, afterwards, to a moonlit night, to record with the utmost accuracy each passing phase of the changing light.

Yet accuracy is hardly the quality that we are most aware of in the presence of Turner's best watercolors. They may be based on acute observation yet they achieve a lyrical quality that one does not associate with realism. In this example the last rays of the sun have spread a rose-colored veil across the upper slopes of the mountain. At its foot, level lines of blue mist spread themselves across the calmness of the lake, and the wooded slopes that come down to its edge are almost lost in the deepening twilight. The sharp accents of three boats break the surface of the water and one of them in the distance emits a trail of smoke that drifts upward into the mist. In the far distance one feels rather than sees the ranges of the high Alps.

From a purely technical point of view, the gradations in the luminous sky from blue to the palest pink are the work of a virtuoso, as anyone who has attempted such effects in watercolor will know. Yet just as Turner makes one forget his realism, so also does he conceal his virtuosity. It is as though he were identifying himself with the sunset rather than describing it.

Courbet. Funeral at Ornans

A HUGE PICTURE, over twenty feet long and containing thirty nearly life-sized figures, entitled Funeral at Ornans, attracted crowds in the Paris Salon of 1850. The crowds consisted of the interested, the puzzled, and the alarmed, for this was a new kind of picture and the French, never indifferent to the art of painting, but conditioned in the mid-19th Century to judge paintings by a set of currently accepted standards, did not know what to make of it. They were interested because no one could deny that M. Courbet, a young man of thirty, was a competent painter; they were puzzled because here was something quite unfamiliar; they were alarmed because the rules had been broken.

Throughout the previous decade, the rival schools of Classicism, led by Ingres, and Romanticism, led by Delacroix, had hotly debated their own relative merits, and the French public, accustomed to the rules of debate, had listened carefully and had decided that both parties were entitled to respect

whichever of the two had earned their vote. But it had hardly occurred to them that there might be a third category. A picture that was neither classic nor romantic was a picture for which one could hardly vote at all. And if it were as large and important and competent as this, it was likely to cause serious trouble.

Courbet's Funeral at Ornans caused a great deal of trouble. How it ever achieved the Salon is a mystery. But to modern eyes it seems perfectly normal and some passages in it are of outstanding merit. One's natural comment on it is a slight surprise that anything so honest in intention and photographic in vision should be required to occupy such a large area. Yet for Courbet it was necessary to produce a large statement because he knew that it was, in the eyes of 1850, a defiant statement. This was "realism"; this was art that neither idealized nor emotionalized the world but accepted it as it was. The picture was a "slice of life," like a play by Chekhov or a novel by Zola.

The slice-of-life theory of art has now become so familiar that we cannot, even in imagination, identify ourselves with those who were surprised by it, still less with those who were outraged. Courbet's battle was won almost immediately, though, being by nature an exhibitionist, he persisted in regarding himself as a revolutionary and the world his enemy. Today we know that the end of the 19th Century was dedicated to slices of life. We look back on the period with approval tempered by boredom. Manet was a realist, so was Monet, so were Degas and Pissarro and a dozen others. Why, then, call to mind the fuss engendered by the first shots in a battle that has been won and has since proved unimportant?

"Realism" as such may be unimportant, but certain "realistic" works of art are masterpieces. Velasquez produced them, so did Rembrandt, and Courbet's picture is at least a near-masterpiece. The long procession of villagers that accompanies the coffin, the priests, the kneeling grave-digger, the long line of hills behind, the dull expanse of sky broken only by the vertical of a black crucifix—all this has a dignity and a sincerity that the noble gestures of Ingres and the passionate gestures of Delacroix could never have achieved.

Courbet did not often achieve dignity. Too often he was so busy proclaiming his own realism at the top of his rather boastful voice that a streak of vulgarity spoils him for us. But here is something so human and so sympathetically observed that its appeal is both immediate and deep. This was part of everyday life in the village, *his* village in which *he* was born. The weeping women, the serious men, the innocent children, the pompous priests were his friends and acquaintances. For once, Courbet was paying homage to his friends instead of trying to impress them with his own originality.

112. *Courbet (1819-1877). Funeral at Ornans (detail). 1850. Oil. Louvre*

113. *Degas (1834-1917). La Classe de Danse de M. Perrot. 1873-74. Oil. Louvre*

Degas. *La Classe de Danse de M. Perrot*

DEGAS possessed, in common with the whole of the Impressionist school of painters, an eye trained to catch every shift of split-second movement. Like Monet, he was a master of the transitory, but whereas Monet studied shifts of light, Degas' eye was tuned to inflections of gesture. It follows that while the landscape painters of his time were evolving the new "divisionist" method of painting, Degas, though a masterly painter, relied on draftsmanship and in doing so took Ingres, the self-confessed master of line, as his model.

There was, of course, a basic contradiction between the static, deliberate draftsmanship of Ingres and the nervous snapshot effects that interested Degas. But in the end the reconciliation between the two was established and Degas' paintings of the ballet at rehearsal and on the stage are among the most satisfying examples of his art.

Degas was born in 1834. This painting, dated 1873-74, was therefore completed in his fortieth year. As a painter his style was by this time mature. There is no hesitation at all either in composition or execution, though in his later pictures he was to introduce a calculated casualness that had not yet appeared. But this is among the earliest of the series of elaborate rehearsal-room paintings of the ballet in action.

The ballet in all its phases was to become the subject for which he is now famous. He approached it in his earliest work (1868) from the front row of the stalls with the orchestra in the foreground. It was not long before this distant view ceased to satisfy his searching eye. In 1872 we find him behind the scenes, making drawings of dancers in the wings, and then, realizing that what ballet really meant for him was not the glamor of the stage but the grueling work of the rehearsal room, he began the series of paintings of which this is a superb example. M. Perrot, the dancing master, leans on his stick in the center of the floor—a martinet, the focal point in a scene in which every figure is almost grimly dedicated to the exacting task in hand. It is a world as concentrated on a task to be done as any conceived by Millet or Courbet.

Degas himself became an expert in the technical side of ballet. This painting could be "read" by any connoisseur of the language of ballet. In the whole picture there is not a single dancer who is not either performing her difficult task or watching her companions with a critical, concentrated eye, awaiting the moment when she herself will go into action.

Spontaneous though the picture seems—the result, one might have thought, of suddenly discovering a scene of immense activity and rapidly noting each flashing movement—it must have been slowly and deliberately evolved, after many detailed drawings of separate figures had been made. The girl seated on the piano was added from one such study after the canvas had been completed, and there is a brilliant separate study of M. Perrot himself.

Rodin. Crouching Woman

THE GATE of Hell, which Rodin first conceived in 1880 and worked on for twenty years but never finished, came to resemble, in the end, an enormous three-dimensional sketchbook to which he added, from time to time whatever new sculptural idea occurred to him and which, later, he used as a quarry when some isolated fragment of it seemed to him worthy to be given a life of its own as a separate statue. It contained innumerable figures and its general plan—originally a kind of sculptural Dantesque Inferno—gradually changed as he worked on it, from a series of specific figures (the Paolo and Francesca and the Ugolino groups were never abandoned) to an assemblage of sensual or tragic symbols of humanity.

The most famous of the "extracts" from the Gate, which were later given a separate existence, were the Thinker, which sat brooding above the lintel of the door, and the three Shades, which formed an apex to the whole

114. *Rodin (1840-1917). Crouching Woman.*
c. 1880. Bronze.
Rodin Museum, Paris

115. Rodin. The Embrace.
Undated. Pencil, watercolor
and gouache.
Metropolitan Museum, New York

design. But among the smaller figures, almost lost in the writing confusion of the whole, were one or two figures of the Damned, among which the Crouching Woman is the most remarkable in its own right and the most typical of Rodin's genius.

Genius is certainly not too strong a word for Rodin's gift of seizing on the meaning of a sudden unpremeditated gesture and of creating out of it a symbol of human emotion or aspiration. One is, of course, reminded of Michelangelo, but Michelangelo was too deeply versed in the classic tradition of sculpture to know the meaning of "sudden" or "unpremeditated." The powerful poses invented by Michelangelo came as a result of brooding and so had to be expressed by the deliberate method of carving. Rodin's gift for snatching a moment out of time demanded the quicker action of modeling and a more pliable medium than marble. His greatest bronzes preserve the nervous surface imprinted on clay by the fingertips. They are Impressionist in the strictest sense of the word and the light plays across their surfaces in exactly the same restless way in which it dances across the façade of Rouen Cathedral in a painting by Monet (see Plate 123). The only comparable works in sculpture are the studies of dancers in action by Degas. But whereas Degas used modeling as an aid to painting, for Rodin it was an end in itself. Degas' ballet girls are documentary; Rodin's nudes are charged with a deeper meaning.

The Crouching Woman is certainly one of those realizations of the unpremeditated gesture from which Rodin could always extract a new meaning. The sudden turn of the head, the sudden clutch of the right hand at the left ankle, the sudden touch of the left arm on the right breast, the grip of the toes on the ground—all these are, as it were, separate movements contained within the general conception of the compact, huddled limbs. The knees are spread out to frame the torso that thrusts itself forward between them, and the slope of the whole figure to the left gives it movement but never suggests a lack of balance.

It is a complex pose and one that Rodin would never have imagined without studying the model in action. Yet no model in action could ever have achieved precisely that rhythmic harmony.

Just as Degas used sculpture as an aid to painting, so Rodin used drawing as an aid to sculpture, or, to be more precise, as an aid to the discovery of sculptural ideas. His drawings, done with a light hairline that seems to capture rather than describe the outline, must have been done with his eye always on the model, never on the paper. The established outline was then lightly colored so as to create a mass as well as a shape. These are not drawings "for" sculpture, but without them Rodin could never have kept his sculptural eye so alert for a new discovery.

Manet.   The Bar at the Folies-Bergère

THIS IS Manet's last major painting and it is the only one that succeeds in reconciling the two conflicting sides of his vision. One thinks of Manet as the oldest member of the Impressionist group of painters who fought for recognition in the mid-Seventies of the last century but did not achieve it till the late Eighties. Certainly Manet was eventually absorbed into the group, adopted their bright range of color and was often persuaded by them to paint in the open air. But at the beginning of his life his style was modeled on that of Velasquez, softer in color, brilliant and direct in execution, with none of the true Impressionist vibration of light and none of their abhorrence of browns and blacks. It was not until 1874 that he began to paint in the open air and heighten his key of color.

The Bar at the Folies-Bergère was begun in 1881 and finished and exhibited (at the Salon) in 1882, the year before his death. One would think that it had been painted in answer to a challenge. It has the steady classic composition of an old master—the symmetrical arrangement of the main masses, the equally symmetrical frontal pose of the barmaid, the deliberate

116. *Manet (1832-1883). The Bar at the Folies-Bergère. 1881. Oil. Courtauld Collection, London*

placing of the bottles, the decisive, smooth silhouettes unbroken by the flicker of light. Yet it could only have been painted by an artist who had served a term of apprenticeship with Impressionists. Not Velasquez, not even Franz Hals whom Manet admired, could have handled paint with the virtuosity that appears when one examines in detail the bottles, the cut-glass bowl, the roses, the swift indication of the girl's lace collar and the crowd in the theatre behind her. All this may not be Impressionist in its strictest sense, but it is a result of new courage and freedom in the application of paint to canvas. "Brilliant" is a word that suggests itself at once, as soon as one attempts to describe the flash and glitter of the lamplit scene of the bar and the crowd at the Folies-Bergère theater.

As usual with the later Manet, the subject is taken straight from life. The tired girl (Suzon was her name) leaning heavily on the edge of the bar and the man reflected in the mirror behind her are portraits; the restlessness of the crowd is the result of acute observation. It is a scene caught by the eye, not the mind, and one does not look for social comment in it or even

223

psychological insight of more than a superficial kind. Yet for all its apparent immediacy, it is a thought-out, highly formalized masterpiece, utterly different in effect from the casual (perhaps deliberately casual) compositions of Monet and his fellow Impressionists.

Renoir. *The Umbrellas*

R E N O I R is the most lovable of 19th-Century painters, and for a good reason. He painted what he loved, and what he loved was a quality we can all understand—radiant optimism. His still lifes have a healthy glow, his nudes are caressable, we can bask in his landscapes. He is never cynical, like Toulouse-Lautrec; he is never the detached, impersonal observer, like Degas; Cézanne could never have said of him, as he said of Monet, " He is only an eye." Renoir was a gourmet for whatever, in ordinary life, contributed to his sense of well-being.

But like all true gourmets, his palate for good things was wonderfully refined and subtle. The opulence in which he rejoiced was never obvious; still less had it the slightest taint of vulgarity. His canvases may seem to us to be visual equivalents of simple and often childlike happiness, but they are *not* simple, and to find Renoir childlike is to underrate his intelligence as a man and his superb sensitivity as a painter. Because he painted so many small and seemingly spontaneous pictures—quick, casual responses to whatever had delighted his eye—he is rarely thought of as a monumental painter with a formidable equipment for picture *planning* and a brooding mind that imposed a discipline on his basic impulsiveness. Yet from time to time, as though to remind himself, as well as us, that the planning of a picture is an architectural problem and not an emotional outpouring, he painted an ambitious major work as deliberately constructed as any Raphael.

The Umbrellas is one of them. It was painted over a period of many years, and at one moment, when less than half of the big canvas had been completed, it was abandoned for a period of at least six years; when he came back to it his mood had changed and with it his style. It is not difficult to see that the little girl with the hoop, and her solicitous mother in the bottom right-hand corner, are painted with a more caressing brushstroke and even a different key of color from the girl on the left with the bandbox and from the complex canopy of open umbrellas above.

The truth is that, in the interval, the influence of Cézanne had intervened, sharpening Renoir's eye to certain problems of structure and certain chromatic subtleties of which he had hardly been aware when the picture was begun. In the interval the world had become a little harder, more vertebrate, less sensuous. The optimism is still there; in fact that optimism is what gives the

225

117. *Renoir (1841-1919). The Umbrellas.* c. *1882-87. Oil.*
National Gallery, London

picture its unity and prevents it from falling into two unrelated stylistic halves. But without that Cézanne-like consciousness of the intersecting domes of the open umbrellas, the monumentality would be lost. We should be left with an "impression" of the moment when the rain is stopping and the spirits of the crowd are rising. As it is, we have a masterpiece that combines the keen, momentary observation of Impressionism with the more permanent, classical values of Cézanne's contribution to Post-Impressionism. In the progress of late 19th-Century French painting this picture is a landmark.

But it is also (how easy it is to drift into the analytical frame of mind of the art historian!) a Renoir. It is not often that a great painter with a long stylistic development like that of Renoir becomes more conscious of structure and less conscious of atmosphere as he grows older. The stylistic development of Titian and Turner work the other way round. And even with Renoir this tension of the artistic muscles was a temporary phase. Atmosphere, sensuousness and the inner glow of color returned in his last pictures.

But at whatever stage we find him in the solution of his purely artistic problems, he is temperamentally consistent throughout. Life must always be an experience to enjoy. The midinette smiles to herself as she carries her bandbox; the mother looks down affectionately at her child; the girl behind her looks up at the sky. The shower is over. Soon the sun will be shining in the streets of Paris. The umbrellas will soon be folded.

Van Gogh. *The Ravine and the Sailing Boats*

E A R L Y I N 1889 Van Gogh left his house in Arles and became an inmate of the hospital at St. Remy at the foot of the little range of hills called the Alpilles. Not much more than twelve months earlier he had moved from Paris to Arles, and during those months he painted like a man possessed. The southern sun not only gave him a new creative vigor but it also intensified the colors on his palette. De la Faille's catalogue of his works lists more than two hundred canvases—an average of four each week—painted between his arrival in Arles and his departure for St. Remy.

In the hospital at St. Remy, despite physical and mental exhaustion, there was no slackening of the creative tempo. His paintings in Arles had been full of the explosive radiance that everyone now recognizes as the mark of his genius. In St. Remy the explosions continued but the dynamic rhythm of his brushstroke became more turbulent. Partly the mountainous landscape itself was responsible for the change, but doubtless a certain lack of security at finding himself in an institution added a new restless intensity to his art during his first few months there.

226   It is to this period that some of his most glowing canvases belong.

118. *Van Gogh (1853-1890). The Ravine. 1889. Oil.*
Kröller-Müller Museum, Otterlo, Netherlands

119. *Van Gogh.*
Sailing Boats.
Drawing. 1888

They were painted in the hot summer of 1889. As autumn passed and winter approached the same dynamic brushstroke continues but a more sinister note appears. It can be seen in The Ravine, of which there are two versions—one done in October, and the one illustrated here, in December. The second version (now in the Kröller-Müller Museum in Holland) is perhaps less vigorous but is realized with greater completeness.

The story of Van Gogh's life is too well known for even a brief outline to be needed here. During his lifetime he was ignored as an artist by everyone but his devoted brother, Theo. Today we find no difficulty in recognizing and welcoming the passionate, colorful expression of a vision that no previous artist had been brave enough to attempt with such spontaneity. It was Van Gogh who made the word Expressionism a necessary addition to the vocabulary of art criticism.

One thinks of Van Gogh primarily as a colorist, but even in his drawings there is the same muscular urgency. The short nervous strokes of the reed pen give to the best of his drawings not only a restless movement but also an illusion of color. In June of 1888 he visited Les Saintes-Maries and for the first time saw the Mediterranean and was enchanted by the boats. "All along the flat, sandy shore," he wrote to his friend Emile Bonnard, "red and blue boats, so pretty in their form and color that one was reminded of flowers." The same rhythm that his brush had discovered in the wind-blown cornfields of Provence were extracted by his pen from the breaking waves at Les Saintes-Maries. With wonderful skill he has used the diminishing thickness of the pen strokes to suggest the distance between foreground and horizon, and has introduced a pattern of dots to indicate the texture of foam among the breakers.

Cézanne.   La Montagne Sainte-Victoire

THE IMMENSE INFLUENCE of Cézanne's painting on the whole of 20th-Century art has been felt by every sensitive eye, yet no one, not even the most analytical of writers, has quite succeeded in explaining it. That he rebelled against the superficial—the purely optical—attitude of the Impressionists is obvious enough. To record the effect of the passing moment did not interest him. Monet or Sisley, setting up their easels in front of the great pyramidal structure of the Montagne Sainte-Victoire, which Cézanne painted so often that one could describe it as his favorite "sitter," would have made us feel that we had accompanied them into its presence. We should enjoy the sensation of the open air, the sunshine, the particular moment of a particular day.

Not so with Cézanne. With him the word "particular" never occurs to us. We are not, as we look at this monumental painting, in the presence of

120. *Cézanne (1839-1906). La Montagne Sainte-Victoire. c. 1890. Oil.*
Baltimore Museum of Art

the mountain. Rather are we permitted to watch Cézanne creating it—building it up, touch by touch, designing its skeleton, clothing it with muscle, analyzing and modifying and feeling his way across its structure as though he were a sculptor creating a new image. With Cézanne we almost always feel that we are sharing the very act of creation. Often he is clumsy and unsuccessful, as though he had attempted a task that was beyond his powers. At his best he is triumphant—as here—as though he were so sensitively attuned to what lay before him that he could perform with his brush the same kind of task that Nature had already performed by centuries of gradual growth and attrition. Perhaps that is what he meant when he said (as reported by M. Joachim Gasquet) "L'art est une harmonie parallèle à la nature."

No artist is less dramatic, less spectacular, more humble in the presence of Nature than Cézanne. In that respect he is the exact opposite of Van Gogh, 229

121. *Seurat (1859-1891). La Poudreuse. 1891. Oil.*
Courtauld Collection, London

whose every brushstroke was an explosive response to the scene or the person he looked at while he painted. Where Van Gogh asserted himself, Cézanne suppressed all idea of an emotional reaction. He neither copied nature like the Impressionists, nor did he intensify her as Van Gogh did. He recreated her in his own terms and, in doing so, clarified her. He makes us more aware of her essence.

Looking at the blue, sculptural mountain and the hard tawny rocks in the foreground we are apt to imagine that Cézanne has invented a color scheme. Yet one visit to Provence, one glance through his studio window at the mountain itself, and we realize that this harmony of the red earth and blue-grey mountain belongs not to Cézanne but to Provence. It is not the effect on the eye but the basic, permanent essence of the Cézanne country.

Seurat.   La Poudreuse

THROUGHOUT THE HISTORY OF ART, the calculating, highly disciplined, classic artist has appeared at fairly regular intervals. Piero della Francesca in the mid-15th Century, Raphael in the early years of the 16th, Poussin at the beginning of the 17th, Vermeer of Delft sixty years later, Ingres at the beginning of the 19th, Seurat at its end, and Mondrian in the Twenties of our own century, all belong by temperament to the same family. What they have in common may not be immediately perceptible, for each of them inevitably carries with him the stylistic mark of his generation. But they would have understood each other. Each was seeking, in his own way, the grand, impersonal generalization. Each mistrusted the overtones of romantic excitement and detested violence or exaggeration. For each of them, the process of creating a work of art was a process of slow, intelligent, often laborious manufacture, in which intuition played no part at all and the excitement of improvisation was unthinkable.

Such artists willingly sacrifice a good deal. Drama, fantasy, the macabre or the humorous, the sensuous and the symbolic are outside their range. They strike no impulsive attitudes; but the best of them can achieve immortality and the worst of them command our admiration because they are perfectionists and because they are prepared to go to surprising lengths in the pursuit of perfection.

The most fanatic in my list of perfectionists are Seurat and Mondrian, and of the two, Seurat is the more adventurous and the more conscientious in his attempts to solve his central problem. It is, of course, the problem of how to discover the exact formal equivalent for what he has to say.

In this case one might have thought that his subject, a portrait of his friend and mistress, Mlle Knobloch, would have tempted him away from such formal preoccupations. There is something unusually endearing in the spectacle of this little dumpling of a woman complacently powdering her nose in the absurd mirror. But Seurat refuses to let the warmth of his feelings take charge. The same intellectual process that had so patiently organized the complex architecture of the Grande Jatte must be used here too. The picture is, of course, less ambitious: the architecture is not that of a public edifice but of a modest dwelling. None the less, it must be planned with care. Mlle Knobloch dictates its main rhythms by the natural exuberance of her contours. But curvature must be Seurat's theme, not because his sitter is plump, but because curvature as such is geometrically appropriate. The swinging folds of her dress, the curved legs of the table and the mirror, the line of her right arm, uninterrupted by the angle of an elbow, all make their contributions. The picture is as consistent in its architecture as any of his larger works.

I have never been able fully to accept the validity of Seurat's pointillism, but it is certainly consistent with his temperament. To sacrifice caressing brushstrokes that travel, like handwriting, along the picture's surface for the little deliberate dot that descends vertically like the letters of a typewriter is part of the sacrifice of sensuousness that the classic artist is always prepared to make. It is the final protest against the seductive qualities of paint itself. Seurat may have persuaded himself that color blending on the retina of the eye of the beholder rather than on the palette of the painter had a more vivid impact. But he does not convince me. Like most temperamentally classic artists he is anything but an eloquent colorist. I suspect that the method appealed to him for the very reason that it was laborious—that it slowed down, as it were, the natural tempo of picture production.

Gauguin.   *Fatata te Mite*

HISTORY HAS NOT been kind to Gauguin. It has built up around him the legend of a proud, angry, aggressive man, whose pride eventually became a persecution mania and who spent his life escaping to remote destinations which always disappointed him on arrival and, in the end, robbed him of hope and of life itself. He died in tragic loneliness, on the island of La Dominique in the Marquesas, in 1903.

The escapist who, having escaped, writes to his former friends in accents of self-pity is never a sympathetic character. And in Gauguin's case the mistaken legend of his life has too often given us a prejudice against his art. Of all that group of men whom we rather carelessly label "Post-Impressionist" because they all rebelled against the pseudoscientific objectivity of Impressionism, Gauguin is the one who has been taken least seriously.

122. *Gauguin (1848-1903). Fatata te Miti. 1892. Oil.*
Chester Dale Collection, National Gallery, Washington, D.C.

The passionate intellectualism of Seurat, the painstaking analysis of Cézanne, the turbulent excitement of Van Gogh seem to us more understandable than the escapism of Gauguin. We tend to regard him as a kind of artistic beachcomber.

Nothing could be more unjust. The story of his escape from Paris to Brittany in 1886, from Brittany to Tahiti in 1891, his dispirited return in 1895, his second and last escape to Tahiti and the Marquesas Islands—all this is well known. But the word "escape" can imply either a "to" or a "from." And what drew Gauguin away from Europe was a genuine desire to discover an authentically primitive life—the atmosphere that Rousseau had once engendered round his concept of the "noble savage." It may have been an illusory concept, but in Gauguin's case it gave birth to some of the noblest and the most human paintings of the late 19th Century.

Fatata te Mite (which means nothing more significant than "Beside the Sea") was painted in 1892, a year after his first journey to Tahiti. It is not difficult to find in it Gauguin's sense of a new-found freedom. This is not the tourist's discovery of the "noble savage" whose body has never felt the constraint of clothes. It is as though Gauguin had used these Tahitians as the basis of a new kind of human mythology, more primitive and more robust than the Hellenic ideal of physical beauty which had dominated Europe for so many centuries. Gauguin managed, as it were, to identify his own life with that of these golden-skinned children of a tropical island in a tropical sea. The two bathing girls are his alternative to the water nymphs of Greek vase-painters and sculptors. They are tougher, more conscious of the need for strength, less of the desirability of grace.

Gauguin was, throughout his life, a great colorist. By simplifying his forms and eliminating shadows, like the makers of Japanese prints that he so much admired, he could divide up his canvas into a series of bold areas and treat those areas as an excuse for the most daring juxtapositions of color.

Gauguin's escape to Tahiti was an escape to artistic freedom in one sense, but in another it was a form of suicide—the suicide of the civilized man who attempts to force himself into the pattern of primitivism and succeeds as an artist but fails as a human being.

Monet.   Rouen Cathedral

NEITHER THE ESSENCE nor the nature of the object painted, but its appearance, and in particular its appearance at a specific moment of time and under specific atmospheric conditions—these were what Monet and his fellow Impressionists were determined to record. This pursuit of the "moment in time" became such an obsession with Monet himself that he felt, at certain periods in his career, impelled to paint "in series," selecting a given subject— a haystack, the railway station of St. Lazare in Paris, the western façade of Rouen Cathedral, water lilies and their leaves on the surface of a pool—and making consecutive records of it as the direction and intensity of the light changed. The light, not the object, was the true subject matter of his paintings, and never have impressions of light, the chords of color evoked by it and the vibrating surfaces produced by it, been observed with greater attention or rendered with greater precision.

The Rouen Cathedral series was produced in the years before 1895, when they were exhibited in Paris together. In many ways, taken as a coherent group, they are his most satisfying though not his most typical, for the problem of differentiating between a magnificently designed architectural complexity and its momentary effect on the eye was more difficult to solve

123. *Monet (1840-1926). Rouen Cathedral.* c. *1895. Oil.*
Chester Dale Collection, National Gallery, Washington, D.C.

than most of his self-imposed problems. The form of haystack has little interest, the artist's eye is not distracted by it or tempted to explore its detail, but a cathedral demands the maximum of sacrifice if it is to be translated from a proud monument of the mediaeval spirit into a set of surfaces whose only function is to reflect light.

Monet had precisely the temperament to make such sacrifices, though even he confessed that he was shocked to find himself, at the bedside of a dying friend, analyzing and memorizing the relationships of tone and color in his friend's pale face. The confession is an extreme instance of the sharp division between the "life of action," in which most of us are involved, and the "life of contemplation" which the artist must strive to attain, even at the cost of common humanity. The romantic artist compromises by emotionalizing his theme; the realist (and Monet was certainly a realist) refuses to make the compromise. His strength lies in his truthfulness; his weakness in his heartlessness. Among the central group of Impressionists who worked in France in the last quarter of the 19th Century, only Pissarro and Renoir are concerned with humanity or compassion. They move us on a different level from Monet and Sisley. Yet truth has its own power to move us, for oddly enough, in the wholehearted pursuit of visual truth, beauty may unexpectedly arrive as a by-product.

That certainly happened in Monet's case. Surface textures of a kind never envisaged before, subtle variations of a color within the narrowest of harmonic ranges, and above all, color relationships that were quite outside previous experience appeared in his pictures. To him they were extracted patiently and searchingly from the spectacle before his eyes as he painted. To us they seem inventions, justifiable in their own right, which altered the whole aspect of painting, making the earlier experiments in realism by the Barbizon painters look a little lifeless and dull. A new radiance that connects the Impressionists with the great colorists of art suddenly appeared in the Eighties, and at once our appetite for color became sharper, more fastidious, less easily satisfied.

Rouen Cathedral, with the morning light turning the gray stone into a fretted rainbow, was something that had not been seen before. Today, with eyes conditioned by Impressionism, it can be seen by us all.

Munch. *The Cry*

THE READER will find in my note on Soutine (Plate 134) a tentative definition of Expressionism as a translation into paint of a disturbed or anxious state of mind. Munch, the Norwegian artist, is certainly an Expressionist; in fact, together with Van Gogh, he could with reason be called the founder of Expressionism. Yet between Soutine and Munch there

124. *Munch (1863-1944).*
The Cry. 1893. Lithograph.
Rosenwald Collection,
National Gallery,
Washington, D.C.

is a difference in kind, for whereas Soutine's disturbance of mind came from within and tended to impose itself on whatever subject he chose to paint, Munch's Expressionism was essentially romantic. For him, the drama that is inherent in most of his art is also inherent in the subject. His was the North European pessimism which sees life itself as something threatening and man as journeying through it beset by fears and under sentence of death. At times this Scandinavian drama becomes, as it does in this print, melodrama.

The Cry is a comparatively early work. Everything is sacrificed to the intensity implied in the title. The lonely road, the lurid light, the almost inhuman creature who utters a terrified scream in the foreground all add up to the effect of a nightmare.

Significantly enough, 1893, the year in which this dreamlike image was conceived, is also the year in which the style now known as *art nouveau* was first seen in a newly erected building in Brussels. Munch's art is full of those elongated glutinous curves that form the basis of *art nouveau*. In architecture *237* and interior decoration they strike us now as mannered. But in Munch's art they can achieve an almost tragic quality.

It is not easy to trace the beginnings of a new style when it arrives as suddenly as this and appears simultaneously in places as far apart as Norway and Belgium. One can only refer vaguely to the mysterious force of the *Zeitgeist* which enables artists to discover new shapes for a new kind of emotion. Other artists have seized on the twisted forms of *art nouveau*—it runs through much of Aubrey Beardsley's illustrations and it can be traced in Gauguin, but none has used them so dramatically as Munch.

Beardsley. The Black Cape

WHEREIN LIES the essence of what we now know as "the naughty Nineties?" Surely in the volumes of *The Yellow Book,* Oscar Wilde's *Salomé* and the earlier drawings of Aubrey Beardsley. The phrase has stuck, but it is hardly descriptive of that period. What strikes us now, looking back on what was once a craze and then became a bore, is not its naughtiness but its calculated preciousness. Its characteristic was rather an affected and an almost scholarly decadence than anything as obvious as "naughtiness."

Salomé (even the fact that the play was written in French) contains the essence of Oscar Wilde's fantasy. And Beardsley's drawings for it contain the essence of *Salomé*. Both are works of genius in that they build up a world as unreal as a harlequinade, yet convincing because, behind the reality, there is a fragile and sometimes a passionate pathos.

The best of the series of twelve full-page drawings ignore the action of the play but uncannily catch its flavor. The moon-imagery with which the play opens inspires the first drawing; then come two that establish the character of Salomé herself—the Peacock Skirt, a sly burlesque of the later pre-Raphaelites, and the Black Cape (Plate 125), a witty reference to the prevailing fashion for all things Japanese. After that the tragic note begins to be heard and rises to a climax in a drawing of Salomé gazing into the eyes of the severed head of Jokanaan.

Through them all runs the exquisitely modulated line, the feeling for the placing of the black accents, and a fanciful love of pure decoration that is now as "dated" as *art nouveau,* but which is never trivial and never detracts from the mood of the drawing.

The best of Beardsley can hold its own with the masters of book illustration in black and white—the woodcuts of Dürer, the woodcuts of the early Florentine and Venetian printed books and the line drawings of Matisse or Picasso. One is tempted to use the kind of Ninetyish phraseology that Wilde and Beardsley would have liked, and to say that the Salomé drawings have the sick beauty of an orchid.

125. *Beardsley (1872-1898).*
The Black Cape.
c. *1894. Drawing*

Henri Rousseau.   Le Rêve

UNTIL HE WAS twenty-seven, Henri Rousseau had never attempted
to paint. He was born in 1844, was called up for military service in his
eighteenth year, served for a time in Mexico, returned to France in 1866,
became a minor customs official in 1871 and made his first tentative experiments as a painter in that year. Self-taught, self-contained, uninterested in the
aesthetic theories that obsessed the Parisian artists of his generation, he relied
entirely on a vivid visual imagination and an instinctive ability to transfer it
to canvas. He was in fact the first "naïve" painter in a city of professional
artists, and by doggedly following the path he had chosen he gradually
attracted the attention of the connoisseurs of his generation.

239

126. *Henri Rousseau (1844-1910).*
The Dream. 1910. Oil.
Museum of Modern Art, New York.
Gift of Nelson A. Rockefeller.
Below: *Full view*

Naïve painters, Sunday painters, *maîtres populaires* as the French now call them, have become a phenomenon to be reckoned with in the art of the 20th Century. They have been made fashionable and the fashion has been exploited by the modern dealer. But Rousseau's innocence of eye and ignorance of technical procedures would not have been sufficient to secure the admiration of his more sophisticated friends had not his imagery been charged with a strange poetry. His early pictures, commonplace enough in subject matter, always had a visionary quality; but it was only in his last years—from 1904 till his death in 1910—that he produced the series of consciously romantic dream pictures of which *Le Rêve,* exhibited at the Salon des Indépendants in the last year of his life, is the latest and most intensely personal.

It may be that memories of Mexican jungles, lush undergrowth inhabited by beasts of prey, tropical birds and conventionally imagined native musicians came back to him in these last years. And, as though to introduce a dreamer into the dream, a mysterious nude, a reconstruction of an early romance in his life with a Polish woman whom he called Yadwiga, lies at one side of the picture on the red sofa in his studio.

All this strikes us as forced and rather childish, but the true meaning of the picture lies in the wonderful sense of crowded, thrusting growth, the claustrophobic tangle of vegetation. To be able to construct an imagined or remembered world so convincingly requires more than naïveté.

Leon Bakst. *Nijinski in "L'Après Midi d'un Faune"*

IT HAPPENS not infrequently that the conjunction of two or more creative minds produces a minor outburst of creative energy. Certainly, in the Nineties, Aubrey Beardsley and Oscar Wilde had stimulated each other. An even more formidable collaboration occured at the beginning of this century when Diaghilev breathed new life into the art of ballet. Diaghilev became the leader of a closely knit team of artists that included as composer, Stravinski, as dancers, Nijinski and Karsavina, and as designer, Leon Bakst.

Bakst, drawing on the oriental traditions of barbaric color and pattern which he inherited from the Russian Byzantine tradition, revolutionized the spectacle of the ballet. He banished the pale, twilight romanticism of its early years and replaced it with a passionate and sometimes orgiastic spectacle which altered the taste of a whole generation, especially in dress and interior decoration.

Bakst was more than a daring colorist. He was a draftsman of great power. His best drawings, originally done as working designs for Diaghilev, remain today as works of art in their own right. Among the most striking of them are his costumes and settings for *Scheherezade,* but one of the most

127. *Bakst (1866-1924).*
Nijinski as the Faun in
L'Après Midi d'un Faune.
1911. Watercolor.
The Sumner Collection,
Wadsworth Atheneum,
Hartford

moving is his wonderful conception of Nijinski as the wild creature of the woods in *L'Après-midi d'un Faune*. The idea for the ballet (which lasted for no more than eight minutes) was Diaghilev's, but the detailed conception of it, as a Greek vase-painting come to life and danced almost entirely in profile, was probably Bakst's. It was produced in Paris, at the Théatre du Châtelet, on May 29, 1912. Most of the audience were deeply impressed by the mood engendered in Debussy's music, Nijinski's dancing and Bakst's designs, though some were shocked by the erotic implications of the final scene in which the faun fondles the scarf left behind by one of the nymphs.

Bakst's drawing is a reinterpretation of the "Wild Men" of mediaeval legend (see Plate 29) and of the inarticulate Caliban of Shakespeare's *Tempest*. Half-untamed, half-tender, half-animal, half-deity, Bakst's interpretation of the faun as he plays with the scarf he has captured is one of his most original contributions to what has already crystallized into the Diaghilev legend.

The Century We Live In

To the art historian of the future, the first half of the 20th Century will be regarded as an age of revolution in the arts, and also as a period of ceaseless and daring experiment.

It began, in France, with Post-Impressionism and a deliberate abandonment of the searching eye and the recording methods of the Impressionists in favor of a vision that was more emotional, more symbolic and more analytical.

Then came a series of experimental movements almost too numerous to tabulate. Cubism, invented and developed by Picasso and Braque; Fauvism, inspired by Van Gogh and turned into a program by Matisse, Derain and Vlaminck : its derivative, Expressionism, which took root more easily in Central Europe and found its leaders in Soutine and Kokoschka; and finally abstract or nonfigurative painting, which began about 1911 with the attempts of Kandinsky to jettison "subject matter" altogether.

Today, abstract art which, in its early manifestations (notably under the influence of Mondrian and Ben Nicholson), was carefully planned and rigidly geometrical, has gradually become freer, more spontaneous and rhapsodical, until we have now given to that aspect of it the general title of "Abstract Expressionism." This final outburst of 20th-Century experimentalism has been boldly developed in America, though some of its most masterly practitioners work in Paris.

How the second half of the century will build on these revolutionary foundations it is impossible to prophesy. What is quite evident is that the illustrations in this book that start with Van Gogh, end with Soulages, and celebrate the inventive genius of Picasso, are marked by an extraordinary courage and a sustained vitality.

128. *Boccioni (1882-1916).*
Continuity in Space.
1913. Bronze.
Museum of Modern Art,
New York

Boccioni's Continuity in Space and Duchamp-Villon's The Horse

THE EXPERIMENT OF Cubism in painting, led by Braque and
Picasso at the end of the first decade of this century, was bound to find its
counterpart a little later in the art of sculpture, but with a rather different
intention: for whereas the painter's aim had been to see and interpret nature
sculpturally, that of the sculptor was to interpret three-dimensional form
dynamically. It was not an easy problem to tackle and it gave rise to very
few successful solutions. Perhaps the most exciting is Boccioni's attempt to
render the swift forward movement of a human figure. It was a part of
the Italian Futurist program to celebrate in art the power and movement of
244   machines. Obviously, painting could tackle the problem more easily than

sculpture, for machines, being themselves essentially sculptural, hardly lend themselves to reinterpretation. But Boccioni's attempt to suggest in solid form the power and speed of the human body was well worth making. The figure consists not so much of limbs as of thrusting shapes that almost suggest the rush of wind through thick drapery. The whole conception is charged with a sense of speed working against the friction of the air.

Boccioni's statue was made in 1913. Duchamp-Villon's dates back to 1914, although the final version of the horse's head was not cast till after the artist's death in 1918 when his brothers, Jacques Villon and Marcel Duchamp, enlarged the original model according to his instructions. Though the idea of movement through space plays a less important part in this than in Boccioni's figure, The Horse, too, is a brave attempt to invent a strictly formalized set of masses that will symbolize the dynamism and strength of the animal.

129. *Duchamp-Villon
(1876-1918).
The Horse. 1914. Bronze.
Museum of Modern Art,
New York*

Bonnard. *Nude Against Light*

IMPRESSIONISM was an inevitable result of the eyes' continuous exploration of the world of visible phenomena. When Degas and Monet concentrated their extraordinary powers of observation on the world they lived in, the former on the rapid gestures of human beings—ballet girls, jockeys, women at work in the laundry—and the latter on the transitory effects of shifting, vibrating light on landscapes and buildings, it seemed as though art had wrung the last, reluctant secrets from nature by means of the eye alone.

Impressionism marked the final analysis of nature by dint of sheer *looking,* and by doing so became a little inhuman. It led into a cul-de-sac from which art could only escape by one of two routes—either by a new kind of warmth of feeling or by a new application of intellectual analysis. The first was achieved by Bonnard and Vuillard, the second by Cézanne. Cézanne abandoned altogether the Impressionist preoccupation with the impact of light. Bonnard used it but combined it with a new humanism. Cézanne's verdict on Monet that he was "only an eye" could never be applied to Bonnard; yet his eye—and especially his eye for tonal relationships—was almost as keen as that of Monet.

In this delightful interior there is a good deal more than the infiltration of dancing light into a bedroom. The picture has a richness of surface that is no longer photographic in intention. It has the beauty of variegated, patterned marble. The girl is no longer merely an object placed there because she makes an interesting silhouette. Color and form are once more used emotionally. The world of the imagination, momentarily banished by the Impressionists, has returned, and with it a new kind of romanticism. It is a very far cry from Turner to Bonnard, yet the haze of dazzling light through which Turner had earlier seen the palaces of Venice is closely related to the light that Bonnard has evoked in this enclosed space. Both artists expressed themselves with a sensuous enthusiasm that takes us far beyond the frontiers of the eye.

Modigliani. *Nude*

MOST OF THE minor masters of early 20th-Century painting found it necessary, whatever their country of origin, to gravitate to Paris, for only in the enthusiastic, excitable atmosphere of Paris could they develop to the

130. *Bonnard (1867-1947). Nude against Light.* c. *1908. Oil.*
Musées Royaux des Beaux-Arts, Brussels

full their own individual talents. Yet they retained the traditions that belonged to the countries in which they were born.

Modigliani, born in Italy in 1884, came to Paris in 1906, the year in which Picasso was making his first tentative experiments in Cubism and in which he fell under the momentary spell of African carvings. Modigliani was temperamentally averse to the three-dimensional view of life implied by Cubism, but African distortions of the human head (see Plates 151-153) appealed to him and gave him courage to experiment with milder and more elegant distortions of his own. Basically he was a descendant of Botticelli, and Plate 131 inevitably reminds us of the finely wrought Botticellian contour, the dependence on beauty of shape, the avoidance of all emphasis on shadow and the consequent sacrifice of volume or weight.

Certainly his line is mannered—more so, even, than Botticelli's—and his art is gentle and lyrical whether he paints a portrait or a nude, but it is a mannerism that springs from purity. He was the least ambitious of artists, the painter of the single figure, isolated on the canvas, dependent for its meaning on its innate, stylish beauty. The absolute assurance of the outline, the extraordinary reticence of the modeling (there is no single tone in the flesh that could count as "shadow") and the oriental economy of the color— pale pink, cool greenish gray and a variegated warm brown to underline the shape of the arm on which she leans—are the simple ingredients on which the picture depends. Yet, for all its simplicity, it is complete.

Modigliani died young and his best paintings, including this one, were done in a brief period during the years just before and after 1917.

Kokoschka. Self-Portrait

IN 1913, when this portrait was painted, Kokoschka was in his late twenties. His father was a Czech who had come to Vienna from Prague. In 1904 Kokoschka entered the Vienna School of Arts and Crafts. From the beginning he shocked his teachers by the violence not so much of his painterly style as of the imagery behind it, even though his subjects, in his early days, were largely confined to portraiture and the mountain landscapes of Switzerland, which he first visited in 1909.

For Kokoschka the mountains of Switzerland were not static objects, they were giants that heaved themselves up from green valleys and assaulted the sky. Portraits were not likenesses but restless souls clothed in flesh. Caricature of a kind was inevitable in such an approach, not merely in the features but in the gestures of the hands. Kokoschka's sitters are not immobilized as they wait for the artist to describe their behavior, they are restlessly alive.

A self-portrait is never painted in quite the same spirit as the portrait of even a close friend. The artist cannot avoid a slightly self-conscious attitude to the task of painting himself. Perhaps Rembrandt alone could see himself impartially with no hint of defiance or self-pity. But Kokoschka, in this portrait of himself painted in the year before the outbreak of World War I, almost achieves objectivity. The head is grave and thoughtful. The hand that points upward seems to suggest that we should look more closely at those roughhewn features.

It is one of his least agitated paintings, yet it is arresting. Color is used emotionally. The cold greenish tones of the flesh against the slightly darker cold background, the flashes of scarlet on the cloak, have nothing to do with appearances. Later in life Kokoschka was to paint with far greater freedom, but even here, in his twenties, it is as a painting and not as a drawing that the portrait holds its meaning. Rembrandt's self-portraits usually look us straight in the eye. Here the eyes have strayed pensively to a point just over the spectator's left shoulder. He is a tough, aggressive young man, but he is abstracted by his own thoughts.

Chagall. *Les Amoureux*

CHAGALL was born in Russia in 1887, but moved later to Paris. The questioning spirit of the Ecole de Paris at the end of the first decade of this century can easily be traced in his paintings, but instead of turning him into a self-conscious experimentalist, as had been the case with Picasso and Braque, Paris merely succeeded in giving him the courage to express his personal temperament.

Puzzled by his strange independence and always anxious to assign a label to its artists, the Ecole de Paris decided that Chagall was a Surrealist and in doing so bracketed him with the early "metaphysical" style of Chirico. But no label could fit him more awkwardly than that of Surrealist, for the strangeness of Chagall's art was never that of the newly discovered imagery of the subconscious mind. It was the strangeness of folklore, of the nursery rhyme in which cows jump over the moon and cats play the fiddle, not because such things happen in the world of fantasy but because they belong to the essence of the waking life of primitive man. To Chagall it is the most natural thing in the world that lovers should float through the air, that they should embrace in the foliage of a flowering tree. For him the laws of nature, and especially the law of gravity, are suspended. Their place is taken by the laws of wish-fulfillment in which everything that happens is the result of a profound conviction that, in an ideal world, that is what *should* happen.

Chagall's art is the art of basic human happiness. Its closest parallel is, 251

perhaps, the lyric art that Blake, and Blake alone, produced in his *Songs of Innocence*. Innocence is the keynote of both artists, though Blake's innocence was that of the visionary while Chagall's was that of the peasant. Consequently Chagall's best painting has a rich sensuousness of color and texture that few artists have ever achieved. His is a world in which happiness has discovered, intuitively, its own appropriate imagery.

133. *Chagall (b. 1889).*
Les Amoureux.
1911. Oil.
Private Collection

Soutine. *Chartres Cathedral*

A LITHUANIAN, born in 1884, Soutine became an integral personality in the Ecole de Paris. Not many of its members' names automatically suggest the label "Expressionist," but Expressionism is Soutine's central characteristic.

The word has been much misused. It is not as easy to define as Impressionism. Usually it indicates a nervous, excitable and often troubled state of mind which the artist, consciously or unconsciously, has translated into paint, so that, whatever his subject may be, the spectator is more

252

134. *Soutine (1894-1943). Chartres Cathedral. 1933. Oil.*
Collection Mr. and Mrs. L. B. Wescott, U.S.A.

conscious as he looks at the picture of the artist's agitation than of the object he is describing. That, of course, is true in the main of Van Gogh's later work, but it is even truer of Soutine's. With Soutine, the state of mind is part of the artist's sensitive temperament. It is only remotely connected with his response to his subject. There is nothing inherently disturbing in the western façade of Chartres Cathedral.

It would have been easy to select a painting by Soutine in which the excitement is more intense and the distortions are consequently more noticeable. For such an artist this picture is, in fact, unusually solid and architectural, yet a comparison between it and Monet's account of the west front of Rouen Cathedral (Plate 123) will tell the whole story of the difference between Impressionism and Expressionism. It is not merely that Soutine has painted in a fine frenzy, but that whereas Monet has used his eye and mistrusted whatever emotions he may have felt while he was painting, Soutine has turned his mind inward and even mistrusted the evidence of his eye. For Monet it is an effect of light that interests him; for Soutine it is an example of Gothic architecture in which the gargoyles hurl themselves outward at the base of the spire on the left. The windows are dark caverns, the main accent is on soaring verticals. Soutine has even suppressed the south transept of the building because it would give the whole mass too broad a base. The sky is caught up in the dynamic rhythms of the cathedral. And in order to give it scale he has introduced two small figures in the foreground.

Klee. *Landscape with Yellow Birds*

IT WAS IN the year 1914 that Paul Klee first began to paint the kind of small pictures which could not have been conceived by anyone but himself. His last painting was done in 1940, in his sixtieth year, the year of his death. Between those two dates he produced several thousand works. He was born in Berne, Switzerland, worked mostly in Germany at the Bauhaus in Weimar and Dessau, and died at Locarno.

It is easy to say that not one of his drawings or paintings could have been conceived in any other mind than his or executed by any other hand. To say that implies a common factor which ought, in theory, to be definable. Yet I doubt if the acutest eye or the most profoundly analytical mind could put into words what that common factor is. In style his works range from the most delicate drawings that suggest the hand of a spider, or water colors that seem to be painted in tinted air, to the boldest and simplest possible statements. In method any medium would serve, provided he used it in the way that came to him naturally, for no craftsman has ever been more of an opportunist. In contrast he ranged through the whole world of sensation or

135. Klee (1879-1940). Landscape with Yellow Birds. 1923. Watercolor. Benziger Collection, Basle

poetic imagination, but always avoided the world of visible fact. He never wandered far from the world of fantasy—usually childlike, never childish— yet he always seemed to be within reach of the deeper levels of experience. Joy, fear, death, passion, mystery, exaltation—all these find their expression in his work, but always on a small scale and always with the equivalent of a gentle, humble, good-natured smile.

But to analyze the inner meaning of Klee's work would be to crack a nut with a steam hammer or use a machine gun to shoot a butterfly. The whole corpus of his work could be roughly divided into categories as far as style or medium or subject is concerned, yet they are all different. No single choice will represent him, yet a single choice must be made. Klee once wrote that the artist draws his creative strength from "life," as a plant draws its strength from the earth. And, as the plant's foliage and flowers bear no resemblance to the earth, so the artist's work need bear no resemblance to "life." But with Klee one could never predict what kind of foliage or what 255 shape or color of flower would emerge after this process of drawing sustenance from the experience of living.

As far as any of his works could be said to represent him, this little watercolor, Landscape with Yellow Birds (fourteen by seventeen and a half inches) is typical. It has all of his surprising naïveté and whimsy (of the seven yellow birds one has perched upside down on a cloud); his ability to create a new world (a forest, dark and claustrophobic, with those four pale sword-shaped leaves weaving their way upward through an undergrowth of primeval vegetation); his innate sense of rhythm (the contrast between lazy curvature and thin, spiny shapes); his unerring sense of color harmony.

It seems to have come to him so easily, like a doodle—but an inspired doodle. It has the odd effect of being at once innocent and profound, as though an elderly philosopher were explaining the universe to a child in words of one syllable.

Braque.   Still Life with a Mandolin

WHEN THE HISTORY of the Ecole de Paris, during the first half of the 20th Century, can be seen in its true perspective (at present we are too near to that most experimental of all periods to judge it objectively) the names of Picasso, Braque and Matisse will occur at once to the minds of everyone as the founders of its traditions. Their temperaments are different, even their conception of the very purpose of painting. But of the three it is already evident that Braque has been, since the end of the First World War, the most serious, the most subtle and the most consistent. Matisse has been more superficially attractive with his natural exuberance, his fluency and his gaiety. Picasso has been more impressive by reason of his passionate Spanish nature and his readiness to experiment with new modes in order to achieve new emotional results. But Braque is neither fluent nor passionate. He himself has said, "Emotion is not something that can be added or imitated. It is the seed of which the picture is the blossom." This is a more searching, a less triumphantly arrogant saying than Picasso's "I do not seek, I find!"

There was a short period when Braque joined forces with the *Fauve* group (1905-09), to which Matisse also belonged, followed by another period in which he and Picasso together forged the language of Cubism (1909-14). That Braque could for a short time belong to both parties is an indication of his central position, for Matisse was never intellectual enough to be a Cubist and Picasso could not have been exuberant enough to join the *Fauves.*

Braque, after those temporary allegiances to both parties (one could roughly label them classic and romantic), began to pursue his own path. It was the path of the pure painter who, using the unremarkable, commonplace

256

136. *Braque (b. 1882). Still life with a Mandolin. 1937. Oil.*
Private Collection, New York

object or group of objects as his starting point, could extract from it new pictorial "meanings" of all kinds. For that reason more than half his paintings—and an overwhelming percentage of his best paintings—are still lifes. For him a table laden with jugs, musical instruments, a dish of fruit, seen in space against a background, are all that he needs. Out of them he can extract new convolutions of form, new textures, new color harmonies. His paintings are not so much like a musician's variations on a theme as what composers call a *passacaglia,* in which a brief sequence of notes can be made to reveal an unsuspected range of moods.

Such revelations, based on the theme of a still life, follow each other in a remarkable sequence in Braque's work from about 1917 onward. The precise flavor of these still lifes at any given period cannot be described in

257

words. One recognizes the firmness of the composition, the exquisite refinement of the color and the interpretation of space in them all.

The particular example chosen dates from 1933, a period when Braque's work was particularly rich and dense in pattern and pure in color. Perhaps it is more insistently decorative than most of his work for it was originally intended as a basis for a tapestry. The paneling of the room and the angular pattern of the wallpaper seem to combine with the objects on the circular table and both steady them and extend them upward.

Matisse. *The Purple Robe*

THE ART OF Matisse requires little comment. When, at the beginning of the 20th Century, the group of Parisian painters who called themselves the *Fauves,* or wild beasts, banded together to produce pictures that were consciously hectic and strident in color, broad and vigorous in design and energetic in the handling of their paint, Matisse, who had previously been an unusually competent late Impressionist, joined them. But alone among them (Vlaminck, Derain and Dufy were all members of the group) Matisse painted *fauve* pictures without seeming at all defiant or wild. The heightened key of the *fauve* palette and the freedom of the brushstroke came to him naturally, and when the movement lost its impetus in about 1907, it became clear that Matisse's Fauvism was an integral part of his temperament.

There was an oriental flavor in his painting that certainly robbed him of profundity or passion but made him a supreme master of the decorative side of painting. Like the Persian miniaturists, he thought and painted naturally in terms of color-pattern. As his style matured he used paint with greater freedom, but the pattern was still exquisite and controlled even when it seemed at its most casual.

Here is a gay but daring harmony of color held together by a linear patterning that is skillfully varied in every corner of the canvas as it breaks up the main masses of color and gives them a sparkle. Broad red stripes cover the area of yellow wallpaper; pale undulating lines carry the striping across onto the blue-green to the right. They are repeated more emphatically on the girl's purple dress, straightened out on the floor at her feet, narrowed down to hairlines that cross each other on the black in the left-hand corner. On the Moorish table they become restless and on the vase they spiral upward.

Against this patterning of line Matisse opposes, in the bouquet of flowers, a pattern of apparently careless, but in reality calculated spots of red and white, thus giving the flowers a different texture from the rest of the picture.

One would suspect Matisse of turning the art of patterning into a

37. *Matisse (1869-1954). The Purple Robe. 1937. Oil.*
Cone Collection, Museum of Art, Baltimore

science if it were not that all his pictures radiate a kind of inner happiness. Matisse never poses a problem. His ambition was to be a popular painter—easily understood, completely without bitterness, but above all elegant, for popular, to the Frenchman, is certainly not synonymous with "plebeian." In Matisse the decorative genius of the East is fused with the painterliness of the West.

Picasso. *Jupiter and Semele*

B O T H Matisse and Picasso were first-rate draftsmen, if draftsmanship implies the expressive handling of line and a refusal to force line to perform more than its proper function. Naturally, in the hands of a creative artist, that function is far more than merely to define objectively the outline of an object. All art is stimulated by experience coming to the artist from the world outside, but all art is generated by the excitement that comes from within. And, in their inward processes, Picasso and Matisse were very different men.

138. *Picasso (b. 1881). Jupiter and Semele. 1931. Etching for Ovid's* Metamorphoses. *Cone Collection, Museum of Art, Baltimore*

Whether Matisse drew or painted, he translated what he saw —and one knows instinctively that he worked in the presence of a model though he was doing nothing so prosaic as describing what was before his eyes. His eye invariably selected what was gay and lively. Matisse's line (as a painter he was basically linear) is full of quick, unpredictable decisions. It pulsates with its own adventurous progress.

Picasso can make those decisions too, but it is not often that he is willing to do so. The drawing of the two classical nudes from Ovid is grave and considered. Even its distortions are the outcome of deliberation. This was certainly not done eagerly, in the presence of the models. The line moves slowly, never hurrying, never slackening. The decisions were all made before the pen touched the paper.

There is no attempt at modeling, yet the lines all enclose the full bulk and weight of the relaxed limbs. There is far more "meaning" in Picasso than in Matisse. There is, for example, a strange tenderness in the relationship of these two impersonal beings. Picasso's woman has exactly the "tempo" of the pen that swings round her knee and her breast and describes the fold of flesh made when she raises her hip. The line is not elegant, like Matisse's. It is, in fact, purposely flaccid and unstylish. But it produces the exact effect he wanted when he drew the Ovid illustrations in 1931 in an attempt to capture the steady rhythms of Latin hexameters.

John Piper.   Stained-glass Window

I T   I S not often that an artist of our own day, truly contemporary in spirit, manages to preserve his own vision and yet master so completely a medium which flourished in the Middle Ages, and which was subsequently either neglected or misunderstood (and therefore mishandled) for five centuries. John Piper is still primarily a painter, romantic by temperament, as often happens with contemporary British artists, but always on the alert to take advantage of whatever medium he works in. His compelling designs for the theater, the freedom with which he tackles lithography and book illustration and his complete understanding of the medium of stained glass prove that he is a craftsman who can steep himself in tradition and yet never become a slave to it.

The three sets of windows, each composed of three vertical lights, which he executed in collaboration with Patrick Reyntiens at Oundle School, England, are the first examples in this century of a professional painter working in stained glass in England. The result, both in sustained brilliance of color and in thoughtfulness of iconography, can take its place confidently beside any parallel example from the 13th Century.

139. *John Piper (b. 1903).*
The Way, the Truth, and
the Life (detail). 1956.
Stained Glass Window
from Oundle School, England

Each of the nine windows contains a single figure. Each figure is symbolic of a different aspect of Christ. The central group illustrates the Vine, the Bread and the Water; the southeast group, the Judge, the Teacher and the Shepherd; the northeast group (a detail from the central figure is illustrated in Plate 139) the Way (with a star), the Life (with a Tau Cross) and the

Truth (with a book). From the head and shoulders of the central figure sprout living branches.

There is nothing self-consciously archaistic in Piper's use of the medium or in his formalization of the nine figures. They have a hieratic dignity that is more reminiscent of Byzantine than of Romanesque design, but in the breaking up of color areas with lead lines and in the subtly varied scale of the patterning John Piper and his collaborator have studied the best examples of early Gothic glass to good purpose, without adopting its mannerisms.

Horace Pippin. The Holy Mountain

S I N C E   T H E douanier Rousseau (Plate 126) accustomed our eyes to the phenomenon of naïveté in painting we are no longer surprised to find ourselves admiring and even, on occasion, being considerably moved by the innocent eye. We are even in danger of assuming that innocence of eye is an enviable possession and that childlike painting must therefore be inherently excellent.

Nothing could be further from the truth. It so happens that painting and writing are the only arts that do not demand a severe craftsmanly discipline in order to make them tolerable. And it must be remembered that spoken language is a means of communication that all of us have practised daily from earliest childhood. It is true that the language of visual imagery, unlike the language of musical composition or of ballet, *can* be achieved by a combination of observation and patience and by a minimum of training or instruction. The naïve painter can, and often does, express himself vividly. But the secret of his power to stir us depends not on his innocence or on his complete independence from the influence of other painters, by which he can always be identified, but on the quality of his visual imagination.

In The Holy Mountain Horace Pippin transports us into a world half-known, half-imagined. It is a world overarched with heavy, embowering trees (reminiscent of the forest in the Indian painting, Plate 160) and inhabited by children and animals—a childlike vision of the Garden of Eden. Such paintings had already been produced in America by an earlier American primitive, Edward Hicks. But it is doubtful whether Pippin—a Negro artist, self-taught and deeply conscious of the meaning of Biblical stories—was aware of Hicks' pictures. The mood of the painting is entirely his own. Like other naïve painters he is intensely conscious of the separate existence of each object, animal and figure in his picture. For what at once distinguishes the "primitive" artist from his more sophisticated contemporaries is his inability to achieve tonal unity or to carry the whole of the picture in mind while he is at work on the isolated detail.

140. *Horace Pippin (1888-1946). The Holy Mountain.*
1944. Oil. Downton Gallery, New York

The flowers, the patterned bark on the trunks of the birch trees, the birds perching on the branches, the animals, the shepherd with his crook and the child in the spotted dress with her doll are all separate items in an addition sum. That the picture strikes us as having a powerful cumulative effect is not the result of any attempt at pictorial unity. It depends entirely on the inherent poetry of Pippin's creative mind.

He was born in 1888 and died in 1946.

Picasso. *Weeping Woman*

THE YEAR 1937 was a vintage year in Picasso's switchback career. It was the year in which, in passionate indignation at the bombing of villages in the Spanish Civil War, he painted Guernica for the Spanish pavilion in the Paris Exhibition. It was also the year in which he made some of his most tenderly lyrical drawings in the series connected with the Minotaur.

Before the Guernica came a series of exploratory studies in which he built up the composition of the panel, and after it another series of drawings, prints and paintings in which the angry mood of Guernica is forced to an even greater pitch of intensity than in the panel itself. Of that series of paintings The Weeping Woman is the most passionate in expression and the most explicit in form.

With Picasso, more than with any other artist, form and expression are so closely linked that one can only be described in terms of the other. Whatever the "subject" of his picture may be, it is by means of his ceaselessly experimental methods of formal organization that it acquires its impact. A woman, a guitar, a bull or a coffeepot becomes a vehicle for a mood, tender or vitriolic, precise or mysterious, according to the kind of linear rhythms, the chord of color, even the tempo of the pencil or brush as it makes contact with the paper or canvas. Every other European artist known to me is the slave of his own stylistic habits. Picasso's restless mind will not permit him to acquire such habits. Ever since his beginnings as a serious artist, in the "blue" period of the early nineteen hundreds, he has discovered for himself a sequence of modes of self-expression. And that sequence has never been the outcome of a logical development, as with all other artists, but of a fearless opportunism in the course of which he has never hesitated to pillage or borrow the stylistic syntax or vocabulary of the art of any nation or culture that could be of service to him. A list of such borrowings would fill this page. The wonder is that behind all of them there is a recognizable personality. And that personality is recognizably Spanish in its passionate, sometimes frightening power. He has lived in France ever since his precocious maturity. But there is in his work none of the stylish elegance of a Braque or a Matisse.

Out of the enormous volume of his work one could select at least a dozen eligible candidates for this anthology. I have chosen The Weeping Woman of 1937 partly because it is unusually powerful even for Picasso, partly because its brave distortions seem so inevitable, given the subject, that it speaks for itself.

The rhythms are, appropriately enough for the theme of uncontrolled grief, fiercely angular, all but the sweep of the hair which seems to enclose the whole structure of the head. Each feature (as in Egyptian reliefs) is seen from its most explicit point of view—the nose from the side, the mouth from a three-quarter angle, the glaring eyes from the front.

The white handkerchief she holds in front of her face (note how its falling corners contribute to the angular rhythms) has become transparent so that it shall not conceal the symbolic tracks of the tears that furrow her cheeks. Above them, the tears themselves hang, like pearls, from her eyelids.

The color, like the form, is harsh and acidulated, and, like the form, it is precise, clear-cut and elementary. This is a cast in which no mystery is needed, nothing but a ruthless isolation of the emotion to be portrayed. *265*

141. *Picasso (b. 1881). Weeping Woman. 1937. Oil.
Penrose Collection, London*

142. *Picasso. Bullfight. c. 1946. Ceramic. Gallerie Leiris, Paris*

Yet, in the same year, Picasso was producing water color drawings as tender as Watteau's and as mysterious, in their symbolism, as Blake's. And they, too, are as unmistakably *his* personal creations as this extraordinary *cri de cœur*.

Picasso.   Bullfight Ceramic

THERE ARE very few serviceable generalizations one can make about Picasso's art except that he differs from almost all other artists in that he has never developed. He has never, like Bellini or Turner, set his foot on the long road that leads to a destination and then gradually, by solving problem after problem, arrived at a summit from which a lifetime's work could be seen as a "progress."

Picasso could be likened to a spider who sits watching, in the center of a web, in every direction. And from time to time he pounces and the direction of his pounce is usually unpredictable. Also, from time to time, he explores

the possibilities of a new medium, never basing himself, except in a purely technical sense, on the achievements of his predecessors but always discovering for himself what can be done in it that has never been done before. It is for that reason that I have been compelled, in this anthology, to represent him three times—as a painter in oils, as a master of pen line and as a decorator in ceramics.

What he must instantly have realized, when he began to experiment with ceramics in the middle Forties, was that here was a medium which offered the richest possible rewards to a man who would dare to be completely spontaneous.

Ben Shahn.   Cherubs and Children

B E N S H A H N was born in Russia but it would be impossible, looking at his paintings, to imagine that they were conceived in any other country but America. It is an America seen through innocent, wondering eyes and a mind easily stirred to compassion or indignation. In 1930 he wrote, "I had seen all the right pictures and read all the right books. But still it didn't add up to anything. Here am I, thirty-two years old, the son of a carpenter. I like stories and people. The French school is not for me."

That was his creed and his art shows his creed in action. The stories that moved him are not mere anecdotes. They are fragments of everyday life, some of which move him to protest—like his series of angry pictures connected with the Sacco-Vanzetti trial—others to pity tinged with poetry. In particular, the lives of children brought up against the hard and often sordid background of a city provide him with subjects. Almost always it is the poignancy of innocence seen against the oppressive urban background that gives his pictures their meaning. Children play, rather desperately, in an environment manifestly hostile to play, or, as here, fall asleep among the rigid lines of steel girders and concrete walls. In Cherubs and Children, however, painted in 1944, a new note creeps in. They lie untidily and uneasily among the golden images of their own dreams, and the dreams themselves seem to protest against the hard mechanism of their waking lives.

Such paintings, in which poetry and pathos are extracted from the spectacle of everyday life, are rare. Only a large heart and a keen, documentary eye could imagine them.

Ben Nicholson.   Still Life (Winter Landscape)

THE PAINTER or sculptor of our own century who dares to reject all reference to the wealth of form contained within the visible world in which we live, has sacrificed much but, in exchange, has acquired a freedom which was never granted to painters and sculptors of the past.

He can no longer say "this line is a recreation of a human head" or "this patch of color is my interpretation of the foliage of a tree in high summer." By rejecting the appeal to association he has impoverished his power of communication. But by that same rejection he has turned himself from an *interpreter* into a *creator,* and having done so, he is free to create formal harmonies and juxtapositions of color never dreamed of in the past, except by artists whose aims were either purely functional (like the designer of the telephone) or purely decorative (like the weaver of a textile).

Today abstract (or nonfigurative) art is a commonplace, but by the practice of it the modern artist submits himself to a far severer test than the artist of the past. Can he afford to sacrifice the advantages of association? Is he strong enough to use his new freedom? Is he rich enough in inventiveness to turn from interpretation to creation?

Certain artists have manifestly passed the test, and in doing so have revealed their own characters more clearly than they could have done had they clung to the tradition of representational painting. A Mondrian can refine   *269*

144. *Ben Nicholson (b. 1894). Still Life (Winter Landscape). 1947. Oil.*
C. S. Reddihough Collection, Yorkshire

on his own puritanism, a Kandinsky on his own emotionalism, a Ben
Nicholson on his own highly developed sensitivity more wholeheartedly than
before. And even though in this example of Ben Nicholson's painting one
can still detect the contours of cups and a beaker, and still agree that these
objects are living their lives in Ben Nicholson's picture, the "meaning"
of the painting is no longer dependent on our previous experience of cups
and beakers.

It is here that the normal methods of criticism break down. There is *no*
means of *proving* to the reader that the world of shape and color created by
Ben Nicholson is one of exceptional beauty, or even that the underlying
mathematics of the picture are based on an unusually satisfying set of tensions
and resolutions. One can no more analyze such tensions than one can explain
why a melody has its own inevitability by analyzing the length of the notes
or measuring the intervals between them. Only the eye or the ear can arbitrate.

We have been familiar with musical intervals and rhythms for long

270

enough to trust our ears. Our eyes are becoming, at last, more and more sensitive to their visual equivalents, but only familiarity will enable us to judge between mediocrity and mastery in any given instance of the difficult process of creation.

Graham Sutherland. Thorn Heads

GRAHAM SUTHERLAND has the power to develop a symbolic image from a fact, suddenly seen and vividly remembered. The series of

145. Graham Sutherland (b. 1903). Thorn Heads. 1945-46. Oil. Colin Anderson Collection, London

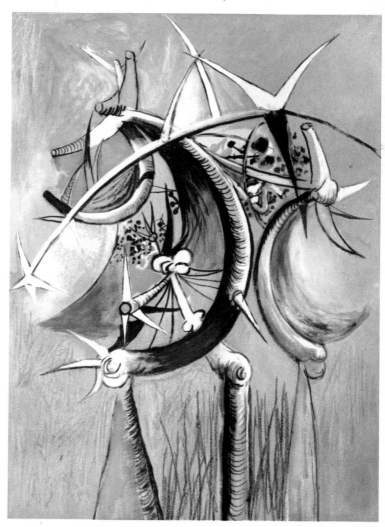

paintings and drawings of thorn heads with which he was occupied in 1945 and 1946 makes this clear. He had been commissioned to paint a large Crucifixion for the Church of St. Matthew, Northampton, England. It was natural enough that he should brood over so responsible an assignment and that in doing so he should think of the Grünewald Crucifixion at Karlsruhe (see Plate 64), for Grünewald was an artist with whom Sutherland has much, temperamentally, in common. Perhaps the most terrifying invention in Grünewald's version of the theme is the crown of thorns. Such a conception could easily become an obsession in the creative mind of a sensitive artist, and for Sutherland it began to sum up the whole meaning of the Crucifixion.

The searing cruelty of the thorn shapes had already appeared in his paintings, but in 1945 it became a central theme. To observe such shapes in nature and then to isolate and intensify them so that the inanimate form begins to have a will and a purpose of its own is the special gift of a visionary artist. Fact and symbol are so closely related that each reinforces the other. Hence the power of this painting. The strong, curved forms whirl like swords; the white thorns emerge purposefully out of them; the notes of orange-red are oblique references to blood; the blue background suggests the abstract space in which the tragedy of the Crucifixion is enacted.

This is a typical example of Sutherland's use of the close-up in isolation. When one compares it with the Crucifixion itself, painted by him in the same year, one finds that the symbolic thorns have almost disappeared. The event itself has made the symbol unnecessary.

Henry Moore.   Family Group

THE GRADUAL EVOLUTION and enlargement of the sculptor's vocabulary of form in the 20th Century can be largely traced to the searching eye and exploring mind of Henry Moore. It would require more than a brief essay to describe each step in his development, from his earliest carvings in the mid-Twenties, through the near-abstractions of the Thirties and the figures of the early Forties in which human anatomy is the starting point for a set of bold experiments in the language of form, to the more humanist and more serene sculpture of which this Family Group of 1945-49 is possibly the most satisfying example.

Perhaps a quotation from an essay by him written in 1934 will best explain what his consistent aim has been. "The human figure is what interests me most deeply but I have found principles of form and rhythm from the study of natural objects such as pebbles, rocks, bones, trees, plants etc."

That reveals, in a sentence, how the formation of a thigh bone, the smooth surface of a waterworn pebble, the jagged shape of a rock, the twisting, thrusting form of a tree trunk, the ponderous, heaving bulk of a range of mountains can all find their way into a carving—or even a drawing—that is ultimately centered on the human figure and is basically concerned with humanity. In short, Henry Hoore, unlike his great predecessors—Michelangelo or Bernini, for example—has enlarged the horizon of the sculptor so that we no longer expect him to limit himself to an interpretation of the skin that covers the muscle or the muscle that half-reveals the skeleton. Man, for Henry Moore, is not the climax of creation but an integral part of it, subject to the same formal laws that are responsible for a shell or a root or a mountain.

Once that has been said, the Family Group becomes charged with a new set of meanings. The theme itself —the unity both of sentiment and of composition dictated by the seated figures of the father and the mother turning toward each other in their concentration on the child, the object of

146. *Henry Moore (b. 1898). Family Group. 1949. Bronze. Museum of Modern Art, New York*

their common affection—is an obvious one. Moore has worked it out in detail in a long series of experimental drawings and maquettes, discovering new possibilities in the rhythms of the four arms that take the weight of the child, the relationship between two torsos, the gentle emphasis on the distinction between male and female, discovering the point at which specific human anatomy is absorbed by generalized or symbolic form.

Notice, for example, the rhythm of the drapery round the woman's knees, suggesting the horizontal swirl of water, and the firm strength of the man's legs, growing like slender tree trunks out of the earth. The whole group, including the treatment of the heads themselves, is full of these oblique references to nonhuman phenomena, yet its innate humanity, the suggestion of maternal tenderness and paternal protectiveness, is not diminished by these distortions.

273

Marino Marini.   Horseman

SCULPTURE HAS ALWAYS thrived along the North Mediterranean seaboard. The tradition that began in the 7th Century B.C. in Greece still continues in the Italian cities, based sometimes on the classic repose of pre-Christian Greece itself, sometimes on the more rigid strength of Etruscan art and sometimes on the grace of the Italian Renaissance.

Marino Marini could be classified as a neo-Etruscan, especially when, as so often happens, his subject is that of the horse and rider. Here, almost geometrically simplified into a series of right angles, is a typical specimen of his powerful art. The thrown-back head and stretched arms of the man; the defiantly thrust-out head of the horse are, like many of their Etruscan prototypes, a little intimidating.

Marini has an unusual feeling for the surface of bronze. The forms are as simple as possible, yet the smooth curves of the man's legs and the cylindrical body of the horse are tense and muscular. Smoothness can easily suggest flabbiness, but never with Marini.

148. *Abraham Rattner (b. 1893). Composition — Don Quixote. 1949.*
Downtown Gallery, New York

Abraham Rattner.   Composition — Don Quixote

RATTNER'S FATHER, a Russian trained as a rabbi, moved, in his middle years, to America. His son was born in Poughkeepsie, New York, in 1895. The Rattner family was always half conscious of racial exile and when the son became a painter after a brief training at the Pennsylvania Academy of Fine Arts, in 1917, he could still write "The Jewishness of way back somehow finds its way into my living moments now."

"Living" is a word that has always appealed to Rattner as providing the motive power of his passionately vital art. He always knew that his pictures must be expressive of the fullness of human experience, but he was less sure of his ultimate means of expression. For nearly two decades he lived in Paris, settling there in 1920 and absorbing the hectic, experimental art of the city, adapting himself to the languages of Cubism and Fauvism, but never content to use them for their own sakes. For him they were means, not an end; the end was basically humanist. It was also basically urgent and sensuous. His humanism is the romantic humanism that never hesitates to use formal distortions for the sake of intensifying meaning and rich, saturated color in order to emphasize emotion. Yet both are subservient—more so than in the art of Soutine—to the readable content of his paintings.

He has been likened to Rouault, but it is more likely that both artists responded to the influence of mediaeval stained glass than that Rattner was influenced by Rouault. For Rattner spent many hours brooding in front of the windows of Chartres Cathedral and their insistent black outlines, framing in areas of jewel-like color, surely provided the impetus for his later style.

This Don Quixote picture is one of a series. It was painted in 1949. The half-crazed adventurer, who saw himself as a noble knight on a fiery charger rescuing distressed damsels and tilting at windmills, must have had a special appeal to Rattner. For Cervantes' Don Quixote was a man pathetically struggling to live the life of a hero in a mocking world. Rattner endows him with a kind of satirical arrogance, while his steed, Rozinante, stands by, equally noble in character and equally an object of ridicule.

Rattner is one of those rare artists who can sincerely use the painterly vocabulary of today in order to communicate the strong, fundamental emotions —love, compassion, triumph—that are common to all human beings. Consequently his style, though full of echoes of the intellectual experiments of the Twenties, has an essential warmth which makes it easily understood, even though it has become, in his more recent painting, less descriptive and more abstract.

149. *Pierre Soulages (b. 1919). Composition. 1958. Oil.*
Collection Capt. Ernest Duveen, London

Pierre Soulages.   Composition, 1958

THE LATER MANIFESTATIONS of abstract painting have
tended less and less to explore the classic geometry of Mondrian and Ben
Nicholson, which emphasizes shape and proportion to the exclusion of the
sensuous elements in painting. What could be called the romantic or expressionist side of abstraction is a comparatively recent discovery. It has led in
two directions, one of which, "action painting," is a record of the muscular
urges of the hand that holds the brush. The other, usually called *tachisme* by
the French, is concerned with the sensuous qualities of paint itself. Form and
rhythm tend to disappear. The *tachiste,* instead of being the master of his
medium, allows himself to be governed or even seduced by it, and in doing so
discovers potentialities that might otherwise have been overlooked.   277

Somewhere between the two one could place Soulages. The immense forcefulness of those broad black strokes, superimposed on one another or crossing each other, is a product of the *act* of painting itself. It is impossible to look at a good Soulages without imagining the artist himself at work. To that extent he is an "action painter." But, in addition, the paint seems to live a life of its own, insisting on its own sensuous consistency and delighting the eye by its texture.

There is a kind of romantic urgency in all that Soulages does. Light seems to glow through the interstices of the prison bars he constructs. Space is implicit in the superimposition of one bar over another. To call him a romantic is to use the term in the same sense in which it was applied to Altdorfer (see Plate 75). There is the same suggestion of a dense forest with light endeavouring to force its way between the branches.

Art and Magic

THE ARTS OF WHAT we call, for want of a more specific word, "primitive" peoples tend to differ in kind from those of civilized man. They are functional in a more vivid sense than anything produced in Europe, Asia or modern America.

This book contains four specimens of such art, the paleolithic bison from Altamira (Plate 1) and the three masks from Africa (Plates 151-153). What is common to all four is that they are neither descriptive, as a Crucifixion or a still life is descriptive, nor do they communicate an emotion, as the mosaic head of Christ Pantocrator in the Cathedral of Cefalù (Plate 16) communicates an emotion. They are ingredients in a magical ceremony. They exist not to please the eye or to stimulate the mind but to placate hostile gods or bring about the fulfillment of human desires.

It is to this complete disregard of the "spectator" and to their reckless disregard of the visible facts of life that they owe their power. They are, in fact, not interpretations of a known world but creations in their own right, and they are called into being from the dark recesses of the creative imagination.

The word "imagination" is based on the word "image"; and we of the 20th Century, who are just beginning to learn something about the mechanism and the meaning of those dark recesses, are at last beginning to understand and admire the imagery that is generated in them.

The plates which follow should clarify this distinction between civilized man's emphasis on emotion and primitive man's creation of an image drawn from the deeper levels of his unconscious mind.

The Human Head

TO ISOLATE the human head so that it carries the whole expressive weight of the artist's message is, in one sense, the final test of man's attitude to mankind. For the Greek sculptor the very notion that a human head was capable of expressing more than a generalized type or the mildest of emotions was unthinkable. The headless Greek torsos that have survived hardly strike us as incomplete, for the Greek artist regarded the human body as a unit in which the head, admittedly more complex in form than the rest of the body, was not more charged with meaning. But for the Gothic sculptor the headless body of, say, a Crucifixion would have seemed meaningless, whereas an isolated head—possible to the classic artist only in portraiture—could actually gain in emotional intensity by its isolation.

The fragment of late Gothic sculpture from Perpignan, with its deep-set eyes, jutting cheek bones, emaciated cheeks and pain-racked mouth, comes as near to the limits of romantic distortion as one could expect to find in early 16th-Century Europe. One has to wait for Picasso in the 20th Century to find a parallel. Doubtless his Weeping Woman of 1937 (Plate 141) was prompted by similar feelings of compassion and indignation.

It is worth noting that both works, though they come from France, strike us immediately as typically Spanish in their acceptance of human suffering. Both, despite their distortions, are essentially realistic in the sense that they do not shrink from the full implications of the tragic event. It is also worth noting that the only other illustration in this book of which the same could be said is by another Spaniard (Plate 110). Goya's etchings of the Disasters of the War have the same grim realism; they are from the same fusion of indignation and compassion.

Yet if the Perpignan head is, by European standards, a masterpiece of expressive distortion, the word distortion itself begins to require a new definition when we turn the page and find ourselves confronted with the ritual masks from Africa.

The comparison between Perpignan and Guro is enlightening; we have made a transition to a world in which not only the purpose of art is different but the very nature of the creative imagination and the creative act itself.

Once this is realized it becomes clear that the word distortion is not applicable to African sculptures, for distortion implies departure from a norm —features exaggerated, limbs stylized or rearranged, colors re-harmonized. For the African there is *no* norm and therefore no departure from it. The African sculptor does not transform a human head into a stylized work of art that begins by observing it and ends by intensifying it. The African creates an

150. *Head of Christ. Early 16th Century. Wood. Perpignan, France*

image, potent and self-sufficient in its own right. If it happens to include two eyes, a nose and a mouth, that is not because he has a particular man or even the concept of "mankind" in mind, but because the image he has made has to perform a magical function that directly concerns the men of his tribe. But if the tribe is connected with or protected by the totem of a cow or a gazelle, then the mask will include horns—not, be it noted, by adding horns to a man's head but by the special act of creating a man-cow or a man-gazelle image.

No race of artists has possessed a more extraordinary power to invent such images than those of the Gold and Ivory Coasts of Africa or of the Belgian Congo. If, at first sight, they have a family likeness, it is not because of a similarity between any two chosen examples but because all of them (and in this they differ from the art of any other geographical area in the world) virtually ignore the normal sculptural form of the human head or the human body. They may refer to basic human features but those features are 281

incidents in a formal design, angular or suave, concave or convex; that is, never a *departure* from the normal but always an imaginative creation which owes little or nothing to observation or visual experience.

The only exceptions to this rule are the baffling heads from Ife and, to a lesser extent, certain Benin bronzes which neither the archeologist nor the art historian has ever satisfactorily explained. Apart from these, the African mask is the formal expression of a magical purpose. It is as much a part of a religious or sociological ritual as a chalice or a piano, and its form is equally an expression of its function as either. It is more vivid than either because its function is, to the African, more urgent and more varied; therefore, its form is not only more varied but more inventive.

No conceivable human head could have prompted the artist to construct that wonderful *S*-shaped curve that runs from the top of the forehead to the end of the nose in the mask from Guro on the Ivory Coast. Eyes can be huge spherical bosses or mere slits; noses can have the ferocity of beaks or the impudent tip-tilted charm of a debutante; heads can be conceived as spherical or concave, swollen or emaciated, flat or hollow. There is no apparent limit to the formal inventiveness of the African carver. Compared to him the caricatures of a Rowlandson or the experiments in distortion of a Picasso are childish attempts to invent a new pattern for the human head.

The reason is obvious, and it points a moral that Europe had for-

151. Antelope Mask from Guro. Wood. British Museum

gotten since the beginning of the Renaissance and that the 20th Century is only just beginning to rediscover—namely that function begets form; that the extraordinary difference, for example, between a gazelle and a hippopotamus is not the outward sign of artistic inventiveness on the part of the creator but of a difference of biological purpose.

In a word, African sculpture is not, in any conscious sense of the word, "art." It owes its shape not to the aesthetic sensitivity of the artist, as does a Greek statue, but to a purpose to be fulfilled, as does a scythe or a lathe or an airplane. This is true to such an extent that the African, who uses such images for magical purposes and finds that they do not "work" as spiritscarers or rain-producers or whatever their purpose may be, will destroy them as readily as a modern engineer will scrap an ineffective machine, with no suspicion that in doing so he may be destroying a work of art.

Exceptional among these ritual masks, which are carved in wood, are the bronzes of Benin which display a rather different kind of creative vision and an excellence in the art of bronze casting that has never been achieved in the West. The head reproduced here, from Bini, despite its bold simplification especially in the delineation of the eye, strikes us at once as more closely based on observation than the others. A personality, not a type, seems to be the artist's intention. But at the other end of the scale the antelope mask from Guro is a wonderful creation of the essence of the

152. *Mask from Guro. Wood. Segy Gallery, New York*

283

*153. Head from Benin. Bronze.
British Museum*

animal, combined with a sense of rhythmic form exceptional even for the
Gold Coast. Evidently a race of sculptors who could design human or animal
symbols with equal confidence can hardly have been conscious that between
the two there is a difference in kind.

East of Suez

THE ART OF THE AREA that covers Persia, India, China and Japan can hardly be summed up in a few superficial generalizations. Yet, to a Western eye, there are certain negative qualities that are at once recognizable in every work of art which comes from the Orient. One looks in vain for the physical magnificence of Greece, the strained tensions of early Christianity, or the intellectual and inquisitive eye of the Renaissance. In their place we discover certain qualities that are never found in their purest form in the West, even though certain artists have been influenced by them.

No paintings of Europe or America have quite the delicacy, the patterned gaiety of Persian miniatures, though one or two French tapestries (in particular the Licorne tapestries, Plate 60) seem to reflect some of their spirit. Nothing from Europe approaches the concentrated romanticism and the poetic symbolism of those little Indian paintings that tell the story of ladies waiting for their lovers. In India, too, there are to be found carvings that have never been matched elsewhere for their voluptuous rhythms or for their explicit use of physical imagery as an equivalent for spiritual meanings.

China and Japan have a cultural history longer than and as varied as that of Europe, and both countries have produced masterpieces of painting, sculpture, and craftsmanship beside which their European counterparts all look clumsy and lacking in sophisticated refinement. In the West, man is the measure of all things; in the East, man is an incident in an environment.

Above all, the artists of China and Japan have preserved an almost mystical attitude to the *craft* of painting and carving. To regard the arts of painting and calligraphy as almost synonymous, so that the control of the brushstroke as it passes swiftly across the surface of silk or paper determines the quality of the work, is a mystic conception that no Western artist could fully understand or successfully imitate. The Western method of using oil paint on canvas could never hope to achieve such subtlety or refinement.

The notion of basing the arts of painting and sculpture on an analysis of what the eye sees—the perspective, the cast shadow, the modification of *285*

154. *Khusrau and Shirin.*
Persian Dish.
13th Century. Pottery.
Freer Gallery of Art,
Washington, D.C.

color by light and the intervening atmosphere—is, in general, repugnant to the artists of China and Japan. What they have achieved by consistently refusing to succumb to visual curiosity can be judged from the illustrations. Perhaps the most appropriate word for the state of mind that produced these works would be "contemplation."

Persian Dish

IN THE 11th and 12th Centuries the Turkish conquerors of Iran gave an important stimulus to Persian craftsmen, and particularly to the Iranian makers of ceramics. Under their patronage were produced some of the most richly and beautifully decorated examples of pottery ever made. In various centers the crafts of luster decoration in monochrome and polychrome became highly developed. In Kashan, during the 13th and 14th Centuries, each potter was proud to sign his name on his best and most elaborate products.

The plate shown here was made for a prince and signed by the potter Shams-ad-din-al-Hasani. It contains an elaborate illustration to Nizami's romantic poem *Khusrau and Shirin* and probably represents Prince Khusrau and a group of court attendants watching Shirin bathing. The delicate, sensitive line and the bold, dense patterning are evidence of a master of the art of combining lively painted illustration with pure decoration. The plate itself, with its grooved rim and deeply sunk and scalloped upright sides, is a good example of the basic form of the best Persian ceramics.

Persian Illuminations

P E R S I A N painting developed late. The art of the Persian illuminated book dates from the 14th Century and does not reach maturity till the 15th. Mogul invasions had laid waste to the country. Tamerlane and his successors brought foreign influence into Iran, but eventually a tradition evolved that makes the best Persian illuminations rank among the most exquisite examples of small-scale painting in existence.

It is an art of the court. Brightly clad personages sit at ease in their gay pavilions, tended by their servants (perhaps the nearest approach to them that can be found in Europe is the " Dame à la Licorne " tapestry, Plate 60), or they hunt wild animals; or, occasionally, they engage in combat with each other. But whatever their occupation, they move in a landscape decorated by trees and flowering shrubs, and they walk or ride on meadows carpeted with a joyful pattern of flowers or in well-kept gardens. They play musical instruments or converse with decorous gestures. No hint of strong feeling disturbs them. Pattern and delightfully harmonized bright color are the essence of the world they live in. None of the strange voluptuousness of their cousins in the art of northern India is allowed to stir their passions. Even in battle they are calm; they behave like puppets.

Art has always divided its allegiance between emotion and decoration and in great art the two are always fused in varying proportions, but in Persian art one feels that decoration has been carried to such lengths that it takes the place of emotion.

The Persian love of opulent landscape enriched with flowers has resulted —as so often in Oriental art—in a complete abandonment of optical perspective. It is not true to say, as has been said by some critics, that the horizon is always high on the picture. Rather does the Persian artist hover, mentally, above the landscape in which his human beings disport themselves, so that there is no such thing as a distant tree or a distant group. What would be, to the European, the distant feature, is merely higher up the picture, which is organized in strips that indicate different areas of space. This gives the *287*

155. *Style of Bihzad (15th Century). Dancing Dervishes.*
Illumination from Jami's Diwan. *Metropolitan Museum of Art*

156. *Style of Ustad Muhammadi*
(late 16th Century). Hunting Party. Persian
Illumination. Metropolitan Museum of Art

Persian artist the enormous advantage of keeping the same scale of pattern throughout. The flowers on the skyline are just as big as those which grow in what we Europeans would mistakenly call the "foreground."

It was at Herat, the cultural center of Persia, where Shah Rukh and his son Baisunkur Mirza established a great library, that the art of miniature painting reached its height, late in the 15th Century. Most of the finest illustrations were to books of poems by Nizami and Sadi. And the most famous of the Herat artists was Bihzad, admired for his brilliance of color-pattern and suave precision of line.

The "Dancing Dervishes" is by an artist of his school and close to him in style, from a book of mystical lyrics by the 15th-Century poet, Jami. Decorative refinement is carried to such lengths that one hardly notices the subject matter of this little painting, yet in the quartette of dancers who 289 occupy the center there is a swinging movement that is carefully balanced by the static figures who stand and watch them.

This belongs to the end of the 15th Century. Almost a century later the center had moved away from Herat, the style had become a little less formal and the colors less brilliant. In Ustad Muhammadi's "Hunting Scene" the figures are distributed with less skill but there is a new hint of realism in them. Typical of the style of this later period is the elaborate decorative border, crowded with animals whose treatment is certainly derived from Chinese art, though the Persian artist somehow contrives to add a touch of decadence to the dragons. His animals are both more elegant and less vertebrate than their Chinese prototypes.

Figure from the Laksmana Temple, India

THE CHRISTIAN ATTITUDE of mind, accustomed as it is to making a fairly sharp division between body and soul and, in particular, between physical and spiritual beauty, finds it difficult to enter into the deeper meanings of the sculptures of the Hindu temple in which a whole world of carved imagery, manifestly erotic in its appeal and often frankly so in subject, becomes entirely and deeply involved in religious meanings. In Hindu art alone the flesh becomes a symbol of the spirit and the union of man's spirit with the deity can only be completely represented by images of human physical desire. The very profusion of such imagery strikes the Western eye as excessive, whereas to the Hindu it seems natural that intensity should be expressed by excess and that voluptuous rhythms should be the visible counterparts of the very meaning of the deity.

Here, the upper part of one of the Celestial Beauties that attend the gods and even release aspects of their power, represents Salabanjika, who is connected with the growth of trees and the exuberance of the forest. She herself, in her spiral, twisting movement, contains all the slow exuberance of tropical growth. She belongs, architecturally, to the structure of the temple itself and should belong to the category of high relief, yet she struggles to exist as a free-standing statue in the round. The marvelously complex sequences through which the axis of her body passes have no parallel in Western sculpture. The surfaces of her curved back, the sweep of her right hip and thigh (which continues downward in an unbroken line to her foot), the snakelike gestures of her arms combine into a single upward-surging rhythm, as though the anatomy of the human body had become no more than the basis for an essay in the shapes of sensuousness made visible. The jeweled armlet, the curving headdress, the scarf that crosses her back and enfolds her breast, even the incised pattern and the jeweled border on her legs emphasize her sinuous bulk.

290

157. *Nayika. Mid-10th Century. Stone. Laksmana Temple, Khayuraho, India*

This is an art that hovers on the verge of overstatement and could easily become repellent if the sculptor had not felt so acutely the need to control his forms and the curvature of his surfaces. As it is, excess is held in check at every point by an exceptional feeling for the hard skeleton behind the voluptuous curvature of the surface. The surface, in fact, is not the surface of skin; it is the tactile surface of a symbol which is essentially a symbol of a religious state of mind.

The figure belongs to one of the group of temples at Khayuraho in central India and dates from the middle of the 10th Century A.D.

Four Indian Paintings

W H E N   W E   T U R N from the illuminated books of Persia to those of India, we move not only into a later development of Eastern art but also into a more human and a more romantic world. The ultra-refinement of the stiff Persian figures is replaced by a race of beings more conscious of their physical beauty, more passionate in their actions and pursuits, more dramatic in their relationship to their surroundings and to each other. Beside these Indian miniatures Persian art begins to look static and unemotional, as though a Persian carpet had been endowed with life.

It is not very long since scholars have been able to distinguish between the various art centers in northern India and to recognize the stylistic signatures of the different regional schools of painting. We now know that there was, from the end of the 17th Century and throughout the 18th Century, an area in the foothills, in the states to the south of Kashmir, that produced an art rather different from that of the most familiar Mughal school still farther south.

Notable among the works of these northern Indian artists are the narratives of the lives and adventures of Krishna, whose life among the Gopis (the damsels who looked after the cows) was celebrated in poetry and legend. Of all these damsels Radha was Krishna's favorite. It is, of course, typical of Hindu legend that the stories of Radha and Krishna should be symbolic in meaning as well as romantic in content. Krishna, the most celebrated of the heroes of Indian mythology, eventually emerges as the Supreme Deity. Radha represents the human soul whose absolute and entire surrender to the godhead is the central meaning of the many legends that relate to the two lovers. Their love and Krishna's playful relationship to the Gopis are not incidents but eternal realities.

The more richly decorative of the two scenes of their legend (Plates 158 and 159) is the earlier. It dates from *c.* 1680 and is a product of the Basholi school. Krishna enters Radha's dwelling and finds her asleep in an attitude of complete relaxation on her bed. The color scheme is of the utmost splendor,

158. *Basholi school. Krishna Finds Radha Asleep. c. 1680. Miniature. Victoria and Albert Museum, London*

including the red surround that frames the bright yellow room with its patterned rugs and elaborate decorations. In Persian art the figures of the two protagonists and the maidservant who beckons Krishna would be lifeless and statuesque. Here there are all the elements of drama. This is one of a series of miniatures illustrating the Sanskrit poem, the *Rasamanjari,* in which Radha and Krishna play, as it were, the part of actors who illustrate the various phases of an earthly love.

Radha and Krishna with Cows was probably painted about a century later. It comes from the Kangra school of painters and in it the influence of the more familiar Mughal school is easily traced. There is a greater degree of naturalism and corresponding diminution in intensity. The lovers seem to have shed much of their mysterious atmosphere of divinity. Krishna has abandoned his symbolic lotus and has exchanged his crown for a turban. This is romanticism on a more terrestrial level, in which the lovers live quite naturally among Radha's cows.

293

159. *Kangra school. Krishna and Radha with Cows.* c. *1780.
Miniature in tempera*

160. Malwa school. Lady Waiting for her Lover. c. 1680. Miniature. Victoria and Albert Museum, London

The portrayal of the lady who awaits her lover in the woods (Malwa School, *c.* 1680) is no longer a narrative painting. It is an illustration to a poem which, in its turn, attempts to express one of the thirty-six "musical modes" of Indian music, whose precise flavor the European-trained ear can hardly be expected to detect. Technically, the "mode" illustrated here is the "Kakubha Ragini," but our Western ignorance of Indian musical categories hardly detracts from the emotive effect of this little painting. The lady, seen against a background of red, symbolic of passionate love, stands embowered among dark trees. The peacocks who attend add an exotic note to her tryst in the forest.

The same preoccupation with images of romantic love can be seen in the Lady with the Hawk (from Guler) painted in about 1760. Here, but in a much simpler composition, is the same symbolic patch of vivid red, placed just where it will have the maximum of effect on the eye. There is a fluent but sensuous purity of line in the contour of the single seated figure. Everything nonessential has been omitted, and essentials—the couch and its canopy—have been reduced to a minimum. Her attendant, introduced as an indication of her rank, is only allowed to appear at the very edge of the painting. The sole concession to the closely packed pattern of the other three examples is the bed of delicately drawn flowers at the base of the picture.

161. *Lady with Hawk. c. 1760.*
Miniature from Guler.
Victoria and Albert Museum,
London

Horse's Head in Chinese Jade

THIS, the earliest example in this book of Chinese art, is surely also one of the most deeply satisfying. As in all good Chinese art the form seems to be dictated by the medium, which, in this case, is a piece of jade of exceptional semitransparent beauty in its own right.

Jade is too hard to be fashioned by the sculptor's chisel; it must be ground to the desired surface and then polished. Every subtle inflection of the surface is made manifest by the impact of light which is half-reflected and half-transmitted. Later craftsmen in jade were tempted by their own virtuosity to worry their semiprecious material into too intricately fretted a pattern. But here is a conception, no more than ten inches in height, of monumental simplicity. The feeling for pure abstraction and simplification of form is the exact antithesis of Bernini's baroque expressiveness (Plate 90) but it finds a close parallel in the noble simplification of Henry Moore (Plate 146). Yet the Chinese artist, despite his close approach to abstraction, never loses sight of the character of the horse itself, the dilated nostril, the quivering, open mouth, the tense muscular curves of the neck. A single groove marks the junction of the neck and the mane; the flat cheekbone and the set of the ear are positively cubist in treatment.

Nothing is known of the origin of this little masterpiece. "Perhaps 4th-5th Century A.D." is the nearest guess that scholars can make to its date.

162. *Horse's Head.* c. *Late 4th Century A.D. Jade.*
Victoria and Albert Museum, London

163. *Emperor Hui-Tsung. Ladies Preparing Silk.* c. *Late 11th Century. Silk scroll. Museum of Fine Arts, Boston*

Sung Copy of a T'ang Dynasty Scroll

ACCORDING TO A 13th-Century attribution, this is a copy by the Sung Emperor Hui Tsung (1082-1135) of a scroll by Chang Hsuan, an 8th-Century painter of the T'ang Dynasty. To the Western mind the notion of copying carries with it implications of a lack of originality in the copyist, if not of downright forgery; but to the Chinese mind to copy was to enter into the creative spirit and therefore to inherit rather than to imitate the genius of the original artist. But in any case, the Emperor Hui Tsung was a connoisseur and an artist of considerable distinction in his own right.

The scroll itself, fifteen inches high and nearly six feet in length, deals with the occupations of women in the palace. Like all good scroll paintings, the essence of it is its continuity, yet it is full of details which, like this group of women preparing newly woven silk, can be "quoted" and still retain their charm.

The gently sagging curve of the length of silk, the two upright figures at either end whose attitudes describe the exact amount of tension necessary to keep it taut and enable the girl in the center to run the heated iron over its surface, the little girl who quietly watches the process and the even smaller child who stoops as she runs underneath it—all this is stated with such simplicity and such completeness that we are hardly aware of the absence of a background or even of a base for the figures to stand on.

The nearest counterpart in European art to this impeccable refinement is to be found in the work of Piero della Francesca, but even Piero looks a little coarse beside the T'ang scroll painter. Held at arm's length, so that subsidiary details can no longer be read, this little group of five women, together with the silk they hold, make a set of pale verticals, joined by a pale horizontal and punctuated by the dark accents made by their hair. It reminds one of a perfect specimen of Chinese calligraphy. Any indication of the floor they stand on or a wall behind them would have been intolerably disturbing.

164. Bird on a Bough. 11th Century. Silk album-leaf. British Museum

Chinese Silk Painting.   Bird on a Bough

NOTHING COULD MAKE the cultural gap between East and West clearer than a comparison between this album-leaf and any work of art produced in Europe at the same period. The name of the artist is not known but he was working at about the same moment that William the Conqueror was invading England and the ladies of Normandy were celebrating the event in the embroidery known as the Bayeux Tapestry. The crude vitality of Romanesque carving—the Isaiah of Souillac (Plate 17) for example —has no stylistic connection with this modest but exquisite painting on silk, ten inches by nine, of a bird on a bough.

It tells its own story of an artist whose sense of line and color were so finely adjusted that no leaf, no twig could be altered. They have their own inevitability, and the bird itself is drawn with a sensitivity that is a monopoly of the best Chinese and Japanese painters.

To the Chinese connoisseur of painting it is something more than a beautiful study of a bird on a bough. Each kind of bush or flower, each species of bird had its own symbolic meaning. Even in China many of these significances have been forgotten today and to draw up a glossary of such meanings would not help a Western eye to enjoy such paintings as works of art. We instantly recognize the quality of this tiny masterpiece and need no additional help from the abstruse Chinese language of flowers and birds.

Chinese "Kuan Yin" in Gilded Wood

ONE MORE STEP in the direction of what a Western critic would describe as a rococo ornamentation would have robbed this magnificent figure of its relaxation. But somehow the calm monumentality of the pose, the set of the head on the left shoulder, the limp right hand, the firmly planted left leg are so dominant that the restless agglomeration of carved detail that clings to the serene body is not too disturbing.

This is the Bodhisattva of Mercy, seated, presumably, on a rockery on the shore of a seagirt island. The role of the deity is that of protector against misfortune. This is an example of later Buddhist sculpture. Its date cannot be fixed with precision but it probably belongs to the 12th or 13th Century. Few European carvings have ever achieved such passive inscrutability; even the expressionless symbols of kingship produced by the greatest of the Egyptian sculptors (Plate 3) seem, by comparison, a little too tense, too conscious of their own power. Here power is effortless.

165.   Kuan Yin. c. Late 12th Century. Gilded wood. William Rockhill Nelson Gallery, Kansas City

Ch'en Jung. The Scroll of the Nine Dragons (two details)

DRAGONS APPEAR in all the major mythologies of the world, but whereas in the West the dragon was a symbol of the devil or at least of a force hostile to man, in China it probably originated as a god of rain and became an emblem of good government, closely associated with the power of the Emperor himself.

"Dragons," wrote T'ang Yiu, "should rise toward the sky through dense mist and layers of clouds, or plunge into the bottomless depths of the turbulent waters." He describes them as having a head "like that of a bull, the muzzle like a donkey's, the eyes like a shrimp's, the horns like those of a deer, the ears like an elephant's, the scales like those of fishes, the beard like a man's, the bodies like a serpent's and the feet like the Feng-Birds [the Eastern equivalent of the Phoenix]." These are the "nine similarities."

The Scroll of the Nine Dragons by the Sung artist Ch'en Jung was painted (according to inscriptions on the scroll itself) in 1244. It is perhaps one of the most complete statements known to us in oriental painting of the interplay of the forces of nature. Caverns and spiral swirls of water stretch across the whole length of the scroll, rising to a climax of whirling movement toward the center. Through them, sometimes plunging into them, sometimes emerging out of them, the nine dragons play, as though engaged in some fierce celestial game. Everywhere this rhythm of natural forces is caught up, varied, repeated, becomes tense, relaxes, develops dissonances, like a harmonic sequence in music that is ultimately resolved. The whole is in monochrome, but so skillfully does the Chinese artist handle the dilution of ink from intense black to palest gray that one is hardly conscious that color is missing.

This oriental sense of rhythmic movement is rare among European artists. The only instance of it in this book that can be compared with the Scroll of the Nine Dragons is the Leonardo drawings (Plates 67-69). Here again the forces of nature resolve themselves into a conflicting pattern. But since Europe has never used the "scroll" method, whereby a continuous rhythmic sequence unfolds itself gradually and the visual arts take on something of the nature of music, Leonardo could only produce a similar effect by making a series of isolated drawings to express the gradual progress of the explosive event he describes. Leonardo's line is even more charged with energy than that of the Chinese artist, but he cannot achieve the cumulative drive of an oriental scroll.

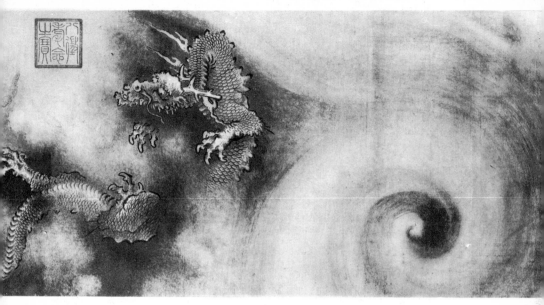

166. *Ch'en Jung. Nine Dragons. 1244. Scroll (two details).*
Museum of Fine Arts, Boston

Hsia Ch'ang.   A Bamboo Scroll

THE CHINESE INTIMACY with nature in all its forms has no parallel in the West. To such an extent did certain Chinese artists study and identify themselves not only with mountains, rivers and torrents but also with flowers and plants that it became normal for them to specialize in the painting of one type of plant or flower, not merely seeing in it one of nature's infinite manifestations, but attaching to it all kinds of human associations, so that a painting of peonies or plum blossoms became far more than a botanical study.

No plant has gathered to itself more associations in Chinese painting than the bamboo. The new shoots spread outward from the parent stock, hence it can be an emblem of filial piety; its stems are easily bent when young and suggest that youth responds to education; its stems can also be used for weaving baskets; its roots are divining blocks for the temple altar; as an evergreen it is symbolic of constancy. Moreover, the character of its growth and the delicate tapering of its leaves lend themselves easily to that sensitive handling of the brush that is typical of the best Chinese painting. It is understandable, therefore, that bamboo painting became a highly specialized branch of art and that certain artists devoted their lives to it. The swift brushstroke that could describe the single leaf required as much control of the hand as a pianist would need in the execution of a difficult sequence of notes.

It is not easy for the Western eye to appreciate these refinements, yet as one studies a series of such paintings one begins to admire the artist's technical virtuosity and the slight calligraphic differences between one artist and another.

167. *Hsia Ch'ang. Bamboo scroll. 1464.*
Freer Gallery, Washington, D.C.

The example shown here is by Hsia Ch'ang, a painter of the Ming Dynasty (1388-1470). It is a portion of a long handscroll painted in 1464. It is noteworthy for the skill with which the stiff, polished stems with their assertive joints are indicated, and the delicate curvature of each leaf as it tapers to a needle point. One feels not only the shape but the direction of each leaf and stem as it points away from or toward the beholder, and the space between the leaves even though their silhouettes intersect and cut across each other.

Wang Shih-Ch'ang. Mountain Landscape

So STRONG IS the power of tradition in Chinese painting—and especially in the painting of landscape—that it is not easy to ascribe even an approximate date to it on the stylistic evidence of any given work of art. The period covered by the Sung Dynasty corresponds roughly to the centuries in Europe that are called mediaeval, while the Ming period in China starts with the dawning of the Renaissance in Italy and ends three years after the death of Rubens. It is therefore a little startling to learn that this romantic landscape, which at first sight would suggest the style of a southern Sung artist of the 12th or 13th Century, was in fact painted by a Ming artist probably contemporary with Botticelli in Italy.

Such considerations, it might be thought, should concern the scholar rather than the layman. Yet it is important to realize that the art of China is dominated by philosophical and poetical concepts rather than by the individual temperament or the personal vision of the painter. This painting is   *305* one among many hundreds of superb expressions of man's insignificance in relationship to Nature, and especially Nature in her more grandiose and mysterious moods. It is a theme developed by the southern Sung landscape painters and continued, with variations, for centuries, always with the same mastery of free brushwork and the same capacity for eliminating the inessential and dwelling on the significant detail.

The great cliffs that rise out of the mist, crowned with fir trees; the distant mountains adumbrated behind them, the lake and the house of the scholar nestling at their base—all these may be part of a formula, but it is a formula kept alive and vivid by the intense feeling of the artist. Man looks upward with humility and reverence at the towering crags. The trees in the foreground form a link between him and the mountains. He is introduced into the picture not because he is the dominant factor in creation, as he would have been in a European painting, but because he is insignificant and yet is filled with awe at the grandeur that surrounds him.

Wang Shih-Ch'ang is not an artist with a resounding reputation. He is known to have been a pupil of the better-known Tai Chin, himself a member of the Che school of painting. None the less, this hanging scroll on silk (twelve feet high), in Chinese ink with faint traces of color, is a splendid example of its kind.

The Burning of the Sanjo Palace

THE HEIJI INSURRECTION began in A.D. 1159 with the burning of the Sanjo Palace near the Tokaido Road, where Hiroshige (Plate 172) ended his journey, and the capture of the ex-Emperor Shirakawa. Three scroll paintings full of military incident survive to tell the tales of heroism and adventure connected with the war. They were done in the early 13th Century and this magnificent example in the Boston Museum is the best of them.

The art of scroll painting, as already mentioned in connection with the Chinese Scroll of the Nine Dragons, has no counterpart in Europe. It is the art of a gradually built up climax—not necessarily a narrative climax, though narrative is the most effective method of describing an incident such as this. It may be the gradual progress of a river from the sea to its source in the mountains, as in the famous Chinese scroll of the Thousand Miles of the Yangtse. Or it may be the gradual intensification of a mood, as in the Nine Dragons. But here, only by means of a long scroll, unrolled slowly and followed as one follows the development of a symphony, could the drama of the burning palace have been presented in purely visual terms. And just as no excerpts from a symphony can reproduce its flavor, so no pair of

306

details, however carefully chosen, can give the cumulative effect of the whole of the Sanjo Palace scroll.

The scroll is in full color, though its main chromatic splendor is reserved for the portions that describe the fury of the flames and the confusion that surrounds them. The narrative starts, quietly enough, with a warrior on an agitated horse, preceded by a solitary bowman and followed by a thickening crowd of soldiers all moving steadily to the left. What matters is the placing of the intervals—like the intervals in a long melody. In sections of the scroll which cannot be shown here there is a gradual crescendo of movement, broken by the heavy accents of chariots and hurrying courtiers, with subsidiary scenes woven into the main headlong flight.

Then comes the palace itself and again a crescendo, this time not of movement but of a tornado of flame. The rhythmic impetus is broken by the diagonal roof of the palace, behind which is an interval of comparative peace with little fire-fighting incidents on its fringes.

The fact that in describing the narrative content of the scroll one is forced to use the vocabulary of an art that exists in time—"then comes" and so on—proves how necessary it is to approach such a work of art in the spirit in which one reads a book. But the meaning of the story is not in the events related but in the artist's instinctive invention of a set of rhythms that will fit into those events. The slow deliberation of the first four figures, like four slow chords before the announcement of the theme, the gradually increasing speed, the contrast between the writhing flames and the steady verticals

169. *Burning of the Sanjo Palace (two details).*

of the architecture, the alternation between compact groups and single figures, the sudden alterations in tempo—it is by these purely aesthetic means rather than by the mere piling up of incident that the unknown Japanese artist tells his story.

Katsukawa Shunsho. Girl with Maple Branch

SHUNSHO WAS FAMOUS both for his prints of actors and his paintings of beautiful women, which were mainly executed at the end of his life. To the European, who instinctively thinks of the human face when the word "beauty" is applied to women, it seems a little odd that artists like Shunsho, in his paintings, and Utamaro, in his prints, should have taken so little trouble to distinguish between one face and another. The girl with the maple branch expresses nothing by her features, yet her beauty pervades the whole painting. It is the delicate flow of her dress, her attitude, in which her turned-back head is balanced by the thrust-out hand that holds the branch, that arrest the eye, and the outline of the scarf that frames the almost feature-less face—even the marvelous placing of the figure within the rectangle that contains her.

In a nation of artists whose instinct for color and the imposition of pattern on areas of color is their greatest asset, Shunsho is exceptional.

Early 13th Century. Scroll. Museum of Fine Arts, Boston

171. *Hokusai (1760-1849). Girl Playing Samisen.*
c. 1820-25. Woodblock print.
Freer Gallery, Washington, D.C.

Hokusai and Hiroshige.   *Woodblock Prints*

I T   W A S   I N   the late 17th Century that Moronobu published the first
woodblock color prints of a new kind, which became known as *ukiyo-e*. The
word meant "the style of the passing hour" but its significance lay in the
fact that such prints could describe scenes from daily life—actors, fashionably
dressed girls, landscapes and everyday incidents of every kind, especially those
which would interest the traveler. After the classical period of Japanese art

170. *Shunsho (1726-1793). Girl with Maple Branch. Late 18th Century.*
Colors on silk. Art Institute of Chicago

which invariably treated of "noble" or "learned" themes, this democratic opening up of new subject matter enormously enlarged the scope of the Japanese color-print makers, and it is not surprising that the names of at least half a dozen of them are famous in the Western hemisphere. To the Japanese they had the same appeal as has the candid camera to us.

Moronobu was the earliest of these color-print artists. Haronobu is credited with introducing the five-block print; Utamaro (1753-1806) is best known for his prints of beautiful women. I have chosen, from an embarrassing wealth of material, Hokusai (1760-1849) and Hiroshige (1797-1858) to represent the whole school.

Both artists were prolific, both covered an immense range of subjects, both produced their prints in series. But beneath the superficial resemblance imposed on them by the traditional conventions of Japanese art and the limitations of the woodblock technique, their styles, indeed their very natures, were different.

Hokusai was brilliant, dramatic, surprising, with an eager eye and a keen sense of humor as can be seen in his drawings from the sketchbooks he filled in the earlier part of his life. Hiroshige was no less inventive but quieter, more subtle and intimate, less decorative in his approach to nature, less anxious to astonish by the introduction of new compositional tricks.

What has already been said about Rembrandt's drawings, that they "pulsate with the essence of the life that they record" is equally true of Hokusai's, though at times Hokusai introduced a note of grotesque comedy that is not to be found in Rembrandt. The drawing reproduced here is not one of these, the line is unusually flowing and the outline of the hand and the musical instrument is unusually deliberate, but the main intention to catch the concentration of the girl as she plays her samisen—is certainly Rembrandtesque.

The works that linger in the memory, in the case of both artists, are the color prints, and mainly those of landscape, almost always with a foreground incident filled with small but carefully observed figures.

The "sets" of prints in Hokusai's case were all done in the last fifteen years of his life. First came the Forty-six Views of Fuji, the sacred mountain; then the Waterfall series, of which Plate 172 is one; later the Bridges and the set called Snow, Moon and Flowers.

The Amida Waterfall (so called because of a supposed resemblance between the hollow from which the water emerges and the head of Amida Buddha) is one of the most striking of the series. With the simplest means Hokusai suggests the immensity of the unbroken vertical fall into an abyss overhung by damp mossy cliffs. The little group of three men on the left gives scale to the whole scene.

Nothing quite as dramatic as this is to be found among Hiroshige's Fifty-six Stations on the Tokaido Road. Taken together, the whole set records   *313*

*172. Hokusai. Waterfall at Amida. c. 1830. Woodblock print.
British Museum*

173. *Hiroshige (1797-1858). The Journey to Tokaido. c. 1850.*
Woodblock print. Metropolitan Museum, New York

stages on the journey from Tokyo to Tokaido which occupies the leisurely
traveler for fifteen days.

Hiroshige's gift for seizing on the essence of a landscape with the
greatest economy of means seems inexhaustible. One is bound to be unjust,
in a selective anthology, to an artist whose genius lies in his variety. Hokusai
sometimes becomes the victim of his own formula; Hiroshige's observant eye
never fails him. Looking at Hokusai's waterfalls and even at some of the
more insistent designs in the Fuji set, we are inclined to doubt whether he
was more concerned with the spirit of the scene or the impressiveness of
the design. In the case of Hiroshige the doubt never arises. Consequently
Hiroshige's Journey to Tokaido is a gentler, more intimate progress, with
less in it of the element of sight-seeing.

Kuniyoshi. *Nichiren Stilling a Storm at Sea*

THIS PRINT IS one of a series of illustrations to the life of the Buddhist priest Nichiren (1222-82). It is magnificent in its monumental simplicity. The great wave that threatens to overwhelm the boat is established in two colors with clawlike, menacing touches of white at the top. Equally simple, and less linear than in the famous Wave print by Hokusai, which looks academic by comparison, are the mountains behind and the almost formless storm clouds. The occupants of the boat make an excited chaotic pattern with their gesticulating arms and contorted faces, while the priest, his robes fluttering in the wind, leans forward and seems to repel the mass of water that is just about to break over the bows.

Kuniyoshi specialized in illustrations of heroic episodes in Japanese history.

174. *Kuniyoshi (1798-1861). The Priest Nichiren Stilling a Storm at Sea.* c. 1835. *Woodblock print. Victoria and Albert Museum, London*

Photographic Credits

*All photographs were supplied by the museums
or collectors except as indicated below.*

1. Nederlandsche Rotogravure, Leiden
10. F. A. Mella
11. F. A. Mella
12. F. A. Mella
13. F. A. Mella
14. Green Studio
16. Alinari
20. Foto Fiorentini
21. Alinari
22. Foto Fiorentini
23. Foto Fiorentini
24. James R. Johnson
25. Osvaldo Boehm
28. Giraudon
29. Larkin
30. *Life* Magazine (c) 1948 Time Inc.
31. Alinari
33. Fine Art Engravers
35. F. A. Mella
39. Giraudon
40. Silvana
41. Oliver Baker
45. Alinari
47. Fine Art Engravers
48. Alinari
49. F. A. Mella
50. Camera Clix
51. Claudio Emmer

52. Conzett and Huber
53. Alinari
54. F. A. Mella
55. Foto Fiorentini
58. Maurice Routhier
59. Oliver Baker
60. Maurice Routhier
66. Fine Art Engravers
74. Fine Art Engravers
75. Roy Bernard-Inter Nationes
76. Roy Bernard-Inter Nationes
77. Roy Bernard-Inter Nationes
78. Roy Bernard-Inter Nationes
79. Foto Fiorentini
83. Oliver Baker
86. Conzett and Huber
88. Maurice Routhier
95. Roy Bernard-Inter Nationes
96. Conzett and Huber
97. Oliver Baker
98. Oliver Baker
99. Hislop and Day
100. F. A. Mella
109. Maurice Routhier
111. Conzett and Huber

112. Maurice Routhier
113. Giraudon
116. Conzett and Huber
118. Francis G. Mayer
119. Roy Bernard-Inter Nationes
121. Fine Art Engravers
127. Emiddio de Cusati
131. Fine Art Engravers
133. Conzett and Huber
135. Conzett and Huber
139. Frank Newens
140. Oliver Baker
141. Fine Art Engravers
142. Laniepce
143. Oliver Baker
144. Fine Art Engravers
145. Fine Art Engravers
148. Oliver Baker
149. Gimpel Fils
155. Oliver Baker
157. Amilcare Pizzi
158. Larkin
159. Conzett and Huber
160. Larkin
161. Larkin
170. Conzett and Huber
173. Oliver Baker
174. Larkin

INDEX